Here Come the Colts

To my dear Friend
Arnie Mellits – One of
the BEST Coaches at
M.C. since the days of the
Great Bob Johnson !!

Yours Truly –

MC Legend

Michael E Ra...

Here Come the Colts

Doug Bennett

To order additional copies of this book, contact:
Xlibris Corporation
1-888-795-4274
www.Xlibris.com
Orders@Xlibris.com
120976

Dedication

This book is dedicated to the memory of ACYA founder Robert M. "Bob" Johnson, Athletic Director and 120 lb. Colt Head Coach from 1965-1976.

INTRODUCTION

"Here Come the Colts !" . . . .

That was the slogan that was written on the side of the team buses, and this is the story of a decade of championship football, the Atlanta Colts of the 1970's, who won 17 of a possible 30 championships in the three age/weight classifications of the Georgia Youth Football Conference from 1970-1979, dominating that league in that decade.

This book is about the players and coaches in the decade of the 1970's for this Atlanta Colt youth football program, the ACYA, based in north Atlanta, Georgia who participated in the three age and weight classifications of the varsity program. It also includes information and recounts about some of the opposing teams and their coaches and players that made up metropolitan Atlanta's most competitive big league youth football organization of the era of the 1970's, the Georgia Youth Football Conference. It is the author's tribute to the ACYA founder and leader, the late Bob Johnson, who is mentioned frequently throughout the book.

The Atlanta Colt Youth Association program, aka "ACYA" was often referred to as the number one "Pop Warner" sanctioned youth football program in the entire US in the 1970's.

The book is written in narrative from the perspective of the author, who participated as one of the Varsity Colt head coaches in the last eight years of that decade (1972-1979) and observed the 1970 and 1971 seasons from an Interleague coaching position within that same famous Pop Warner program. The chapters detail the author's recollections and opinions and most of the detail centers mainly around his own players' and teams' experiences.

The author provides season by season summaries of each of the varsity Colt teams, highlighting some of the most important games in which his own team participated, with capsules of many others. He also reveals some of the strategies employed in detail and the actual on the field rationale and logic behind many of the significant plays and events in some of those games.

The author is Doug Bennett, who was a head coach for the "varsity" Colts for nine years, and participated in the ACYA program a total of 12 years from 1969-1980. In the subject decade of this book, the 1970's, Bennett was a varsity Colt Head Coach for the years 1972-1979. His teams won six consecutive GYFC championships from 1972 to 1977, finishing second in 1978 and third in 1979.

Using a combination of research from written historical material, actual game films and the author's memory, as much detail as possible is written, including the author's recollection of specific game circumstances, situations and plays, with emphasis on individual player and team performances, etc.

There are chapters describing the program's and author's philosophies and strategies on Offense, Defense, Special Teams, Practice and Game Preparation providing written description and analysis of how these championship teams were built from the first day of practice through the end of a season as it was learned from the legendary Coach Bob Johnson.

The ACYA program was not only a football program for the children, it was almost a society within the society of the Dunwoody area and surrounding neighborhoods in the northern suburbs of Atlanta, Georgia, particularly in the decade of the '70's. It was run totally by adult volunteers, whose dedication allowed the program to prosper and flourish from its inception in 1965.

The ACYA program was the annual focal point in the lives of these families from the start of football tryouts in early August until the last bowl games in December, for all of the years they were involved. Lifelong friendships were formed there, among the children football players and the adult parents and volunteers in those families.

The program still serves the community today and many of the volunteers who have been involved in recent years are former players from the era discussed in this book.

SECTION 1

Background: How It All Got Started

CHAPTER 1

Robert M. "Bob" Johnson, 1936-2004

It was Saturday, June 4, 2004, and I was sitting on my back porch relaxing and reading the Saturday paper as I was waiting to leave for the airport to go on a rare Saturday departure for a business trip to Philadelphia, Pennsylvania.

As I turned through the pages of The Atlanta Constitution, I discovered some terrible news. Bob Johnson had passed away earlier that week. Many thoughts immediately raced through my mind, the most pleasant memories of a special friendship that had begun in 1971. I had a huge amount of admiration and respect for this wonderful man that I looked up to and that I had learned so much from in my early adult life.

Some of my fondest memories are recalling the times with him at Colt Field in Murphy Candler Park in North Atlanta watching his Colt football team play, or him watching mine. I was deeply saddened by this news of his death, and disappointed when I realized that I would likely miss his funeral due to this important business trip which involved too many other people to postpone or reschedule.

Since I had a mid-afternoon flight that very day, I had to finish packing and leave around noon. On my way to the airport, I called Bob's home, hoping to speak with his wife Meredith or one of his three grown children, all whom I knew very well. I still remember his home phone number today.

Meredith actually answered the phone that day and told me the details of the circumstances which led to Bob's death. He had gotten very sick the last few weeks and his system finally gave out after a lifetime of fighting kidney disease. Bob was only 68 years old. Before the conversation ended,

I was driving though the Atlanta expressway connector and sobbing, and Meredith was consoling me. She was that strong and had been with Bob for so long, she knew and felt the pain he had dealt with through the years due to his health. He was finally at rest and in a better place.

I had last seen Bob at another unhappy occasion, about a year earlier, at the funeral of his former player, Jimmy Blake, who had died at a very young age in his early 40's. Many of Bob's former players remained friends into their adult lives, so I saw and talked to a lot of those former Colt players that day at Jimmy's service. Parts of Bob's legacy are the friendships and teammate bonds that were developed on the sweaty practice and game fields of Murphy Candler Park and the positive impact the ACYA program had on so many North Atlanta families, many of whom Bob never actually knew. The Blake family was very typical of an ACYA family with a son, three daughters and husband and wife all involved in ACYA.

These North Atlanta families, from various walks of life, many who had transferred into the area from all over the country, came together and worked together in a team effort toward the common goal of building and administering this program that was so helpful in the growth and development of their children. There was a diversified group of families that included corporate CEO's, professional athletes, and gas station owners. Some also came from poorer surrounding areas and those that could not afford the fees were "scholarshipped" or not required to pay the fees. Bob Johnson was the leader and inspiration in those families' cumulative effort to build and maintain the ACYA.

After seeing Bob at Jimmy's service that day from across the other side of the church, I was unable to get to him to speak before he left, but I did call him at home that night, just to say hello and catch up a little bit. We had a good talk that night, mostly about the past, but I was able to tell him how much his friendship had meant to me for so long. He agreed and used the word "Godly" to describe the bond between us. That phone call was the last time I ever spoke with him.

How I loved hearing that from this man I so admired! I had also been to his Sunday School classes at Wieuca Baptist Church many times over the years, and he was as good a Sunday School teacher as he was a football coach. Other circumstances had led me (and my wife, Cathy) to another church, but there would never be another teacher like Bob. In fact, as far as I'm concerned, there will never be another man like Bob.

I first met Bob and got to know him on a personal basis in 1971. As I will explain in the actual football coaching chapters of this book, I started in the ACYA Interleague in 1969, while I was still a college student. I knew who Bob was, as the leader of the program, but never got to know him personally until the '71 season.

In 1971, I had just graduated from college, but after coaching in the ACYA Interleague for the two previous years, I knew that I wanted to continue with coaching as I had enjoyed it so much. I knew a little about the varsity Colts, from having seen them play once or twice in 1970, but I decided that I wanted to learn more about this important and most focal, "Varsity" part of the ACYA program.

So, I started to stop by and watch an occasional 120 lb. Colt practice. The first time I went to a 120 lb. Colt practice, there was Bob Johnson, coaching an Oklahoma drill while sitting in a folding lawn chair. His other coaches were up, coaching and shouting encouragement to the players in the drill, and as each play started, Bob would have some calm words of advice and encouragement for whichever one of his running backs that was in the drill from his chair.

One thing I remember was a running back named Billy Todd was in the drill at this particular time, and I could not tell exactly what he was doing wrong, but something was not going right for him. The other thing I noticed was that Billy had a huge black eye, almost swollen shut, but that he would not get out of the drill until he made the perfect play the way that "Coach" Bob wanted.

Bob let him stay in the drill and kept coaching him and encouraging him to do his best. Watching Bob at work taught me an immediate lesson about conducting practice and how to push players to give their best efforts, yet how to be patient at the same time. I learned many similar lessons from watching Bob's practices over the years and tried to model my team's practices as much like his as I could. Details of these practice methods are in Chapter 15.

When Bob would be unhappy with a player, he would not yell or berate the player, he would simply and calmly teach and motivate. I can recall hearing him say things like: "son, I'm really disappointed by that effort." He would always tell that player exactly what he wanted done, tell the player how to do it and motivate the player to give his best effort. If further exasperated, Bob's most stern words would be something I've heard him say, like: "son, I'm about to lose my patience with you." That's when you knew you better get it right!

Simple phrases like that, calmly spoken were Bob's way of motivating and coaching. He was a tremendous motivator. His players and also his assistant coaches looked up to him in such a way that he could motivate without raising his voice or being very critical. He did the same things with me when I began coaching for him as a varsity Colt coach. He was my "boss" at this football coaching and I looked up to him and respected every word that he spoke about it. He could say a lot with just a few words.

I later learned that Bob was restricted to the lawn chair at this time because he had just had surgery, and although he was restricted from activity, he was going to coach his practice however he could. That demonstrated to me how serious he was and dedicated to his team and this coaching craft. I also learned for the first time that Bob had a chronic kidney disease and that he would eventually be going on dialysis.

As we went into the 1971 season, I thought I had what would be a good Interleague team, and I also took interest in Bob's 120 lb. Colt team, and started going to a few of his games and practices. I wanted to learn more by simply watching and observing this great coach and his team at work. Bob took note of this and started talking to me whenever he had time, about the Colts and the league they played in, the Georgia Youth Football Conference (GYFC).

Later in the year, as most of the entire program of ACYA players were boarding buses to Athens, Georgia for an outing to a complimentary University of Georgia home game, I was talking to Bob before boarding the bus, and he casually asked me if I might ever want to coach with him on the varsity Colts. I immediately said yes, but I didn't really think he was being as serious as he was just being friendly and making conversation, so I didn't really give it much thought at the time. Little did I know at that time, that he was in fact looking to the future. Bob was always thinking and planning about the future of the ACYA.

I recall his 120 lb. Colt team's most important game in that 1971 season was with the Midway Mighty Mites, his arch rival, on a Thursday night at Midway, so I drove to Midway Park in the Avondale area of DeKalb County for the game. I knew Midway was the toughest team in GYFC at the time and I expected a close game that night. It was very close and Bob's Colts pulled off a squeaker, winning in a tightly contested game. The atmosphere was very much like a high school game. A loud, but smaller crowd, both teams with bright, colorful uniforms, PA announcer etc.

The winning TD that night came on a play Bob called 28A, a backside option that Bob later explained to me that he knew would only work against a defense deploying a 3 deep secondary. Midway had been in 2 deep all night, and for this play, Bob called for a different than normal formation which caused Midway to roll their secondary into the 3 deep Bob that wanted to run against. The play went for a TD from about 20 yards, and I was taught a valuable lesson about play calling when Bob later explained to me how he had carefully set that play up all night, and patiently waited for the right time to call it by using a new and different formation to set up the opponent's defense. In addition, his team had been coached and taught exactly how to execute the play to perfection.

That 1971 team went on to a perfect season as GYFC Bobby Dodd Bowl champs for the second year in a row. I went to my first ever Bobby Dodd Bowl game that year and helped cheer Bob's team to victory. In fact, all three varsity Colt teams won the GYFC championship that year, a first in GYFC history. I spent that whole day at Forest Park's Kiwanis Stadium watching all three games and thought to myself how exciting it would be if some day, I could be a coach in one of these games.

Bob had had much success in the old DeKalb Youth Football Conference, the predecessor to the recently renamed GYFC, winning the Championship in 1967, but he had lost key games to Midway in 1968 and 1969. Analyzing those important losses, he felt it had happened because his offensive line could not block the Midway defensive stunts and he knew it was up to him to teach his linemen how to do that properly. Bob was very competitive and hated losing. Those two losses cost his team the championship both years, and he immediately recognized something needed to change with his Offense. You will see later how a similar thing happened to me in my first year as a varsity Colt Head Coach. This GYFC was a very tough and competitive conference and had a lot of very good and knowledgeable football coaches.

In order to figure out how to correct this blocking problem, Bob went to Leonard Jones, a very successful high school coach at nearby North Springs High School for advice and help during the off season between 1969 and 1970. When Bob would later recall and describe to me that first meeting with Coach Jones, he would recount it like this (Bob had a very entertaining dialect): he went to Leonard Jones and said emphatically "What are we gonna doooo ? We're gettin' beat!" What that really meant was "We can't block Midway's defense and I need help with my offensive line blocking schemes."

In Bob's dialect, again describing that meeting to me in his way of speaking, he quoted Coach Jones's reply "we're gonna do this right h-e-e-e-re, and we're gonna wi-i-y-i-in !" What that meant was Coach Jones really said "I can show you an offensive system that can block those stunts."

What all of that boiled down to was that Coach Jones showed and taught Bob a whole new Offense based on the Offensive Line being able to block stunts (defensive linemen and linebackers shifting and moving) and to also always give the offensive line and backfield an advantage on their blocks. So, unselfishly, Bob subsequently taught this to me in 1972 as I will describe later. I will also elaborate more on the specifics of the Offense later in Chapter 16. Bob also taught it to Mac Scoggins when Mac began his varsity coaching in 1974, and Mac was very successful using it as well, as you will also read later.

I will mention Bob Johnson's teachings and lessons frequently throughout the chapters of this book. The most significant things he did for my coaching career were: (1). Taking an interest in my coaching career and asking me to be a varsity Colt coach in 1972, (2). having the patience to see me through an up and down first year in 1972, then (3). teaching me his offense at the end of '72, and finally (4). to ask me to replace him as 120 lb. Coach upon his retirement at the end of 1976, which was the ultimate honor for me.

That is not to mention all of the personal advice and counsel he provided me with for many, many years. The subjects of his wisdom were limitless but included football coaching, other sports, business, personal and certainly religion. He actually climbed around in the attic of my first house prior to my purchase of it to confirm for me that he thought it was well built and worthy of my investment. And that was two years after he had retired from coaching. He absolutely lived an exemplary life and was a great person to have as a friend.

Bob and Meredith had three children, I believe in order of age (oldest first) Deane, Jenny and Cyrus. The boys participated in the ACYA program as players, with Jenny cheerleading. Bob would not allow them to receive preferential treatment from their coaches. I know that for a fact, as Cy played for me in 1975.

Deane was a very good player, particularly for his size. He was a star at Ridgeview, his high school and even played at least one year at Auburn as a walk-on. Cy was always so large for his age group that he would be the youngest on his ACYA teams, and not mature enough to be a starter on the Colts. But then he turned out to be a very good lineman on his Woodward Academy high school team and also played at a small college.

Bob Johnson was sick for a lot of his adult life, with many surgeries related to his kidney disease. Many nights after practice during football season, or just an occasional night during the off season, I would go to Bob's house and sit with him during his dialysis, and exchange football ideas or just talk as friends. He was a very wise man.

After retiring from coaching, he also had to have heart surgery in the mid 80's, and he finally received a kidney transplant within a year or two of the heart surgery.

He invited Cathy and me to be his guest at his church service one Sunday in late 1987. It turned out that he was to give his testimony in front of the entire Wieuca Road Baptist Church, a very large church. True to his inspiring way, he told about his life long battle with kidney disease and the circumstances leading to his transplant, which ultimately would extend his life almost twenty years. But rather than dwelling on himself, he turned it into an opportunity to teach the love of Christ for everyone else.

After he concluded, I just turned to Cathy with a tear in my eye and nodded what a special man this was that I could call my friend.

I could go on and on about Bob. He was an inspirational figure and could motivate people of all ages. He was smart, a talented and charismatic entertainer, witty and funny as a storyteller. He was a good businessman as a home builder and land developer, and in his final business effort, helped his youngest son Cyrus build a land development company that was very successful. But most of all, Bob was a Christian man of character and integrity, and he sought to influence that in those around him.

I could say that Bob was a mentor to me, and he truly was a mentor in football coaching. I learned almost everything I ever knew about how to coach kids from him, and most of the modest success I was involved in was due to his teachings and the strength of his ACYA program. But in reality, he was far more that that as he was a true inspiration from the way he conducted himself on the field, and in his business, to the way he handled his illnesses. I am proud to write about him, and prouder to have been his friend. He was truly a great man.

My first major career job that I started in 1973, in the healthcare field was with Crawford Long Hospital, now known as Emory Midtown, which was part of Emory University Hospital System, now known as Emory Healthcare. At the time, I knew who Bob's kidney specialist (Nephrologist) physician was, an Emory Physician, Dr. James Wells. Bob just called him Jim.

I ran into Dr. Wells in an Emory elevator one day early in my time there, probably around 1974, introduced myself, and told Dr. Wells that I was a friend of Bob Johnson. Dr. Wells, who was a short man, and a man of few words, simply smiled as he looked up at me, sort of chuckled to himself and nodded, and said "he's certainly one of a kind!"

That single statement sums up Bob Johnson.

CHAPTER 2

The Atlanta Colt Youth Association (ACYA)

The ACYA was a brainchild of Bob Johnson. He started it in 1965, at the age of 29. I understood that he chose the name "Colts" because the Baltimore Colts were one of the NFL's most successful teams at that time in the era of the mid 1960's. The team colors were Burnt Orange and Navy Blue, but I never heard why those colors were chosen. Bob went to school at Georgia Tech, so that was obviously not the reason for the color choice.

Bob had been a successful coach at the famous Buckhead Red Devil program at Chastain Park in the Buckhead area of Atlanta, but he wanted a program of his own, and he wanted things done his way, children first with very high ethical and behavioral standards for all involved. Bob was a perfectionist and had very high personal and business standards. As a very successful land developer and home builder, he saw the suburbs of Atlanta moving into farther out Fulton and DeKalb counties and felt that Murphy Candler Park in North Atlanta in DeKalb County would be the ideal location. There was already a vibrant and growing baseball program in place there.

He worked it out with DeKalb County, owner of Murphy Candler Park, where by permit, ACYA would have permanent use and control of the athletic fields during football season, and exclusive rights to Colt Field, the primary football arena, year round. The rest of the arrangements were that buildings would be permitted for dressing, equipment and eventually a stadium for seating. ACYA would have to fund those buildings, but the buildings would belong to DeKalb County, as they were on county property.

The program, as designed and led by Bob Johnson, placed emphasis on the fact that it was a children's program, and that the adults were there out of necessity to build, supervise and lead by example. The ACYA was built around the Varsity Colts. There would be three Colt teams, in three age/weight divisions The Colts would play in the very competitive DeKalb Youth Football Conference, which would later be re-named Georgia Youth Football Conference. The Colts would have a schedule of away and home games against other conference opponents. The rest of ACYA would be built of intramural teams (called the Interleague) who would play each other with all games always to be played at Murphy Candler.

Bob Johnson wanted the varsity level experience to be very competitive with the emphasis on winning games and conference championships. There were minimal mandatory playing time rules in DYFC, and all of the programs placed a premium on their competitiveness at the varsity level. The DYFC used high school rules and game officials and the conference was designed to provide a competitive experience for smaller kids, as will be explained in the next chapter.

Girls were invited to participate as the Varsity Colts and Interleague teams all had cheerleaders. There was also a marching drill team called the Coltettes, who performed to music at halftime of many of the Colt games, home and away, and at special events such as the season opening "Family Night" and the postseason bowl games.

Early on, Bob Johnson emphasized to me, and I'm sure to others before me, to always remember that the ACYA was a children's program and to always keep the emphasis on the players, and away from ourselves, the adults as coaches. Bob led by example and he had a couple of simple rules he went by that he felt de-emphasized the adults' involvement and kept emphasis on the players.

Rule One. Adults should not accept or handle trophies. When trophies are won they are won by the kids and should be accepted and handled by the kids. We want to avoid any possible perception that adults are using kids for personal gain and gratification.

Rule Two. Do not lead the team on the field and run out ahead of them. Youth football coaches should walk onto the field to the sidelines after the team is introduced. This is a kids' game and the adults should never be in the spotlight. The adults are there out of necessity as supervisors, leaders and chaperones.

The program grew rapidly and by 1969 they were playing Interleague games on four different fields at Murphy Candler. There were so many teams, that some teams had to practice at borrowed industrial facility lawns in areas away from, but not too far from Murphy Candler. In 1969, financing was arranged, by several ACYA families pledging to guarantee a loan, to conduct a concrete stadium with about 12 rows of seating by about 60 yards with capacity of about 3,000, a press box, meeting room, dressing rooms and equipment storage rooms. A higher and larger press box was added a year or two later. The stadium was unnamed until 2004 when it was renamed after Bob Johnson. Until then, it was simply called "Colt Field". The stadium was often completely filled to capacity with spectators, particularly for the arch rival GYFC games like Glenwood or Tucker, and almost always for the post season Thanksgiving weekend Colt Classic and Toys for Tots Bowls.

I started coaching in the Interleague and it was competitive and fun. The years I was there, it was run by John Ramsey, and he ran it like a dictator, with Bob Johnson's full support. The ACYA was set up with an operating board of directors, called "The Staff". It was made up of several positions, each of a specific responsibility and the program ran efficiently like a business. The board voted on rules and matters of policy, and John Ramsey and Bob Johnson, along with whomever the current year's President might be, ran the program and enforced the rules. Believe me, rules were rarely broken.

Each Staff member had their job such as fields and grounds, concession stands, football equipment, public relations, enrollment etc. Many of these jobs were manned by successful career and business people, men and women. Others were filled by stay at home Moms that wanted to participate and help and be involved with their kids' activities.

They all performed their jobs with vigor and they all watched with pride as the program grew year after year, and their children all loved it. It was a great place for total family involvement. The voluntary Staff appointments were yearly and many remained in their jobs more than one year. It was an honor to be asked to serve on The Staff. There was a President, turning over annually and Bob Johnson was Athletic Director permanently.

The Interleague had very specific rules and the teams were fairly divided and placed. Rules were followed to the letter and it was a privilege to be able to coach there. There were five levels of Interleague play called Yearling, Pinto, Pony, Mustang and Stallion, increasing in age from 7 to 13 years.

The program was set up for the players to learn football and become good players in the Interleague, and then be prepared to try out and make the "varsity" Colt teams when they became of age. It was intended to be similar to a professional baseball team, where the major league franchise has a minor league system to develop their young talent and prepare it for the majors. Here in ACYA, the Interleague would develop the talent for future Varsity Colt teams. There were 33 roster spots on each Colt team, the maximum allowed by conference rules. Those players either not quite skilled enough for varsity or who preferred a less competitive playing experience continued to play Interleague

At the varsity level, the DeKalb Youth Football Conference became the Georgia Youth Football Conference in the later 60's as teams were added in Fulton, Gwinnett, Clayton and Cobb counties. It was very competitive with many very good coaches from all over the Metro Atlanta area.

The Colt teams were very successful from the beginning. Being from an affluent part of Atlanta, and with the Johnson brothers (Bob had a younger brother David, also a home builder and an excellent coach himself) also being very successful businessmen, there was some resentment of that affluence from some of the other conference members. We heard rumors through the years that others in GYFC believed that the Colts had highly paid coaches, and that they took bowl trips to places like California, Hawaii, etc.

Although the Colt teams did travel by air to the post season bowl game (the farthest ever was Dallas, Texas) most of this was not true, although there were many wealthy or certainly upper class families in the program. But I believe that Bob Johnson saw this as a potential distraction to the competition and thus an advantage which he never really attempted to down play. For example, we were the only program to always take our teams on chartered MARTA busses to the GYFC Championship Game, aka, "The Bobby Dodd Bowl." This was not that expensive but it did further that image, and create a little envy against us, as we arrived with much fanfare.

By the way, the Colts usually won those Bobby Dodd Bowl games too, playing in 23, and winning 17 times resulting in championships, losing only five resulting in second place, and tying one resulting in a co-championship out of 30 possible in the 1970's.

CHAPTER 3

The Georgia Youth Football Conference

The GYFC was a very competitive youth football conference in the metropolitan Atlanta area. The participating teams came from county or city parks, but for the most part they were privately funded football programs led by volunteer coaches. There were at least one or two exceptions to that. The East Point Vols did have some City Parks Department employees as coaches, assisted by other non-employee coaches. I believe the cities of East Point and Roswell both promoted their programs as a function of each of those city's Recreation Department and at least provided some funding for them. Their employee coaches appeared to be very dedicated and I suspect would have volunteered as coaches, even if they had had other jobs in a different profession.

The league was set up to be as fair and balanced competition as possible. There were always at least 16 teams in three age/weight classes, with each program required to field teams in all three age/weight classes. The 16 teams were broken up into two eight team divisions, American and National, with two subdivisions in each comprised of four teams. Subdivisions were re-aligned every two years. Each of the programs involved entered their "varsity" teams with their best players into the GYFC. Each program also had an Interleague (like ACYA) or provided a lesser competitive aspect of their program for the other younger and less experienced players to learn and train to be varsity players.

The weight classes got larger through the years, as humans, at least football players, seem to be getting larger with time. Even though in this book for simplicity sake, I will continuously refer to the three weight classes as 80, 100 and 120, in reality they began as 78, 98 and 118 in 1972, and were around 85, 105, and 125 by 1980. They had actually started at 75,

95 and 115 in the 1960's. The weight classes were matched up by age (as of July 31) as follows: 80 lb./11 years old, 100 lb./12 years old and 120 lb./13 years old.

These weight classes were actually geared toward smaller kids. For example, a 120 lb kid could be 14 years old after August 1 that playing season, and in the 9th grade, and the average 9th grader would have actually been much larger. This allowed older, more mature kids who were small, like Mark Wheaton and Richie Guerin, among many others, to be star players, but at the same time, they were way too small to be on their 8th or 9th grade teams.

Wheaton played for the 120 lb. Colts at about 90 lbs., and often was the best player on the field. He definitely was the best pound for pound. Yet he was 14 and in 9th grade that year. This meant something else. That meant that it was unusual for a GYFC star to go on and play in college due to lack of size. A player like Tracy Soles at Central DeKalb was an exceptional kid. He and our Kevin Anthony happened to be late growers, in fact Kevin wound up to be about 6'3" and around 200 lbs as a college player.

The kids most likely to be successful in high school and college were those kids that were good enough to play a larger weight class as an underage player. Chuck Trense was one of our best players ever, and he played close to the weight limit, but was one year under age as an 11 year old 100 lb player and 12 years old as a 120 lb player. Cy Johnson was large, but younger by two years (10 years old/100 lb. team) and therefore not as mature as the older kids on the team, thus he was a reserve GYFC Colt player, yet he went on to be a star lineman at Woodward Academy in high school and played at a small college. Clayton Watson, youngest son of Coach Warren Watson, was another larger kid who had an ACYA, high school and college career similar to Cy Johnson. He was also a very good high school offensive lineman that went on to play at a small college.

The best and most accomplished player that I know of that ever played for the Colts would have been Troy Sadowski. Troy was underage as a 12 year old 120 lb player that was a reserve for our 1978 team. But he became an all state high school player, an all SEC and All American Tight End at Georgia and played 9 years in the NFL. His father had been a major league baseball pitcher, so Troy had an athletic background. He also grew to be 6'5" and around 250 lbs.

I probably saw close to all of the games Troy played in at UGA in person. If you asked Coach Vince Dooley, Troy was probably the best blocking Tight End ever, especially on their "toss sweep" play, and Georgia's NFL caliber running backs like Rodney Hampton, Tim Worley and Lars Tate have Troy to thank for many of the TD's they scored on that play in 1986-1988. When Georgia got inside the 10 yard line, a toss sweep was almost an automatic TD with Troy leading the way.

Troy was a good player for us but at only 12 years old, not quite good enough to edge out the two 14 year olds ahead of him. A year or two of age and maturity are very significant at that pre-teen young age, especially as a 12 year old 7th grade kid, when competing against 13 and 14 year old high school teenagers.

The GYFC subdivisions were re-aligned every two years in an attempt to keep the competitive balance in place and try and ensure that each program had their best opportunity to win a subdivision, and as I said through the years the weight classes got larger. Also, within every season, the players were allowed to gain weight during the year every few weeks, progressing by a pound every couple of weeks. A season that started at 80 lbs., 100 lbs. and 120 lbs in September would end at something like 86 lbs., 106 lbs. and 126 lbs by season's end in November.

The players had to weigh in and present a birth certificate as proof of age once in pre-season to be certified and eligible for the GYFC season, and then weigh again before every game. Players were rarely disqualified for being overweight, in fact I do not recall ever having one of our players miss a game due to being overweight but it was always a possibility.

The conference had a four team playoff system in each weight class, with each subdivision winner participating so the primary goal going into each year was to win the subdivision championship. The American subdivision winners would play each other as would the National, and the winners of those games advanced to the championship game, known as the Bobby Dodd Bowl. The Bobby Dodd Bowl was always played at Forest Park's Kiwanis Stadium, a large municipal facility where the Forest Park entry in GYFC played as their home field.

There was one exception. In 1974, the Bobby Dodd Bowl was played on the Astroturf of Grant Field, Georgia Tech's home stadium. The legendary Coach Dodd was in attendance most years as the game was an honor to bear his name.

The first round playoff game became known as the Jim Brazier Bowl in 1974. Mr. Brazier was a GYFC officer and board member, who had passed away in 1974, and the first round game was named in his honor and memory. The game was usually played at one of the local high schools, most often at St. Pius X High School.

The on the field game Officials used by GYFC were from two groups, Dixie High School Officials and I believe the other one was called the UYOA or "United." Many were high school officials whom we might see on a Friday night at a high school game, and then at our games the next day. There were many fine referees, Frank Murphy, Randall Barnett, John Dodson, Dick Davis among others. One of the absolute best was Robert Rouggieaux, (not sure of the spelling, but pronounced Roo G O) whom I have recently seen call games at UGA, and heard on TV as a SEC replay official. He was an outstanding football official as evidenced by his progression into the SEC.

Like the ACYA, the GYFC was ruled by a Board of Directors, but GYFC was chaired by a Commissioner. As in most sports organizations, the Commissioner was the final say on all matters. The member organizations also each had one vote and voted on matters of policy. In GYFC, there was a new Commissioner every two years. The actual playing rules followed the GHSA (Georgia High School Association) rules except the GYFC played four 10 minute quarters whereas the high schools played 12 minute quarters.

I always found the GYFC Board and Commissioners to be very fair and unbiased. Although there was some jealousy among other programs of the Colts due to our consistent winning and the fact that the ACYA was in one of the most affluent areas in Atlanta, it never appeared in GYFC rulings that I could see.

The following are the programs that made up the GYFC from 1972 to 1980:

Atlanta Colts	Buckhead Bandits
Sandy Springs Saints	Roswell Hornets
North DeKalb Chargers	Northeast Mustangs
East Point Volunteers	DeKalb Yellow Jackets
Tucker Lions	Midway Mighty Mites
Glenwood Panthers	Central DeKalb Cardinals
Smyrna Roadrunners	South Cobb Vipers
Forest Park Vikings	Clairmont Raiders
Briarcliff Eagles	Gresham Park Rattlers
North Decatur Rebels	Jonesboro Cardinals
Stone Mountain Pirates	

Each participating program had a conference representative. The Conference had mandatory meetings the first Monday night of every month throughout the year and the Representatives had to be there in case a vote was needed to determine the outcome of an issue, rule or policy change. The conference was very well run, efficient and organized.

I was the ACYA representative to GYFC from 1974 thru 1980, and David Johnson, Bob's younger brother and long time 100 lb. weight division Atlanta Colt Coach, was my predecessor.

The following volunteers with their prior GYFC program affiliations next to them, served as Commissioner of the GYFC between 1972 and 1980:

Eric Johnson, Roswell
Kline Pugh, Northeast
Bill Brandon, Midway
Bill Edmondson, Forest Park
George Chowning, Midway

The job of Commissioner or any other conference board member was, in my opinion, a thankless one. It took many hours of personal time and no doubt some hours out of the business day as well throughout the entire year. These men did not get the exciting part of GYFC which was the on the field coaching.

There was never a conflict of interest situation because the Board of Directors and Commissioner were not allowed to coach at the same time as serve in that capacity.

Their jobs were strictly administrative, and they were truly volunteers whose only gratification or reward was to serve the youth of metro Atlanta. They all did an outstanding job, each and every one, exhibiting a spirit of unbiased fair play, and with very little acknowledgement and recognition from either within or outside the Conference. They knew that the GYFC, like the ACYA, was a program for children.

I want to commend and thank them now for a job well done.

CHAPTER 4

The Atlanta Colt Players and "All Decade" Colt Teams from the 1970's.

80 lb. "Player of the Decade" Preston Coleman gaining yardage against Tucker in the 1973 Chattahoochee Bowl GYFC Playoff Game

The football players have always been the most important ingredient of the ACYA's success, and the kids (players and cheerleaders and Drill Team) were and still are what the ACYA is all about.

It was Bob Johnson's philosophy that hard work, thus demanding, but well organized and time efficient football practices, made for winning football, and player and character development. Colt players were subjected to grueling and demanding practices by all of the coaches, and that resulted in the winning record described in the following pages. Bob Johnson stressed a high emphasis on teaching during practice, thus so did the rest of our Colt coaches, continually teaching fundamentals every day. See Chapter 15 on Practice.

Colt players of that era were a proud and dedicated group, many of them still associate with one another today, and they were always willing to pay the price of hard work to achieve the lofty goals and expectations placed upon them by their predecessors. I know, because I pushed them very hard, and sometimes possibly a little too hard because of those expectations.

The Cheerleader and Drill Team squads worked just as hard in their own way, spending many hours in practice and rehearsal.

Bob Johnson was convinced that the teaching of competitive football to kids of this age was of great value to the physical and mental development and maturity of those kids, and those that chose to try out for a Colt team deserved the best efforts we adult coaches could give them. Bob always reminded us that it was ABOUT THE KIDS.

The following are what I believe were the most outstanding players from each weight class, position by position from all of the teams of the 1970's. Obviously, this is completely subjective on my part, and I tried my best to not show too much favoritism to those that played for me versus those that did not. I did not know as much about the 1970 and 1971 teams, but I was able to select some from those years based on what I observed, remembered and read in "The Mouthpiece." I certainly remember seeing Eddie Jackson, 120 lb. Colt Tailback (and the 120 lb. Player of the Decade) from Bob Johnson's great 1971 team. He was the complete player, big, fast, strong and tough. I also recall Running Back Blake Mitchell, and read a great deal about his outstanding play in "The Mouthpiece."

The 100 lb. Player of the Decade had to be Brian Jager. As I will say in following chapters, he was a once in a lifetime Running Back, and had an outstanding year in 1977 when the Colts swept all three GYFC weight divisions. The 80 lb. Player of the Decade is Fullback/Linebacker Preston Coleman. Not only did he have an outstanding offensive season in 1973, gaining over 230 yards from scrimmage in that year's Bobby Dodd Bowl, but he was also a very good blocker at Fullback, and a great defender as well where he played Outside Linebacker in Coach Doug Perreault's 4-4 scheme.

The success of each year's team had some bearing on the various positions awarded. I also factored in how many years the players played for the Varsity Colts, and a player that played both ways could have been awarded a position on either Offense or Defense, but not both.

For example, Kevin Schmidt and Mike Yancey were both very good Quarterbacks, but made the all decade team on defense. Kevin Anthony was a great Quarterback, but only played one year as a Colt. He was obviously a great player as he went on to be a starting QB in the Atlantic Coast Conference in college. Phillip Ebinger was an outstanding lineman for Bob Johnson's great 1974 team, but also only played one year as a Colt.

Another example of the difficulty of this task is that there were many outstanding Tailbacks for the 100 lb. Colts over the years, starting with 1970. I personally coached three in 1974, 75 and 76 that could have made it in Neil Brewer, Mike Coveny and Mark Wheaton. But as stated before, Brian Jager was probably the best of all and therefore earned the "All-Decade" designation. Mike Coveny made all decade based on his performance on the 1974 80 lb. team and Wheaton and Brewer made it on their defensive ability.

I also had some flexibility with many of these great players because some played as many as four years with the Colts. For example, no one was included from the 1976 120 lb. team, but many of those same players had made it from the 1975 100 lb. team or the 1974 80 lb. group, thus were not eligible to repeat as 120 lb. players. That made it easier to include as many different players as possible. No player made it more than one year and none at more than one position.

Note there are two 120 lb. Quarterbacks. These two, Blake and Reese were both great players, just too good to leave either one off this team. Also, Don and Ron Scott share one Linebacker position on the 100 lb. team. They were both great defensive players and identical twins. I literally could not tell them apart.

There were several other sets of brothers on these three all decade teams in addition to the Scott twins. The others were the Campbells, David, Clay and Mike; the Passarellas, Donnie and Kenny; the Chathams, Robert and Richard; and the Colemans, Preston and Craig.

Make no mistake about it, any player good enough to be a starter on a Varsity Colt team or even to make the team was a very good football player in their age and weight class. Certainly, many great players are not included on the all decade teams, and no slight was intended toward anyone. I repeat the story of Troy Sadowski, reserve Colt player, but then

All SEC/All American Tight End at Georgia with a 9 year NFL career. He must have been pretty good! QB Todd Rampley took his Peachtree High School team to the Georgia High School AAAA championship game, and then started for Georgia Tech in a NCAA Bowl Game, and there are likely many other similar stories of Colt players who went on to greatness that are not on this "All Decade" Team.

Like any all star team, it was extremely difficult to select, fun and challenging for the author, but impossible to be 100% accurate. But in my opinion, based on my own observations, and some research from "The Mouthpiece" yearbooks, the following pages show at least many of the best and most memorable from each weight class, and one player from each age/weight class (player of the decade) whose performance on that particular team stood out the most in my mind and in the "theoretical" record books.

*   *   *

Atlanta Colts 1970-79 "All-Decade" Team, 120 lb. Class

OFFENSE	Name	Year
End	Jimmy Costlow	1977
End	Chip Dickens	1974
Tackle	Frank Baynham	1973 @@
Tackle	John Hardie	1974
Guard	Pete Stephens	1977
Guard	Deane Johnson	1973
Center	Don Passarella	1972
Quarterback	Jimmy Blake	1974
Tie	Brad Reese	1970 @@
Fullback	Chris Welton	1971
Tailback	Eddie Jackson	1971* * *
Halfback	Blake Mitchell	1970

DEFENSE

End	Randy Smith	1978
End	Wade Doss	1972
Tackle	Robert Chatham	1973
Tackle	Ray Carlisle	1979
Nose Guard	Steve Oxford	1977
Linebacker	David Campbell	1971 @@
Linebacker	David Newby	1974
Linebacker	Tom Love	1973
Cornerback	Roger Rubinson	1977
Cornerback	Eric Kruel	1979
Safety	Kevin Schmidt	1973

Coach of the Decade, 120 lb. Class Bob Johnson 1974

*   *   *120 lb. Colts Player of the Decade Eddie Jackson, TB 1971

@@ Pop Warner All American

Atlanta Colts 1970-79 "All-Decade" Team, 100 lb. Class

OFFENSE

End .... Tommy Schreiber 1970
End .... Phillip Reeves 1974
Tackle .... Steve Noles .... 1975 @@
Tackle .... Tommy "T-Bird" Rose 1974
Guard .... Roger Shadburn 1978
Guard .... Mike Campbell 1972
Center .... Richard Chatham 1974
Quarterback .... Jeff Rummell 1971
Fullback .... Matt Putnal 1972
Tailback .... Brian Jager .... 1977 # *   *   *
Halfback .... Jimmy Wilson .... 1971 @@

DEFENSE

End .... Mike Ahern 1976
End .... Scott Young 1975
Tackle .... Chuck Trense 1976
Tackle .... Pat Standard 1979
Nose Guard .... Clay Campbell 1972
Linebacker .... Mike Sellers 1971
Linebacker .... Ron Scott/Don Scott 1975
Linebacker .... Petey Frye 1974
Cornerback .... Mike Yancey .... 1976 @@
Cornerback .... Neil Brewer 1974
Safety .... Mark Wheaton 1976

Coach of the Decade, 100 lb. Class David Johnson 1971

*   *   *100 lb. Colts Player of the Decade Brian Jager, TB . . . . 1977#

Pop Warner National Championship Team

@@ Pop Warner All American

Atlanta Colts 1970's "All-Decade" Team, 80 lb. Class

OFFENSE

End .... Frank Doherty........................ 1977#@@
End .... Scott Willis............................. 1972
Tackle........................... Richie Combs .... 1977#
Tackle........................... Ken Passarella 1973
Guard........................... Ron Barto .... 1973 @@
Guard........................... Steve Dodgen 1978
Center .... James Reinstein .... 1976#
Quarterback .... Frank Coulter........................ 1976#
Fullback .... Preston Coleman................... 1973 *   *   *
Tailback........................ Mike Coveny.......................... 1974
Halfback .... Craig Goldberg 1978

DEFENSE

End .... Phillip Barlow 1971
End .... Wesley Clark 1979
Tackle........................... Mike Stovall 1974
Tackle........................... Chris Sheffield...................... 1977#
Nose Guard.................. Craig Coleman...................... 1976#
Linebacker.................... Jeff Lineberger...................... 1973
Linebacker.................... Jim Caudill........................... 1975
Linebacker.................... John "Bubba" Rushing 1972
Cornerback .... Neil Gifford 1974
Cornerback .... Derek D'Alonzo .... 1977#
Safety .... Richie Guerin........................ 1973

Coach of the Decade, 80 lb Class Mac Scoggins . . . . 1976#

*   *   *80 lb. Colts Player of the Decade Preston Coleman, FB 1973

Pop Warner National Championship Team

@@ Pop Warner All American

CHAPTER 5

The Coaches

Colt Coaching Staff, L-R Fred Amtower, Doug Bennett, Warren Watson, Jim Lineberger, Frank Reeves

This chapter will be devoted to the coaches of the GYFC, starting with the other coaches from the Varsity Colts of the ACYA and then the coaches I knew the best from the rest of GYFC, and finally those that assisted me for the years I was a Head Coach . . . .

Bob Johnson, Atlanta Colts (1965-1976) . . . . Since all of Chapter One was devoted to Bob, I will not repeat much here. Suffice to say, I would state (with acknowledged bias) that Bob would be the best of all youth football coaches anywhere. Since installing his new Leonard Jones Offense in 1970, he was virtually unbeatable four of his seven final years, and very good the other three, while battling his kidney disease and on home dialysis most of that time. He was a great motivator and teacher. He stressed fundamental football, and paid great attention to details. He was conservative, but not afraid to take a risk at the right time. His players loved him and he taught them many lessons on and off the field. He was simply the greatest.

All successful football coaches have great assistant coaching staffs. Bob's long time assistants were Frank Greene, Chuck Willis and George Copelan. Frank was the Defensive Coordinator and an expert on the 5-2 Defense. Chuck was a backfield coach and worked primarily with the secondary. They were both very good coaches, and both Georgia Tech grads.

1974 120 lb. Colt Coaching Staff, L-R Chuck Willis, Tim Mitchell, George Copelan, Bob Johnson, Frank Greene

George Copelan was a true character as the Offensive Line Coach. He had a heavy southern accent, and always yelled the line splits to his players as a reminder before every scrimmage play in practice. He would yell "twenty foah, thutty, thutty six" reminding the players to split 24 "between Center and Guards, 30" between Guards and Tackles, and 36" between Tackles and Ends. He was a great teacher and motivator, continually emphasizing "have praaahd (pride)" in your work and strive for perfection to the players. He always kept the players in good spirits even in spite of the tough practices they were going through.

Larry Adams, 80 lb. Atlanta Colts, 1970 . . . . Larry was the head coach of the 80 lb. Colt team for one year, and had a record on 9-1-3, but did not qualify for the GYFC playoffs. I did not personally know him.

Mike Sellers, 80 lb. Atlanta Colts, 1971 . . . Mike coached the 80 lb. team for one year and brought home the GYFC Championship, and his team also was victorious in the Colt Classic. That 1971 80 lb. Colt team had an overall record of 11-2. He was a very nice and soft spoken man, but he looked like a Marine Drill Sergeant, thick shouldered with a flat top crew cut.

David Johnson, 100 lb. Atlanta Colts (1965-1971) . . . I believe that David was very much like his older brother Bob in most respects. He had similar success, but retired at an early age. I think he may have actually had a slightly better overall winning percentage than Bob did and he won the GYFC (and DYFC) 100 lb. weight class four consecutive years from 1968 to 1971. David basically disappeared from ACYA for a few years when his children were born, but he came back and coached them through the ACYA Interleague. He was a great coach and doubtless would have continued his winning ways had he remained with the 100 lb. Colts instead of retiring.

Jim Wilson, 100 lb. Atlanta Colts (1972-1973) . . . . Jim coached the 100 lb. Colts for only two years, undefeated and GYFC champs in 1972, and just falling short in 1973. I actually had the unenviable task of following Jim as 100 lb. Coach after his two year stint. Although we won the 100 lb. GYFC three consecutive years, we never managed the perfect season as Jim did in his first try. His undefeated 1972 team was one of the best Colt teams ever in any weight class.

1977 100 lb. Colt Coaching Staff, Clockwise from top: Mac Scoggins, Bob Carpenter, Alton Conway, Pat Eder, Charlie Ragan

Daniel McKee "Mac" Scoggins, Atlanta Colts 80 lb. (1974-1976) and 100 lb. (1977-1978) . . . . Mac was a very successful veteran of the ACYA Interleague and replaced me as 80 lb Varsity Coach in 1974 when I moved up to the 100 lb. Varsity level. He began using the Leonard Jones/Bob Johnson Offense from the start, and had instant success with a 10-0 regular season, but fell just short in the Jim Brazier Bowl first round playoff game, ending his first season 11-1 and finishing 3rd place in the GYFC. He had a co-championship the next year in 1975 with a 0-0 tie in the Bobby Dodd Bowl as the GYFC had changed from the GHSA Penetration Rule to settle ties, to a co-championship. He followed with GYFC and Pop Warner National Championships in 1976 with the 80 lb. Colts and in 1977 with the 100 lb. Colts. His 1977 team may well have been the greatest of all Colt teams, going 14-0 and a National Championship, and scoring over 450 points for the season. MAC SCOGGINS TEAMS NEVER LOST A REGULAR SEASON GYFC GAME and had a perfect 50-0 regular season record in his five year tenure in the GYFC, an absolutely incredible feat. HIS OVERALL RECORD AS A COLT HEAD COACH WAS 61-4-1 and he is the only ACYA coach to ever win back to back Pop Warner National Championships which he did in 1976-77. He was a great coach.

He also had a very good group of assistant coaches, led by Charlie Ragan, who ran the defense and Pat Eder, who coached the lines. Jim Awbrey, Bob Carpenter and Alton Conway assisted them, as well as a few others over the years. While completing this book, Coach Pat Eder passed away from Prostate Cancer in mid-December, 2010. In reading the funeral announcement, I recognized the names of his wife (Katie) and children. One of his daughters is married to former Colt player Dean Farber, another example of the "life long" relationships that begun in ACYA. Coach Pat Eder was a great guy and a great coach as well.

John Ramsey, 80 lb. Atlanta Colts (1977-1978) . . . . John was an original ACYA President and Staff member and coached in the ACYA Interleague. In 1975, he moved over to rival North DeKalb to start his GYFC coaching career. He won the GYFC 100 lb. subdivision championships in 1975 and 1976 losing to my Colt teams in Round one Jim Brazier Bowls both years. In 1977, he moved back to ACYA, coaching the 80 lb. Colts to the GYFC and Pop Warner National Championships in 1977 and just falling short in 1978.

Bill Sanders, 80 lb. Atlanta Colts 1979 . . . . Bill was a true Head Coach, in that he delegated play calling duties to coordinators Buddy Ragsdale on Offense and Jay Williams on Defense. He was a very successful businessman and a sound fundamental football coach. He became ACYA Athletic Director and did an excellent job in that role as well. His only team in the 1970's was in '79 when his team went to the Bobby Dodd Bowl and lost to rising power Glenwood. His was the coaching staff of the future, and they led the ACYA into the 1980's.

*   *   *

As you will see throughout the book, there were many outstanding coaches and competitors in the programs that made up the GYFC. Among the best in the 1970's were:

Virgil Sorrels, Glenwood . . . . I knew Virgil to be an intense rival of Bob Johnson, but also a friendly one. Bob had a lot of respect for Virgil. Glenwood was a team that would always give Bob a good, close game, and catch the occasional rare win. My 1977 120 lb. team faced Virgil's Glenwood team in the 1977 Bobby Dodd Bowl, with our side prevailing 15-6 in a tough, hard fought, but cleanly played game. He was very gracious after that loss. I would consider Virgil to be one of the best ever in GYFC.

C.K. Braswell, Midway . . . . Coach Braswell was probably Bob Johnson's all time arch rival. It was his stunting, twisting defense that defeated Bob's teams in 1968 and 1969, causing the retooling on offense that created Bob's dynasty of the 1970's. Bob's 120 lb. Colts scored the only points Coach Braswell's Midway team allowed in 1968 in two Midway victories that year. Coach Braswell's son was a kicker for the Georgia Bulldogs, and in order to attend his son's games, and also to avoid conflicting with Friday night high school football, Coach Braswell scheduled his home games on Thursday nights. Both Mac Scoggins and I learned that same new offense from Bob, so we have Coach Braswell (and Coach Leonard Jones) to thank as well.

Jerome Roberts, Briarcliff and Northeast . . . . Jerome was a very quiet man, but he was a smart, fierce competitor, and an excellent coach in football. Like Virgil Sorrels, his teams always played well against Bob Johnson's and Bob had a great deal of respect for Jerome as well. I also knew him to be very successful in baseball where I ran into him in the summers as I helped my friend Tom Haire with his travelling baseball team that was based in Roswell. Jerome was also very popular with his players and always recruited good ones. I recall facing his Northeast teams in 1978 and 1979 where he defeated us 7-0 in '78 and played to a tie in '79.

Dee Stanley, DeKalb Yellow Jackets . . . . Coach Stanley was another I did not know or ever compete against, but I had heard about him from Bob Johnson. In the 1971 Bobby Dodd Bowl, his team lost to Bob's Colts, 7-0, which was Bob's narrowest victory of the year. That in itself means that Coach Stanley was a very good coach.

Bill Eakin, Joe Cunningham, Central DeKalb . . . . These guys were consistently the toughest I faced. I never actually knew which was Head Coach, but they worked so well together. They coached great defense and sound, conservative offense. They actually defeated Bob Johnson in the

1976 120 lb. Bobby Dodd Bowl in Bob's last GYFC game. Three of my games with their Central DeKalb teams are highlighted in later chapters.

Charles Cook, Smyrna . . . . We faced Charles Cook teams a few times and they were always ready. His teams were very well coached and made very few mistakes. They always played very good defense. He gave us our worst loss ever on Colt Field, 24-0 in 1978 in the game that inspired our turnaround that year. He was very kind in defeat after we came back and won over his team two weeks later.

Jack Moore, Northeast . . . . Jack was the GYFC rep for Northeast and I got to know him well. We faced him a few times and every game was tough. He ruined our perfect record in 1974 with a 7-7 tie. His teams always defended us well, as he was a very good game planner and defensive coach.

Larry Rakestraw, Tucker . . . . Larry held many of the passing records at the University of Georgia for 30 years prior to Eric Zeier who played at UGA from 1991-94. Larry had set those records in the early 1960's. Larry was a QB for Coach Wally Butts at UGA, who was known as a very innovative offensive coach in the 1940's and 50's. Larry also played several years in the NFL as a QB, thus he had a brilliant knowledge of offensive football. As Tucker's offensive play caller, he gave us fits in many games, but most of all in 1974 GYFC Playoff round one, where we slipped by 21-20, and again in the 1975 regular season opener when his Tucker team prevailed 27-7. Tucker had many other fine coaches. Among them were "Jap" Keith, Eddie Sheppard, Mickey Grimmett and Jim Bell. Grimmett, Bell and Sheppard were GYFC representatives at different times. Tucker had an outstanding program with first class leadership, very good community support and nice facilities.

Jerry Gulledge, Midway . . . . Jerry had been an outstanding high school player at Avondale High in DeKalb County, which was a perennial power in the 50's, 60's and 70's and the school where most of the Midway players would go, so I suspect that Jerry may have played for Midway himself. His 1978 120 lb. team gave us our only loss ever in a Bobby Dodd Bowl in seven tries, so he makes the list based on that.

Paul Zarynoff, North DeKalb . . . . Paul joined the Chargers in the later '70's and was an instant success. He was a large red-faced man, and an intense competitor and rival, but he also was friendly and a very nice individual. He was a very good recruiter, which was very important in the 120 lb. class, and he successfully recruited the fastest 120 lb. player I ever saw, Mario Williams in 1978.

Mitchell Gibson, Emmitt Mullins, East Point . . . We always heard East Point coaches were city recreation employees, but I am not sure whether these two were or not. But they were very good coaches and Bob Johnson respected their teams greatly. They always played close, tough and hard hitting games.

Jack Aaron, Forest Park . . . Jack was a former Clemson Tiger and Philadelphia Eagle player. He coached with various teams at Forest Park through the years. I also knew him from business and he was a heck of a nice guy and obviously knew a lot about football.

* * *

Saving the best for last, the following are the coaches who assisted me through the years, in chronological order;

Don Whitehead, Assistant Coach, 1970-1971, ACYA Interleague Jets . . . . Don was a great guy, and in those early Interleague years, every coach coached everything. Don's son was a very good player and Don a very good assistant coach as well. Our teams were very successful and Don's steady advice had a lot to do with that success.

Warner Head, Offensive backfield, 1970-71, ACYA Interleague Jets, 1972-1974 Varsity Colts . . . . Warner was very serious, but the players liked him very much as well. He was an excellent QB coach, stressing the fundamentals of footwork, arm angle, release point etc. He also was very good with offensive play execution and special teams play. We started our coaching careers together and learned a lot together over the years. I was sad when he had to give up coaching due to career and family responsibilities. We had a great time working together and we remain good friends today.

Richie Guerin, Assistant Coach, 1971, ACYA Interleague Jets . . . Everyone knew that Richie was a named assistant in order to comply with rules that allowed little Richie to be placed on our 1971 Interleague team. As Head Coach of the NBA's Atlanta Hawks, he had very little time as his preseason and then regular season conflicted with ours. But he had committed to give it his best to participate as much as he could, and when the Hawks were in town, he came to our practices and participated in the actual practice. The players knew who he was and loved it and so did I. He was a very nice man, and had a great supportive family. He was a good friend to all of us for many years, and after retiring from the NBA coaching and GM roles, he moved back to his home city of New York. His son Richie was on my team for five years, two Interleague and three Varsity Colt.

Doug Perreault, Defensive Coordinator, 1972-1973 Varsity Colts . . . . Perreault is truly a one of a kind individual. He is very smart and has immense knowledge of football, and I learned quite a bit from him over the years. He has a great personality, and the players loved playing for him. In football, he possesses the perfect blend of kidding and having fun, combined with being tough and hard nosed with the players when needed. His 1973 defense gave up 15 points in 13 games, and his defenses only gave up 6 points in four GYFC playoff games and 0 points in two Colt Classic Bowl games.

Doug Perreault is a very smart guy, and he reveals that as a journalist, as he now writes a "good old boy" type column for a Dothan Alabama, newspaper with some funny and occasionally serious, but rarely cogent personal thoughts and observations, almost like an Alabama version of a "Seinfeld" TV show.

Steve Galezeski, Line Coach, 1972 Varsity Colts . . . Steve was a good all around coach, but primarily worked with the lines in 1972. He taught the fundamentals of blocking extremely well and our line showed continuous improvement throughout that year, finishing as GYFC champs.

Warren Watson, Offensive Line 1973-1978 Varsity Colts . . . Warren was a great offensive line coach. From the time we learned our new offense (the afore-mentioned Leonard Jones system), we had consistently strong performing line play. Warren taught the fundamentals of the offensive line play in every practice throughout the year, and the line always improved throughout every year due to that continuous teaching of fundamental blocking techniques and assignments. Warren was also a very good game scout and always helped scout upcoming opponents and assisted with game planning. He was a retired High School Football Official, and thus had very good knowledge of rules which also was very helpful in teaching individual techniques and interpreting rule enforcement, penalty calls etc.

Jim Lineberger, Defensive Coordinator, 1974-1978 Varsity Colts . . . Jim knew the 5-2 Defense like no one else. He taught the fundamentals of line (along with Coach Watson) and Linebacker play. In his defense, he liked to stunt a lot and had an uncanny ability to plan where the stunt needed to go to combat the upcoming play. Coaching defensive stunts is similar to coaching offensive plays as the timing and spacing of the involved players is vital. He also scouted for us, and we spent many hours reviewing game film, scouting reports and game planning at his house over the five years we coached together. Jim was Head Coach of the 1979 100 lb. Colt team, where they made it all the way to the Bobby Dodd Bowl, falling just short of the Championship with a close loss in that game.

Jim Lineberger, from Macon, Georgia was a brilliant man. He was a small college football player at Carson Newman College in Tennessee and a career BellSouth engineer, and he could fix anything, mechanical or otherwise. He also had a couple of funny sayings that I repeat often today. First, when going over scouting reports and talking about an upcoming opponent's tendencies, he would often say "A leopard don't change his spots!" In other words meaning the opponent will continue to do the same things they've always done to be successful. I still use that saying occasionally in everyday life.

Another famous Lineberger quote that I often repeat in the current life: when we were discussing a player's performance in post game and I would suggest that one of his defensive players had played a very good game, Jim's usual preliminary comment was "He done all right!" He was not ready to hand out real praise until he had reviewed the game film and made sure the assignments were properly carried out.

Today, when discussing someone's performance whether an athlete or someone in business, a colleague or friend might praise someone else's performance and I will often simply say "As Coach Lineberger used to say "He (or She) done all right!" "Or, if pertaining to myself I might say "I done all right."

Fred Amtower, Defensive Secondary, 1974, 1976-1978 Varsity Colts . . . Fred had played football at Georgia with the afore-mentioned Larry Rakestraw of Tucker, as an Offensive and Defensive Halfback in the era of one platoon football. He was a true jokester and the players loved to kid with him, but he knew his job and did it well. He was very good at teaching secondary footwork, keeping proper angles in coverages, and open field tackling to the individual players. He also was a good punter and was instrumental in helping our punters with their techniques.

"Freddie" was a true character. He was a very cool guy, a former UGA player of the rough and tumble Wally Butts era that produced carousing characters like Pat Dye, Norman King, Fred Brown, Cicero Lucas and on and on. Freddie was one of the lesser known but I'm sure more popular of that crowd. A very successful straight laced IBM'er of the dark suit and white shirt and tie era during the business day, but a different person away from the business world.

He had a couple of funny things about him that stand out in memory. The first was a pair of white patent high heeled platform shoes, right out of the disco days of the '70's. I'm sure they were quite fashionable when they were new and he wore them to the disco joints like Elan' and others. But he kept them forever and a few years later I saw him wear them to football practice, doing yard work and the funniest of all was he actually waded in the Chattahoochee River trout fishing in them. The other thing was his car "Old White," a white wood-grained Pontiac Station Wagon (about 1973 model) that was expensive and beautiful when new, but he drove it forever. His wife Beverly urged him to trade for a new model after a few years but he refused to give up on it as it aged, like a badge of honor. Thus as it grew older, "old White" became more and more significant as a name. Freddie was a true friend to all, and a very good football coach as well. I drive a 10 year old Jeep today in memory of Old White.

Frank Reeves, Offensive Backfield, 1975-1978 Varsity Colts . . . Frank was more of a part time coach as he traveled internationally for his job with an apparel manufacturer. He was very helpful, particularly on game days as he was our press box game day scout. He consistently provided me with useful information assisting with play calling for offense, and did the same for Jim Lineberger's defense. I suspect that if I saw Frank and we had time to talk about the days of the Colts, he would remind me of the 4th and 2 pass play call in the 1974 Bobby Dodd Bowl. At least he usually talks about that. His son Phillip caught that pass for the opening TD in a 21-0 win.

Billy Martin, Ends and Linebackers, 1979-1980 Varsity Colts . . . Billy had been an All-American one platoon (playing both ways) End at Georgia Tech for Bobby Dodd and played several years in the NFL. He was a storehouse of football knowledge, likely having forgotten more than many would ever know. He was a valuable resource as we rebuilt our coaching staff in 1979. Billy was very good at coaching individual skills, breaking down opponents' tendencies and preparing game plans, and he was an extremely nice guy and a joy to work with.

Doug Cooper, Defensive Coordinator, Secondary Coach, 1979-1980 Varsity Colts . . . Coach Cooper was another true character, I can't really talk about most of his exploits, but he certainly knew his defense very well. He had given us strategic advice in the past year prior to joining us just as an observer, and I was anxious to have him run our defense when Jim Lineberger left. Doug was also a one platoon player for Coach Dodd at Tech and in the NFL as well. Both Cooper and Martin were a few years older than me and I had actually seen them play in games at Tech as a young fan. I believe Doug really could have coached at any level, and he was very good at teaching his players tackling, pass coverages, how to read their keys and diagnose opposing offenses.

Both Cooper and Martin with Georgia Tech faced Fred Amtower and Larry Rakestraw of UGA in actual games in their college careers.

Bill Schmitz, Offensive Line, 1979-1980 Varsity Colts . . . Coach Schmitz was a perfect replacement for Warren Watson. Although he had a completely different style, he would turn his hat around backwards and get down on the ground and demonstrate the actual techniques he was teaching. He had excellent knowledge of our system and did a great job for us. He was an exciting personality and beloved by his players.

Bob Thomas, Ends, 1980 Varsity Colts . . . Coach Thomas was a veteran Colt Coach, actually having coached with Bob Johnson in Bob's last year. He was very athletic himself and was an excellent teacher of the fundamentals of pass receiving, blocking and defensive end play.

There you have the list of outstanding men and football coaches that made up the ACYA and GYFC that it played in. There are many more good ones that unfortunately were omitted, but these are the ones I knew the best.

SECTION 2

What Happened on the Playing Fields in the "Decade of the Colts"

Author's Note: The following chapters provide a summary of the varsity Colt teams seasons at the beginning of each chapter and explain how each team fared that year in GYFC competition. Then after the summary, there are several pages with a lot of detail on my own team's seasons and our teams' individual performances for the years 1970 thru 1979. Most of the details are from my own recollections and reviewing game films, with some information coming from the ACYA's Yearbook, which was titled "The Mouthpiece."

CHAPTER 6

The Beginning of the Decade, 1970, 1971

1970 Varsity Colt Summary

The Varsity Colts won GYFC Championships in the 120 and 100 lb. weight Classes, led by Bob and David Johnson.

The 120 lb. Colts scored 314 points and allowed only 26. They won the Bobby Dodd Bowl over arch rival Midway by the score of 19-0, holding Midway to net yardage of minus 10.

In post season, they won over Vienna, Virginia 28-6 in the Colt Classic and then fought the always tough Ft. Myers Rebels to a scoreless tie in the Rebel Bowl in Ft. Myers, Florida, finishing the year with 13 wins and 1 tie.

This team was coached by Bob Johnson and Bob was assisted by Bucky Jenkins, George Copelan and Chuck Willis. They had an outstanding Quarterback in All-American Brad Reese and Running Back in Blake Mitchell.

The 100 lb. Colts were also victorious in the third consecutive Bobby Dodd Bowl by defeating Sandy Springs 21-0. Their post season was perfect, with wins over Vienna, Virginia 35-6 and the Ft. Myers Rebels 47-6. They were coached by David Johnson, assisted by Tim Mitchell and Ronnie Brown.

They were led by QB Mike Killeen, and Running Back Billy Todd in the backfield and linemen, Alan Neal, Bob Chamberlain and Mark Adams. This great team suffered one regular season loss to tough East Point, but finished 13-1.

The 80 lb. Colts also had a successful season, going 7-1-2 in regular season, but just fell short of the subdivision championship and thus did not qualify for the GYFC playoffs.

They also had a good post season, defeating Alexandria, Virginia in the Colt Classic and playing Roswell, Georgia to a 14-14 tie in the Powder Springs Charity Bowl.

Larry Adams was the head coach of this team and he was assisted by Pat Eder, Jim Boulware and Mike Sellers.

The overall varsity Colt record for 1970 was 35-2-4.

*   *   *

1971 Varsity Colt Summary

The Varsity Colts had a clean sweep in 1971, winning the GYFC Bobby Dodd Bowl in all three weight classes.

The 80 lb. Colts were coached by Mike Sellers and had a 11-2 record, losing to powerful Midway and East Point in regular season. However, they won their subdivision and defeated Tucker 7-0 in the GYFC Semi-Final Chattahoochee Bowl.

They went on to defeat Smyrna 20-0 in the GYFC Bobby Dodd Bowl Championship game, bringing home the championship trophy in the 80 lb. weight class, for only the second 80 lb. Championship in ACYA and GYFC history. They also defeated the Kendall Cowboys from Miami in the post season Colt Classic by the score of 42-7.

The 80 lb. Colts were led all year by Billy Huntley, the Interleague superstar that I will mention in the following pages, who had played for Mac Scoggins's ACYA Interleague Cowboys the previous year. That was proof positive that the Interleague functioned as Bob Johnson had designed it, as a training ground for future varsity players.

The 100 lb. Colts won their fourth straight GYFC Championship led by Head Coach David Johnson. They had a perfect 14-0 record, outscoring the opposition 286 points to 47 allowed.

The 100 lb. Colts squeaked by the tough East Point Vols 7-0 in the Chattahoochee Bowl, and then easily handled the North Decatur Rebels 27-7 in the Bobby Dodd Bowl. They were led all year by QB Jeff Rummell and Running Back Jimmy Wilson.

They also defeated Kendall of Miami 10-6 in the Colt Classic, and went on to beat the Ft. Myers Rebels 14-0 in the Rebel Bowl, held in Ft. Myers on December 9, 1971.

The 1971 120 lb. Colts were certainly one of Bob Johnson's very best, going 14-0, and scoring 408 points while allowing 63. They won every game by more than 10 points, except for the Bobby Dodd Bowl, where they won over the stubborn DeKalb Yellow Jackets, 7-0. They easily defeated Tucker 28-0 in the GYFC Chattahoochee Bowl.

In post season, they beat Kendall of Miami 28-6 in the Colt Classic and the very tough Ft. Myers Rebels, 24-8 in the Rebel Bowl.

They had a fantastic backfield led by Quarterback Mike Killeen. Killeen was not very big, but he was like a magician with the ball. He was joined by 120 lb. "Player of the Decade" Tailback Eddie Jackson, the best ever and Halfback Billy Todd, a clutch performer. The Fullback was Chris

Welton, a future Peachtree High School left handed Quarterback. Welton went on to be a starting defensive back on the Georgia Bulldogs' 1980 National Champions. David Campbell was also a super Linebacker that led the defense all year.

Thus, 1971 was a banner year for the Atlanta Colts and a first in history, as the Colts swept the GYFC championships. The 100 lb and 120 lb. teams were undefeated and a combined 28-0. Adding the 11-2 record of the 80 lb. Colts, the overall record was an incredible 39-2.

After attending the Bobby Dodd Bowls and Colt Classic games as a spectator, I was proud to be part of this program as an Interleague coach. When asked by Bob Johnson to join the 80 lb. Colts in the Spring of 1972, I could not say yes fast enough!

*   *   *

1970 120 lb. Atlanta Colts Record, 13-0-1

GYFC Champions
Atlanta Colt Classic Champions
Rebel Bowl Co-champions

Colts 21 North DeKalb 0
Colts 27 Central DeKalb 0
Colts 20 DeKalb
Yellow Jackets 0
Colts 20 North Decatur 0
Colts 28 Forest Park 6
Colts 26 Briarcliff 6
Colts 21 East Point 0

Colts 27 Clairmont 0
Colts 19 Midway 7
Colts 27 Smyrna 0

GYFC Championship, The Bobby Dodd Bowl, Kiwanis Stadium, Forest Park, Georgia

Colts 19 Midway 0

Atlanta Colt Classic, Colt Field, Murphy Candler Park, Atlanta, Georgia

Colts 28 Vienna, Virginia 6

Rebel Bowl, Fort Myers, Florida

Colts 0 Ft. Myers 0

1970 120 lb. Atlanta Colts Complete Roster

Cody Canarro	Tommy Dutton
Gene Geeslin	Blake Mitchell
Scott Shattuck	Eddie Jackson
Frank Hovey	David Campbell
Mickey Maynard	Tom Sheahan
Clay Herzwurm	Bruce Walters
Tom Baynham	Drew McKay
Jeff Addington	Mike Samples
Tim Hickman	Mike Reed
Forrest Lee Logan	Rob Bruce
Bill Halbert	Jimmy Grissett
Doug Hoechst	Bucky Vaughn
Brad Reese	David Silkner
Randy Greene	Scott Balfour
Tom Higgins	Bud Schreiber
Tim Bright	Kim Reitman

Coaches

Bob Johnson Head Coach
George Copelan
Chuck Willis
Bucky Jenkins

1970 100 lb. Atlanta Colts Record, 13-1-0

GYFC Champions
Atlanta Colt Classic Champions
Rebel Bowl Champions

Colts 52 North DeKalb 0
Colts 57 Central DeKalb 0
Colts 20 DeKalb
Yellow Jackets 0
Colts 27 North Decatur 0
Colts 44 Forest Park 13
Colts 30 Briarcliff 0
Colts 27 Midway 13
Colts 13 East Point 21
Colts 46 Clairmont 0
Colts 28 Smyrna 0

GYFC Championship, The Bobby Dodd Bowl, Kiwanis Stadium, Forest Park, Georgia

Colts 28 Sandy Springs 0

Atlanta Colt Classic, Colt Field, Murphy Candler Park, Forest Park, Georgia

Colts 35 Vienna, Virginia 0

Rebel Bowl, Fort Myers, Florida

Colts 47 Ft. Myers 0

1970 100 lb. Atlanta Colts Complete Roster

Mark Hagen
Bubba Combs
Mark Adams
Jeff Rummell
Paul Bradford
Mark Geeslin
Steve Clifford
Billy Todd
Cary Henderson
Doug Olds
Todd Shattuck
Ray Arkey
Jim Hart
Mark Elliott
Mike Killeen
Mark Barre
Gregg Roy

Billy Spruill
Tommy Schreiber
Scott Doster
Paul Scott
Danny Arnhart
Don Passarella
Jimmy Carter
Chris Eidson
Brent Treadway
Clay Silkner
Mike Veselick
Bob Chamberlain
Alan Neal
Richard Panachida
David Balfour
George Brown

Coaches

David Johnson Head Coach
Tim Mitchell
Ronnie Brown

1970 80 lb. Atlanta Colts Record, 9-1-3

Atlanta Colt Classic Champions
Powder Springs Charity Bowl Co-champions

Colts 40 North DeKalb 0
Colts 18 Central DeKalb 0
Colts 26 DeKalb
Yellow Jackets 0
Colts 6 North Decatur 6
Colts 20 Forest Park 0
Colts 13 Briarcliff 0
Colts 0 Midway 0

Colts 0 East Point 16
Colts 25 Clairmont 0
Colts 39 Smyrna 0

Atlanta Colt Classic, Colt Field, Murphy Candler Park, Atlanta, Georgia

Colts 19 Alexandria,
Virginia 0

Powder Springs Charity Bowl, Powder Springs, Georgia

Colts 14 Roswell 14**

** Roswell wins by GHSA Penetration Tie Breaker Rule 16-15

1970 80 lb. Atlanta Colts Complete Roster

Rich Wampler
Walter James
Joe Jensen
Rob Van Gorder
Dirk Spier
Tom Arckey
Mike Surman
Jeff D'Alonzo
Bill Browne
Don Fuller
Mike Campbell
Wade Doss
Jerry Romberg
Jim Blake
Arthur Hood
Mark Love

Rodney Combs
Tony Jackson
Mike Higgins
John Conway
Bart Pangburn
Brian Bazemore
David Dayton
Ricky Carter
Don NeSmith
Tony Scoggins
Mark Grisset
Daryl Batson
John Rushing
Jimmy Myers
Brent Hendricks

Coaches

Larry Adams Head Coach
Pat Eder

Jim Boulware
Mike Sellers

1970 Atlanta Coltettes Drill Team

Sheril Powers
Jody Levine
Vangie Thomas
Karen Krauss
Jenny Hampton
Best Regelis
Mary Robinson
Karen Davis
Barbara Lavoie
Cheryl Buchannan
Holly Matthews
Kathy Grissett

Susan Rushing
Pam Davis
Nancy Autrey
Vicki Davis
Patsy McGhee
Lori Kumin
Mary Scaramellino
Linda Dioguardi
Reba Young
Lynn Powers
Cynthia Elliott
Vesta Schillaci

Directors

Meta Ramsey
Karen Johnson

1971 120 lb. Atlanta Colts Record 14-0

GYFC Bobby Dodd Bowl Champions
Atlanta Colt Classic Champions
Rebel Bowl Champions

Colts 39 South Cobb 0
Colts 27 Buckhead 7
Colts 33 Roswell 0
Colts 21 North DeKalb 0
Colts 20 Midway 7
Colts 35 Northeast 0
Colts 24 Glenwood 7
Colts 35 East Point 7
Colts 56 Briarcliff 21

GYFC Semi Finals, Chattahoochee Bowl, Roswell High School, Roswell, Georgia

Colts 28 Tucker 0

GYFC Championship, The Bobby Dodd Bowl, Kiwanis Stadium, Forest Park, Georgia

Colts 7 DeKalb
Yellow Jackets 0

Atlanta Colt Classic, Colt Field, Murphy Candler Park, Atlanta, Georgia

Colts 28 Kendall 6

Rebel Bowl, Ft. Myers High School Stadium, Ft. Myers, Florida

Colts 24 Ft. Myers 8

1971 120 lb. Atlanta Colts Complete Roster

Randy Olday	Billy Todd
Chris Eidson	Steve Fallon
Mark Elliott	Tim Underhill
Greg Lambert	Tom Schreiber
Tommy Ellis	Bruce Walters
Billy Spruill	Bill Turner
Ken Fody	Eric Roberts
Rusty O'Shields	Chris Welton
Joe Hovey	Dale Dean
Mike Killeen	Kevin Thompson
Jimmy Carter	Mac Broughton
Bob Chamberlain	Eddie Jackson
Steve Schwartz	Richard Panachida
David Balfour	John Boyle
David Campbell	Alan Neal
George Brown	Mickey Dolan

Coaching Staff

Bob Johnson Head Coach
Frank Greene
Chuck Willis
George Copelan

Cheeleaders

Jenny Johnson	Leslie Ragan
Ann Chamberlain	Kathy Ward
Debi Surmay	Beth Markley
Jan Markley	Julie Gaar
Robin Rummel	Nancy Carter
Susan Rushing	Susie Willis

1971 100 lb. Atlanta Colts Record, 14-0

GYFC Bobby Dodd Bowl Champions
Atlanta Colt Classic Champions
Rebel Bowl Champions

Colts 35 South Cobb 0
Colts 17 Buckhead 0
Colts 20 Roswell 12
Colts 21 North DeKalb 0
Colts 21 Midway 0
Colts 14 Tucker 6
Colts 48 Northeast 6
Colts 10 Glenwood 0
Colts 14 East Point 7
Colts 7 Briarcliff 3

GYFC Semi-Finals, The Chattahoochee Bowl, Roswell High School, Roswell, Georgia

Colts 7 East Point 0

GYFC Championship, The Bobby Dodd Bowl, Kiwanis Stadium, Forest Park, Georgia

Colts 27 North Decatur 7

Atlanta Colt Classic, Colt Field, Murphy Candler Park, Atlanta, Georgia

Colts 10 Kendall of
Miami 6

Rebel Bowl, Ft. Myers High School, Ft. Myers, Florida

Colts 14 Ft. Myers 0

1971 100 lb. Atlanta Colts Complete Roster

Dan Arnhart
Tony Jackson
Mark Love
Mike Sellers
Tim Nix
David Roberman
Walter James
Vic Harper
Don Passarella
Steve Hardy
Bill Griffith
Paul Scott
Roger Logan
Joe Jensen
Jimmy Wilson
Robert Chatham
Bill Asip

Allan Cummings
Eric Spitler
Ricky Carter
Frank Baynham
Steve Clifford
Skeet Pinkerton
John Conway
Jeff Rummell
Mark Grissett
Clay Silkner
Brett Perkins
Todd Shattuck
Matt Putnal
Mike Perdue
Mike Romano
Mike Campbell

Coaching Staff

David Johnson Head Coach
Tim Mitchell
Ronnie Brown

Cheerleaders

Aileen Griffith
Susan Passarella
Tricia Hickman
JoEllen Hough
Tobie Pinkerton
Sharon Eikey

Cristine Jensen
Pam Mathis
Pam Pillert
Laurie Hooker
Susan Moddelmog
Rita Romano

1971 80 lb. Atlanta Colts Record, 11-2

GYFC Bobby Dodd Bowl Champions
Atlanta Colt Classic Champions

Colts 2 South Cobb 0
Colts 12 Buckhead 0
Colts 13 Roswell 6
Colts 6 North DeKalb 0
Colts 0 Midway 21
Colts 14 Tucker 6
Colts 20 Northeast 6
Colts 13 Glenwood 0
Colts 6 East Point 20
Colts 13 Briarcliff 0

GYFC Semi-Finals, The Chattahoochee Bowl, Roswell High School, Roswell, Georgia

Colts 7 Tucker 0

GYFC Championship, The Bobby Dodd Bowl, Kiwanis Stadium, Forest Park, Georgia

Colts 20 Smyrna 0

Atlanta Colt Classic, Colt Field, Murphy Candler Park, Atlanta, Georgia
Colts 42 Kendall 7

1971 80 lb. Atlanta Colts Complete Roster

Billy Huntley
Steve Thielen
Paul Markley
Kirby Davis
Jamie Roberson
Jimmy Arnhart
Wade Doss
John Rushing
Jeff Matthews
Robert Holgate
Randy Addington
Jim Blake
Bobby Fink

Rich Wampler
Mark Davis
Jimmy Myers
Scott Willis
John Loughery
Scott Clayton
Gerry Romberg
Reed Barlitt
Phillip Barlow
Robert Van Gorder
Deane Johnson
Mark Howard
Bill Brown

Coaching Staff

Mike Sellers Head Coach
Carl Harris
Tom Hartley

Cheerleaders

Lynn Rushing
Beth Doss
Cindy Wilson
Kay Connano
Carolyn Romberg
Lisa Rowlette

Libby Wampler
Kathy Anderson
Cindy Zembzuski
Beth Blake
Lisa Balfour
Jeanne Blake

1971 Coltettes Drill Team

Tracey Husband	Kathy Goodwin
Sherrill Powers	Jody LeVine
Ellen Morrissey	Debbie Hope
Diane Hope	Karen Pahl
Jennifer Newberry	Janet Newberry
Susan Neal	Diane Odom
Renee Lambert	Valerie Wigginton
Kathy Davis	Stephanie Wildes
Carolyn Cathcart	Linda Dioguardi
Reba Young	Kathy Grissert
Cheryl Healy	Susan Schultz
Mary Scaramellino	Lynn Powers

Director

Meta Ramsey

*   *   *

1970-71, Two Years Pinto League (ACYA Interleague) Jets

As I mentioned earlier, I started in 1969 as a 21 year old with the Yearling League Jets, 7 and 8 year old kids and I was an Assistant Coach that first year along with my friends Doug Perreault, Warner Head and a parent on that team, Warren Watson. Steve Galezeski was the Head Coach. We had a successful year which I thoroughly enjoyed. We carefully scouted every opponent, and devised game plans to stop their best plays. The young players were eager to learn. Almost all Touchdowns came on long runs and if you could stop your opponents best play, your defense could usually pitch a shutout, which we did winning all but one game.

After a fun and successful year in '69, I didn't really expect to continue in ACYA. Doug Perreault had moved to Miami, and Warner Head was married and busy with business travel. I was about to graduate college and my primary concern at that time was graduating and starting some kind of business career. My other hobby was fishing, mostly freshwater bass, which I did as often as possible. I also had a beginning interest in golf, which is my primary hobby today.

However, that summer of 1970, I received a call from John Ramsey, ACYA Interleague Director, who asked me to consider being Head Coach of the Pinto League Jets, 8 and 9 year old boys.

I wasn't sure I was up to it, and I was very reluctant and even a little scared, but after talking to friends, Doug Perreault and Warner Head, whom I had coached with the prior year, I decided to give it a try and Warner agreed to be my top assistant coach. We got together with Don Whitehead, another great guy who would be our other assistant coach, and his son Dal would be our quarterback. They had been on the previous year's team. That was a good head start, as Dal was a very good player and QB is always the most important player to identify.

The Interleague was set up very fairly, each team could have only two pre-chosen players, which were coaches' sons. That was imperative to allow interleague coaches to coach their own kids. As volunteers, a coach might not be as ready to spend the time required to do a good job of coaching if they could not coach their own child. Almost all of the interleague coaches had sons in the program. Many also had daughters who could be involved as cheerleaders.

So, to avoid "stacking" of teams, it was the rule that the first two coaches, head coach and first assistant, could set aside their sons in place of the first two automated draft choices. Neither Warner nor I had sons, so we only had one pre-selection and that was Dal Whitehead.

Since most of the coaches' sons were good players, we were a little set back to begin with. Including the first two coaches' selections, all players were graded A thru C in tryouts and assigned to their teams by a computer system, evenly distributing the grades A thru C, again very fair. There was no draft, except as assigned by the computer.

John Ramsey ran the Interleague like a dictator, and he was totally focused on fair competition, no favoritism and 100% rule enforcement. Bob Johnson, as Athletic Director, echoed and supported those philosophies and Bob and John were completely in synch when it came to running the interleague.

So we started practice in early August with our eyes on the opening game in early September. We used basic I formation offensive plays and a 4 front defense. We called blitzes "storming" which I copied from Coach Hank Stram, whose Kansas City Chiefs had won the previous season's Super Bowl.

One thing we did that I believe was always very instrumental in our success was heavy emphasis on individual player skills of blocking and tackling. That always served us well, and we worked on these fundamentals all year long in practice, virtually every day.

As luck would have it, my brother Don was getting married to his wife Susan at the University of North Carolina the same Saturday as our first game, so I actually missed my first game as a Head Coach. I called Warner later that day as he had filled in for me, to learn we had won, something like 12-6. He gave me many details which I cannot remember at all.

But one thing is easy to remember and that was I am sure that our TB Stuart Holloway scored touchdowns as he had many long runs that year. We were lucky to have gotten Stuart Holloway straight out of a computer, and he proved to be every bit as good as any player in our league, with the possible exception of one named Billy Huntley, son of Bill and Gladys, and older brother of Chet.

The most memorable games for me are always losses, so my most vivid memory of 1970 was our only loss, which was to Mac Scoggins's Cowboys. I remember three things most about that game:

1. Mac had Billy Huntley clearly the best player in the Pinto League that year and he hurt us with long runs, even though we knew

about him from scouting, and thought we were prepared to defend him,

2. We scored one of our touchdowns on a throw back delay pass from Dal Whitehead to our weakside end Scott Willis from about 40 yards,

3. I had a casual acquaintance who was a parent on the Cowboys. His name was Max Frye and he was next door neighbor to a good friend of mine, Joe Fowler. Max's son, Max II "Petey" was on the Cowboys. Max was a volunteer on the chain crew this day and he kidded me after Billy Huntley's first long TD run on the Cowboys' first possession, and said "don't worry Coach, you haven't even had the ball yet."

"Petey" Frye would become an integral part of our first three years of varsity Colt teams.

We wound up losing 20-13, but it was very exciting and I was proud of our team for coming back. In fact, we came back twice in that game. I think we went 6-1-1 that year, but missed playoffs due to the Cowboy loss as the Scoggins led Cowboys had gone undefeated and would win the championship.

Other players from that team other than Stuart, Dal and Scott were Lineman Scott Clayton, Center Marshall Gaines, FB Rich Papineau, LB Ricky Jennings, OL Kevin Cornett, HB David Nesmith and DB Preston Coleman (a future Colt superstar). We worked hard all year, practiced in heavy rain at times, but were rewarded with moderate success, and a determination to improve.

So, in 1971, Warner, Don Whitehead and I agreed to coach the Jets again, but Dal Whitehead had to move up to the Pony league because of his age, so we had no coach's son to start our team with. Then came another pleasant surprise, as I received an unexpected call from Richie Guerin, the Head Coach of the NBA's Atlanta Hawks.

We had coached 7 year old little Richie in 1969 and he wanted to play for us again. The only way to ensure that little Richie could be on our team was to make big Richie an assistant coach, and therefore we could have little Richie on our team as a Coach's son. Richie was a very good player and we built our team around him. Richie would then play the next three Colt years with us. Big Richie was a great guy as well, and actually worked with us in practice even after the Hawks season started.

We had another celebrity on our team, Atlanta Braves pitcher Pat Jarvis's son, Kent. He had a fireplug build like his dad, and he was a tough and steady linebacker for us all year. We were also joined by Jeff Amtower, whose dad, Fred was a former UGA player, having played for Wally Butts and then Butts's successor Johnny Griffith. I think he missed playing for Vince Dooley by one year, maybe two.

Jeff Amtower was also a good player and played in the offensive backfield and defensive backfield, and would also play the next three Colt years. Fred became a very good friend and a valuable Colt assistant coach as well. Preston Coleman came back and played another Jets year and then the next three Colt years, so I had a very close continuing relationship with those three kids. Preston improved every year and turned out to be a truly great Colt performer, gaining over 200 yards in one game in 1973. In Chapter 4 of this book, Preston Coleman is named 80 lb. Colt "Player of the Decade."

In 1971, we also had LB Paul Thacker another tough kid as a "B" rated player. Jeff Coats, was a FB and LB and was the hardest hitter of all of them. I had film of him "pancaking" an opposing Linebacker on an off tackle play against Scoggins's Cowboys clearing the way for a Coleman TD which was the only score in a 6-0 victory in that game. That allowed me to even my record to 1-1 against Mac and fortunately we were always on the same side after that.

The 1971 Jets also had great defensive tackles, Donnie Rutledge, who Doug Perreault called a "Junior Bob Lilly" and Steve Dinapoli, who was very quick and fast for a DT.

The 1971 Jets went 7-1-1, with three memorable games. The aforementioned win against the Cowboys, a midseason win against the Vikings, another good team, in the rain, where we won 7-0. That game was highlighted by a long TD drive, directed by QB Chuck Hart about 10 plays and 60 yards, for the game's only score. That was quite a feat at any time in 9 year old football, much less on a sloppy day.

The other memorable game was a loss to the Broncos, 18-0. The Broncos were a great team, coached by Attorney Bill Hurst. Their best player was his son John, another just like Billy Huntley, big, fast and mature for the age group. They also had David Nesmith, who had played for my 1970 Jets team. Both would play for the 80 lb. Colts in 1972.

The loss was devastating. It was a late season showdown of undefeated teams, the winner to be league champion. They were 8-0 and we were 7-0-1. We drew first blood with an 80 yard TD by Guerin on a punt return, but it was called back by a clipping penalty. The call back took the starch out of us, and shortly after, the Broncos went ahead 6-0 on a long run by Hurst.

Then Bronco player David Nesmith stole the ball from one of our backs and ran it in for a TD. It was simply a great play by David giving the Broncos a two TD lead, insurmountable against their great team.

It put a damper on the year for a day or two, but we had a great year nonetheless, finishing 7-1-1. Another highlight of that year was that we had a very special guest speaker at our post season banquet. In addition to Greg Brezina, Atlanta Falcon LB as our guest, Richie Guerin brought in "Pistol" Pete Maravich, one of the all time great college basketball players, who was a first year Hawks player. He was a great speaker, told funny, clean jokes and sat next to me for the entire dinner, a truly delightful guy. He later died a very premature death at around 40 years old in the early 1990's.

Also, earlier during the season of 1971, Bob Johnson had mentioned casually to me about maybe someday coaching with the Colts, maybe on his staff. I really didn't give that much thought at the time. But some time, I don't remember what month, he called and asked me to coach the 1972 80 lb. Colt team. I immediately accepted and thought "what an opportunity!" And then thought "maybe I CAN coach in a Bobby Dodd Bowl some day."

CHAPTER 7

1972, Our First Varsity Year

1972 was an unusual year for Bob Johnson and his 120 lb. Colt team. They started off winning the first seven games in a row, scoring an average of 37 points per game. Then, something unfortunate happened when starting QB Jeff Rummell, a great player, was injured, and they lost the next three in a row, scoring only 14 points in the three losses. These crucial losses cost them the subdivision title and they actually missed the GYFC playoffs.

They did rally to win the two post season games, the Colt Classic over Charlotte, 9-7 and a hard fought 7-6 victory over Hialeah, Florida in a game played in chilly and windy Lakeland, Florida.

This team was led by All American TB Jimmy Wilson and QB Jeff Rummell. Wilson would later become an all state performer at Marist and play for Georgia Tech. The lines were anchored by All American Tackle Frank Baynham, and Donnie Passarella, a very good Center and Linebacker.

They finished with a 9-3 record, a good season, but not up to Bob Johnson's usual standards. Barring that injury to Jeff Rummel, I believe they would have been undefeated and won it all. But, nonetheless, they would bounce back with vengeance in 1973.

Jim Wilson's 100 lb. Colt team blitzed through their season, as easy a 14-0 as you could imagine, scoring 477 points and giving up only 33. They defeated East Point 21-6 in the Chattahoochee Bowl and the DeKalb Yellow Jackets 21-0 in the Bobby Dodd Bowl.

They also easily won the two post season Bowl games 42-0 over Charlotte in the Colt Classic and 46-0 over Lakeland, Florida in Lakeland. Jim was ably assisted by an outstanding coaching staff of former high school coach Ed Newby, NFL player Bob Chatham and previous year's 80 lb. Colt GYFC Champs Coach Mike Sellers, a truly great coaching staff.

This great team was led by Quarterback Kevin Schmidt and Running Backs Mike Sellers and Tony Jackson, the younger of the fabulous Jackson brothers. They had good line and special teams play led by Clay Campbell, Mark Grissett, Robert Chatham and Robert Van Gorder all year.

So with our 80 lb. Colt victory described in the following pages, and the 100 lb. Colt Victory in the Bobby Dodd Bowl, we had captured two more GYFC championship trophies and banners for ACYA. The overall Varsity record for 1972 was 32-7.

*   *   *

1972 80 lb. Atlanta Colts

After I received the call from Athletic Director Bob Johnson and knew I would be head coach of the 80 lb varsity Colts in 1972, I was confident that I could do this job. Even though I had never won an ACYA interleague championship, I did have a decent 13-2-2 overall record as an ACYA Interleague Head Coach in two years. The first task for me was to assemble the best, most qualified coaching staff I could find, so I went with the three close friends I started with, Steve Galezeski, Warner Head and Doug Perreault.

Doug Perreault was recently married to Kathy Arnold, an Auburn grad from Abbeville, Alabama, and they had just relocated to Atlanta from Miami where they had met. Perreault knows football as well as anyone and he is a great communicator, and quite a character. He is the perfect blend of a football coach, popular with the players, a good teacher and just a fun guy to be around, but he could be tough and demanding when it came to his team's performance on defense. He coached his players to be tough, hard hitting and how to diagnose an offensive play. The stunts and blitzes he used were simple, but effective.

Warner's wife Shirley was about to have their first child, who would be named Brian. Warner had been a high school quarterback in Atlanta and also was a lot of fun and a good friend. He was a good quarterback coach, teaching footwork, arm angles, release points etc. all parts of the fine art of being a ball handler and passer. Steve already had kids and had been coaching in ACYA for a few years. He was a good blend of being aggressive when needed, but also calm under fire, with his maturity and coaching experience.

I was 24, single, unattached, and totally focused on coaching this football team. My first big break in business (Healthcare) was a year away. Warner and I talked a lot of football constantly year round, and he was also a good observer of the college and high school games, as I was. So, he and I would formulate the strategies from offensive play calling, kicking and special teams formations, etc. Perreault would put the defenses together, based on a 4-4, including stunts and blitzes. He would call all defensive signals in the games. I thought we had a good group and I was confident with our staff.

These guys were very dedicated to the tasks at hand. We had several preseason planning sessions and talked about what we wanted to accomplish. We were all young and energetic, so we were eager and ready to go when tryouts started in early August. The ACYA was probably at its peak enrollment in 1972 and we had around 150 ten and eleven year old boys try out for our 33 man roster.

It was very difficult to cut anyone, but especially the last 10 or so. To make one of the three Colt varsity travelling squads was the ultimate goal for nearly every boy that was the right age/weight for one of those varsity teams. There were 99 spots, 33 on each team and probably around 500 eligible for the 99 spots.

This was a big advantage over most of our GYFC competition and we hoped to capitalize on it, but at the same time, there were a lot of disappointed kids who did not make varsity. The good thing about ACYA was that they could still play a full 8 or 9 game schedule on an Interleague team, have fun in a competitive football experience, improve as a player and try out for varsity again the next year, and many did.

The great Bob Johnson was head coach of the 120 lb. Colt team. Jim Wilson, a very successful ACYA Interleague veteran had just taken over for Bob's younger brother, David Johnson, as head coach of the 100 lb. Colt team. David had been very successful, just like Bob, but at the 100 lb. level, while Bob had always coached the 120 lb. level. David had won four straight GYFC Championships from 1968-1971 before retiring I was the head coach of the 80 lb team at 24 years old. I had two years of head coaching experience in the ACYA Interleague, no championships, while these other men were mature adults with families and each had a lot of championship coaching experience.

I might add at this point that Athletic Director Bob Johnson had very high expectations of all of his varsity coaches, and he did not like losing. The ACYA had advantages over the other GYFC programs in numbers, money and facilities, and Bob wanted and expected the Colt teams to dominate. Early on, I heard Bob refer to the league championship game, aka the "Bobby Dodd Bowl" as "our" game, and he wanted to win every one at every age/weight level and every year. The Colts had won all three weight classes in 1971 and two of the three in 1970. Bob wanted and expected that domination to continue and he expected me to do my part. Beginning with my first Bobby Dodd Bowl in 1972, I told my team every year that this is "our game" and we expect to win, and we always did, except the last one.

Practice and tryouts began in August, it took a full week to cut the roster down to the 33 magic number doing double tryout sessions every night that week, and then we started serious regular season preparations.

The Colt uniform colors were six combinations. We had two sets of jerseys, white with navy numbers trimmed in orange, and navy blue jerseys, with white numbers trimmed in orange.

We had three sets of uniform pants, orange, navy blue and white, and any of the combinations looked very good, as all of the jerseys and pants had complimentary striping. The Colt helmet, was orange, with blue and white stripes and an interlocking AC decal on each side, styled similarly to Auburn's AU.

The 1972 season came fast and we started just fine, a 20-0 win over South Cobb. The most memorable play was a long punt return for a TD by Safety Richie Guerin. Starting that year, and for most of the 9 years I coached the Colts, we used a twin safety punt return where the two safeties criss-crossed and either faked or handed off on a reverse.

The play was called a pre-determined direction, left or right return, so whichever returner was headed in that direction on the criss-cross wound up with the ball, no matter which side the ball was kicked to. The rest of the return unit would set up a picket line or blocking wall on the side of the field to which the return was pre-called. Details of how the punt return actually worked are in Chapter 18.

We scored many touchdowns with that return play and formation over our 9 years.

I learned that play from watching Decatur High School in the 1950's as a grammar school kid.

We won our second game over Jonesboro 42-0. They were new to GYFC and not yet very competitive. Then we hit the wall. We lost to Midway, 12-0, and as I recall we probably did not come very close to scoring.

We then lost three more times out of the next seven games, and finished with a 6-4 regular season record, dreadful by Colt standards, and far worse than any of the three coaches who had preceded me, Combs, Adams and Sellers. I had scouted Midway, we always scouted every opponent and I liked to personally watch them if I could. I do not remember Midway's 80 lb coach's name, but I will state that they were a very well coached team and they looked the way I wanted our team to look. They were quick, fast, played low, hit hard and did not make mistakes. I have no idea how they ever lost that year, but they did and they lost to Forest Park in GYFC Playoff Round 1, called the Chattahoochee Bowl.

We sort of limped into the playoffs, winning our last game (and subdivision Championship) of the year over Briarcliff on two big plays, a kickoff return for a TD by speedy Gary Newsom, from one of the ACYA's most involved families who had four sons to play in ACYA. Gary was a great placekicker for all three weight level Colt teams, who later became a very good baseball player at Georgia Tech. Very late in the game, we were tied 7-7, and had to score to win the game which would allow us to win our subdivision. We threw a throwback screen pass to the weakside end, played by David Nesmith and he took it the distance on a great run from about 50 yards out. Colts win, 14-7 and are subdivision champs, qualifying for the four team championship playoffs.

We were to play East Point in the First Round Chattahoochee Bowl. At that time they were a perennial GYFC power, and not particularly liked by Bob Johnson. At least some of the East Point coaches were city Parks Department employees, thus they had paid coaches. They had beaten us a couple of weeks prior, and Bob really wanted us to win, and we did, 13-7.

We scored one TD to take the lead in the first half, after recovering a fumble deep in East Point territory. It was on a first down play action pass from QB Randy Addington to Scott Willis. The game was tied 6-6 at halftime and then we had a long scoring drive in the second half, culminated by a short TD run by Neil Brewer. As I said, Forest Park defeated Midway, much to my relief, and so we planned to play Forest Park in the GYFC Championship Game, The Bobby Dodd Bowl. We had a chance to win the championship without facing that great Midway team. That was a bit of great luck, in my opinion.

At that time, and most years, the Bobby Dodd Bowl was played for the three weight division championships the Saturday before Thanksgiving at Kiwanis Stadium in Forest Park, a large municipal facility, that seated around five or six thousand. Our game was at 10 A.M., so by playing Forest Park at their own stadium, we faced an opponent on their home field. We always took chartered MARTA buses from Murphy Candler to Forest Park for the Bobby Dodd Bowl, and arrived with much fanfare, to the displeasure of our opponents. That was one of the ways we displayed our financial advantage, which was part of a Bob Johnson psychological ploy, I suspect.

That year, we did not have what I would call a legitimate offensive system, we just had a bunch of plays, mostly from the I formation, and a couple of other formations, not very well conceived strategy on offense. I knew how individual offensive plays worked, but I did not really know at this point in my career exactly how an offensive SYSTEM worked or was designed.

With Doug Perreault running our defense, exclusively using his 4-4, we had a very good defensive system all year, but our offense was inconsistent and not very well planned or coached. But we did have very good talent. I decided to try something different on offense for the Forest Park game. I knew we needed some kind of actual system, so I put in a wishbone offense.

Anybody knows that you can't do that! To run a wishbone in 11 year old football is stupid, and to install it in one week for a championship game is more stupid. But we did, and it actually did pretty well with a few long runs, gained well over 100 yards, but no touchdowns.

The game ended in a 0-0 tie thanks to the Perreault defense led by Linebacker Bubba Rushing, and I assumed that we would be co-champions. But we were immediately told by the conference officials that the GHSA (Georgia High School Association, whose rules GYFC played by) "Penetration" rule would be applied to determine a winner. (I believe this was the only time in GYFC history that Penetration was used to break a tie in the Bobby Dodd Bowl, see 1975).

The Penetration Rule works like this, one point is awarded for each of three categories:

1. Most first downs, won by Forest Park, they get a point,
2. Most total yards, won by Atlanta Colts, we get a point,
3. Most penetrations inside the opponents 20 yard line, one each, tied, no points awarded.

So, after the first round of Penetration rules were applied, we were still tied, 1-1.

We then find out that in the event of a further tie, the GHSA Penetration Rule states that the team with the most yards wins. That silly wishbone Offense had done the job! Randy Addington and Gary Newsom had collaborated on one wishbone option play that made a long gain that probably made the difference!

The Atlanta Colts 80 lb. team were crowned GYFC Bobby Dodd Bowl Champs despite our less than stellar regular season record and a tie in the actual championship game! Bob Johnson was ecstatic and gave me a huge hug and I was very happy and proud. It happened very fast, for a minute or two, we thought we were tied and co-champions, then all of a sudden, we find out that we had won the game and Championship.

I can still remember Bob Johnson's words from almost 40 years ago. He said something like "They're over there arguin' and talkin' 'bout the rules, and we're standin' over here holdin' the Championship Tropheeey!!! Heeh-heeh-heeh-heeh-heeh." Bob usually chuckled rather than laughed. I remembered from that day forward how happy these GYFC championships made Bob, even when it wasn't his own 120 lb. Colt team. He wanted our team and kids to win as much as he wanted his own team to. He felt ownership of and took pride in any victory by any of the three Colt teams, and deservedly so.

Then, as GYFC Champions, after a one day reprieve and celebration, the following Monday we prepared to play in the annual Colt Classic. The Colt Classic was a post season bowl game, officially sanctioned by Pop Warner (Pop Warner was the official sanctioning body for much of Youth Football, sort of like the NCAA), and played on Colt Field the Friday after Thanksgiving Day, usually before the largest crowds of the year. Visiting teams came to play the Colts from all over the country.

There was a good amount of pageantry involved as the Thanksgiving weekend culminated the entire year for the ACYA's home season. The Interleague Championships were held Thanksgiving Day, with U.S. Marine Corps sponsorship with a "Toys for Tots" theme. The Colt Classic was the next day, the Friday after Thanksgiving and local celebrities, either Atlanta Falcon players or high school football coaches would be there to select MVP's from each team who would receive a "Governor's Medal" in recognition in all three Varsity Colt Classic games.

This year's opponent was the Charlotte Bears, and we were able to defeat them 7-0 by capitalizing on a mishandled punt return, leading to a Touchdown by Governor's Medal winning Fullback Bubba Rushing on a pass from Jeff Lineberger. The 100 lb. and 120 lb. teams also won, and the Colt Classic was a clean sweep as it was in most years.

The Colts rarely lost a Colt Classic game and we were 9-0 in our Colt Classic games from 1972-1980.

We finished our first varsity season at 9-4, as GYFC and Colt Classic Champs after a very bumpy mid-season period of losing 4 of 8 games. Shortly afterwards, thinking back about the season, I knew, despite the fact that we had won the GYFC, that we were going to have to do something about our Offense and put in a true system if we were to compete with teams like Midway and East Point in the future. I loved doing this and I wanted to continue for a few years and be as successful as Bob Johnson expected me to.

So, the next week I did what Bob Johnson had done in 1970. I went to an expert for advice. The expert I went to was Bob Johnson himself, and I asked him to teach me the Leonard Jones system. I learned it two ways, first Bob drew everything up on paper for me, taught me the play numbering and offensive line blocking rules. They were very simple and easy for me to understand and I picked it up quickly.

Then, as another piece of luck turned out, Bob's 120 lb. Colt team was going to play a rather late in the year post season bowl game in Lakeland, Florida on December 16, so I went to every practice for the three weeks between Thanksgiving and the mid-December game. I watched the offense in scrimmage and drills and saw the offense operate and being coached first hand. Combining the practice experience and what I had seen drawn on paper, I had it figured out!

That was the most important three week period in my coaching life. Not only did I learn this fantastic offense that incorporated aspects of the I, the option and the split-T Veer, but I learned how to prepare for and run efficient practices, and as far as I am concerned, I learned from the master, the best of all kids football coaches, Bob Johnson.

We had a good nucleus of players returning for next year's 1973's 80 lb. Colt team. We had kept ten 10 year old players on the 1972 team, planning for the following year, but we lost Coach Galezeski to part time status, so I needed another coach. I remembered what a good coach Warren Watson was from the Interleague Jets, and I asked him to join us and put in this fantastic new blocking system, and coach the offensive line for 1973. What a good decision that would turn out to be for years to come . . . .

*   *   *

1972 80 lb. Atlanta Colts Key Performers

John "Bubba" Rushing, FB and LB . . . . Bubba Rushing had played a key role in the previous year's 80 lb. team and we had heard how great he was before seeing him play.

He was every bit as good as advertised and was a consistently outstanding player on offense and defense all year.

Scott Willis, End and LB . . . Scott was a tough kid, and very smart. He caught a key TD pass against East Point in our playoff game and played a consistent Outside Linebacker all year.

Reed Barlitt, HB and LB . . . Reed was one of our bigger players. He was an excellent runner and defender and played well in both positions all year.

Gary Newsom, HB and PK . . . Gary was an outstanding athlete and played a key role all year as a runner and kick returner. He returned a kickoff for a TD in our regular season finale against Briarcliff in a win which helped lead us to the subdivision title. He was an outstanding placekicker and took great pride in that job also. Gary went on to be an outstanding college baseball player at Georgia Tech.

Randy Addington, QB . . . I had coached against Randy in the ACYA Interleague and knew he was a good player and leader. He did a very good job all year passing, running and operating our offense.

David NeSmith, End . . . David made the most important play of the year for us, taking a screen pass and going the distance in the season finale against Briarcliff for the winning TD. This was a must win game and the victory clinched our subdivision title, allowing us to advance into the playoffs and eventually win the Bobby Dodd Bowl and GYFC Championship.

1972 80 lb. Atlanta Colts Record 9-4-0

GYFC Bobby Dodd Bowl Champions
Atlanta Colt Classic Champions

Colts 20 .... South Cobb 0
Colts 42 .... Jonesboro 0
Colts 0 .... Roswell 6
Colts 14 .... North DeKalb 6
Colts 7 .... Tucker 13
Colts 0 .... Midway 12
Colts 13 .... NorthEast 7
Colts 21 .... Glenwood 0
Colts 7 .... East Point 13
Colts 14 .... Briarcliff 7

GYFC Semi-Final,
The Chattahoochee Bowl, Pebblebrook High School, Smyrna, Georgia

Colts 13 East Point 6

GYFC Championship, The Bobby Dodd Bowl, Kiwanis Stadium, Forest Park, Georgia

Colts 0* Forest Park 0
* Atlanta Colts win by GHSA Penetration Rules

1972 Atlanta Colt Classic, Colt Field, Murphy Candler Park, Atlanta, Georgia

Colts 7 Charlotte, NC 0

1972 80 lb. Atlanta Colts Starting Lineups:

Offense:

LE	David Nesmith
LT	Doug Maihafer
LG	Jeff Smith
C	Andy Gastley
RG	Brian Williams
RT	Trey Garner
RE	Scott Willis
QB	Randy Addington
FB	John "Bubba" Rushing
I IB	Gary Newsom
HB	Tommy Varner

Defense:

LE	Robert Holgate
LT	Robert Rudder
RT	David Harrison
RE	Bobby Fink
LB	Jeff Coats
LB	Bubba Rushing
LB	Reed Barlitt
LB	Jeff Smith
CB	Neil Brewer
CB	Richie Guerin
S	John Hurst

Coaching Staff: Doug Bennett, Head Coach
Doug Perreault, Defensive Coordinator and Linebacker Coach
Warner Head, Offensive and Defensive Backfield Coach
Steve Galezeski, Offensive and Defensive Line Coach

1972 80 lb. Atlanta Colts Full Roster:

Gary Newsom
Brian Williams
Ray Spurlock
John Hurst
Phillip Reeves
Tim Duren
Neil Brewer
Bobby Fink
Doug Maihafer
David Harrison
Randy Addington
Kevin Companik
Richie Guerin
Tommy Varner
Tim Hartigan
Jeff Lineberger
Jeff Smith

Trey Garner
Andy Gastley
Kenny Passarella
Jeff Coats
Robert Rudder
Chet Huntley
Rich Papineau
Preston Coleman
Scott Willis
John "Bubba" Rushing
David Nesmith
Reed Barlitt
Petey Frye
Jeff Amtower
Ron Barto
Robert Holgate

Cheerleaders

Kate Spitler
Hunter Foster
Berri Beers
Stacy Hough
Lisa Crosby
Lori Perkins

Kim Perkins
Ann Holdridge
Elizabet Fink
Lynn Rushing
Stephanie Humin
Tina Sutter

1972 120 lb. Atlanta Colts Record, 9-3

Atlanta Colt Classic Champions
Holiday Festival Bowl Champions

Colts 54 South Cobb 0
Colts 56 Jonesboro 6
Colts 28 Roswell 0
Colts 42 North DeKalb 0
Colts 35 Midway 12
Colts 10 Tucker 7
Colts 35 Northeast 0
Colts 0 Glenwood 7
Colts 7 East Point 10
Colts 7 Briarcliff 13

Atlanta Colt Classic, Colt Field, Murphy Candler Park, Atlanta, Georgia

Colts 9 Charlotte 7

Holiday Festival Bowl, Lakeland, Florida

Colts 7 Hialeah, Florida 6

1972 120 lb. Atlanta Colts Complete Roster

Tim Meyer	Greg Lambert
Frank Baynham	Richard Reynolds
Richard Woolford	Mike Romano
Kacey Dolan	Clay Silkner
Ricky Carter	Brett Durham
David Cochran	Billy Asip
David May	Buddy Wilson
Alan Cummings	Jimmy Wilson
Mark Love	Jeff Morris
Joe Jensen	Jeff Rummel
Roger Logan	Andy Harris
Steve Hardy	Tim Miltner
Jeff Dodd	Mike Lobertini
Eric Spitler	Jon Been
Charlie Braswell	Skeeter Pinkerton
Dale Deen	Don Passarella

Coaching Staff

Bob Johnson Head Coach
Frank Greene
Chuck Willis
George Copelan

Cheerleaders

Laura Ramsey	Teri Lineberger
Pam Mathis	Lee Barlitt
Mary Platford	Lisa Fallon
Cathy Ward	Lauri Hooker
Sharon Eikey	Pam Pillert
Debbie Gurr	Susie Willis

1972 100 lb. Atlanta Colts Record, 14-0

GYFC Bobby Dodd Bowl Champions
Atlanta Colt Classic Champions
Holiday Festival Bowl Champions

Colts 41 South Cobb 0
Colts 49 Jonesboro 0
Colts 34 Roswell 0
Colts 34 North DeKalb 0
Colts 34 Midway 7
Colts 21 Tucker 6
Colts 80 Northeast 0
Colts 21 Glenwood 7
Colts 14 East Point 0
Colts 29 Briarcliff 7

GYFC Semi-Finals, The Chattahoochee Bowl, Roswell High School, Roswell, Georgia

Colts 21 East Point 6

GYFC Championship, The Bobby Dodd Bowl, Kiwanis Stadium, Forest Park, Georgia

Colts 21 DeKalb
Yellow Jackets 0

Atlanta Colt Classic, Colt Field, Murphy Candler Park, Atlanta, Georgia

Colts 42 Charlotte 0

Holiday Festival Bowl, Lakeland, Florida

Colts 46 Lakeland 0

1972 100 lb. Atlanta Colts Complete Roster

Scott Wilder   Alex Alford
Robert Van Gorder   Barron Smith
Billy Huntley   Kevin Schmidt
Jimmy Wood   Tony Jackson
Mike Sellers   Matt Putnal
Jeff Baker   Gerry Romberg
Clay Campbell   Rich Wampler
Jimmy Welter   Jimmy Blake
Mark Grissett   David Newby
Neil Johnson   Ricky Rogers
Deane Johnson   Wade Doss
Jimmy Arnhart   Terry Burnette
Nyle Bishop   Brian Cromie
Robert Chatham   Mike Campbell
Gregg Davis   Chip Dickens
Jim Johnston   Peter Youtt
Tony Scoggins

Coaching Staff

Jim Wilson Head Coach
Ed Newby
Bob Chatham
Mike Sellers

Cheerleaders

Diana Cribbs   Paula Rook
Lisa Thompson   Lisa Rowlette
Nancy Wilson   Libby Wampler
Susan Perdue   Tobie Pinkerton
Sharon Hensley   Cathy Anderson
Sharon Farrell   Jenny Johnson

1972 Coltettes Drill Team

Judy Beers	Mary Payne
Kathy Davis	Allyson Polk
Renee Lambert	Lori Williams
Sandra Patterson	Kelly Dempsey
Jeanne Craig	Tracy Husbands
Stephanie Davis	Peggy Moody
Pat Fody	Christine McNabb
Libby Williams	Susan Neal
Mary Ann Caudill	Darci McClure
Ellen Morrissey	Lisa Balfour
Karen Pahl	Carol Bentley
Debbie Hope	Melinda Waring
Peggy Fody	Karen Summers
Diane Hope	Allison Stokes
Cindy Wilson	Dianne Odom

Director

Dodie Healy

CHAPTER 8

. . . . 1973

Colt Running Back Neil Brewer gaining yardage in the 1972 80 lb. Bobby Dodd Bowl GYFC Championship Game

1973 saw two of the three Colt teams with perfect records. I will elaborate on the success of our 80 lb. team later in this chapter, and Bob Johnson's 120 lb. team also ran the table to a perfect record.

Bob's 120 pounders tallied 428 points, and allowed only 61. They won all but two of their games by large margins and had two close calls with

Briarcliff, 14-7 and Glenwood, 14-6. These two opponents had two of the best coaches in GYFC at the time in Jerome Roberts and Virgil Sorrells.

They played a very tough opponent from Piscataway, New Jersey in the Colt Classic, but still prevailed by 31-15. The team was led by QB Kevin Schmidt, an outstanding runner and passer. They had excellent running backs in Tony Jackson, Matt Putnal and Mike Sellers, and a very good line led by Frank Baynham, Deane Johnson and Robert Chatham.

This team was so good they were virtually unbeatable, and I enjoyed watching them practice and play very much.

The 100 lb. team was also good, but not quite as perfect as the 80 lb. and 120 lb. teams.

They had a respectable 7-2-1 regular season and split the bowl games, winning two games in Dallas, Texas in the Safari Bowl games, played in the old 70,000 seat Cotton Bowl Stadium, but they dropped the Colt Classic to a fine team from Mamaroneck, New York.

120 Ib Colt team in a no pads practice session in the brand new at the time Texas Stadium in Dallas. The next day's bowl game will be played in the Cotton Bowl stadium in Dallas where Colt Tackle, Number 74, Robert Chatham recovers a fumble for a Touchdown and receives a Cowboy jersey from legendary Cowboy QB Roger Staubach as a promised reward.

They just missed winning their subdivision in GYFC and thus did not qualify for the GYFC playoffs, but were a very good team nonetheless.

They were led by QB Sammy Long and RB's John "Bubba" Rushing and Jimmy Blake.

Their line was anchored by Mitch Rushing, Clay Campbell and Tommy "T-Bird" Rose.

Jim Wilson had a very good coaching staff with Assistant Coaches Ed Newby, Bob Chatham and Jim Lineberger.

The overall Varsity record for 1973 was 37-3-1.

*   *   *

1973 80 lb. Colts, The Perfect Season

As already stated, we had a good nucleus of returning players for the 1973 season's 10 and 11 year old 80 lb team. Ten players had made the 1972 GYFC Championship team as 10 year olds (like "underclassmen"), and now they were primed to return, like "Senior" players, gain starting positions and become team leaders. They were Jeff Amtower, Petey Frye, Preston Coleman, Richie Guerin, Jeff Lineberger, Ron Barto, Tim Hartigan, Kenny Passarella, Neil Brewer, and Phillip Reeves.

Brewer was a gifted natural runner at Tailback out of the I formation, fast and shifty, could read blocking and cut on the move without losing a step. This style of running ability was a huge asset to the new offense which required the backs to read blocks at the point of attack and make the correct cut around the block. Neil had been a good performer for us in 1972 as a 10 year old, so he already had significant varsity experience.

Lineberger was an excellent QB, good passer, runner and ball handler, and was even better as a Linebacker on defense. He had also played a lot in 1972. Amtower, Frye and Coleman, three tough, versatile players at HB's and FB's were interchangeable at the two positions, and also good runners and outstanding blockers as well as pass receivers.

Hartigan, Barto and Passarella were the nucleus linemen, quick, strong, tough and aggressive blockers and defenders. Reeves was a great pass receiver and blocker as well, and Guerin was a terrific free safety, punt returner and could also play any backfield position. Almost too much talent.

We also added key players like End/Linebacker Chris Whitley, Center Richard Chatham and little, but speedy Jimmy Awbrey, a future SEC Decathlon Champion at Auburn University, who were good players, but less experienced as first year Varsity players.

The defense, coached by Doug Perreault, was literally (and statistically) awesome. Barto and Hartigan at Ends, Passarella at Tackle, Frye, Coleman and Lineberger at LB's and a secondary led by Safety Guerin gave up only 15 points in 13 games. Newcomer Scott Wallace, only 10 years old, was also a terrific Inside Linebacker as was another 10 year old newcomer, Mike Stovall at the other Tackle. Steady returning veterans Amtower and Brewer rounded out the secondary at the corners.

The Defense posted eleven shutouts, giving up points in only two games. One field goal in game one by Scott Young of North DeKalb, who would be our 100 lb. kicker two year later, in a 14-3 Colt win, and two touchdowns in a game against Glenwood where we scored 32 and won easily 32-12.

We were excited about the new offense that we had learned from Bob Johnson. We were confident that the blocking schemes could handle any alignments, stunts or blitzes we might ever face from an opposing defense. The assistant coaches, Perreault, Watson and Head picked up the blocking assignments quickly in preseason meetings before the first practice and it was pretty easy to teach to the players. We were intent and determined to be a coaching staff worthy of the Colt brand, despite the fact that we were the youngest staff in GYFC.

I was 25, Perreault 26 and Head 25. Warren Watson was the oldest in his 30's. His maturity added the needed stability to this youthful group. Warren Watson, an Auburn man from Rome, Georgia, was a great coach and we all looked up to him and greatly respected his knowledge of the game as he was also a high school football official.

The new offense was designed to always give an advantage at the point of attack, one of five ways, by either a double team block, an advantageous blocking angle, or an option block on basic running plays. There were also QB pitch/run option run plays, and QB bootleg pass/run options on pass plays. There were even plays where we could call an audible or an automatic play change at the line based on what the QB saw from the defense he was facing. We could line up in strongside right or left to influence a defense to line up a certain way to set up a play to go in the direction that we wanted to run.

The only thing I did not like in the Leonard Jones system was the play numbering, so I modified it to make it what I thought would make more sense, as well as to be easier for the kids to learn and remember. When Mac Scoggins came up in 1974 to coach the 80 lb Colts, he used the exact same play numbering as Bob Johnson and Leonard Jones did, but I changed it for our purposes anyway.

I guess when you don't lose in a year, losses aren't the memories. So, one of the wins I best remember was the afore-mentioned home game with Glenwood, 32-12. They scored touchdowns on a long kickoff return and a blocked punt. Blocked punts are a pet peeve of mine and I hate them. They usually get you beat, but not our 1973 80 lb Colts. We worked hard from the following Monday for seven more years to avoid having any more of our punts blocked. As you read on, you will continuously see how important the kicking game was to our success.

Defensive Coordinator Coach Perreault had to miss that Glenwood game due to a family obligation, so I called the defensive signals that day. Since the only TD's scored against us that entire year were on the day I called the defense, needless to say, I never called another one the rest of my career. Although I did always enjoy working with the defense in game planning, especially in crucial regular season intra-division games or playoff situations. So, Doug Perreault called defensive signals in 12 games in 1973, allowing one field goal for a total of 3 points.

We scored 350 points that season with our new offense, in 13 games. We never got out of the I formation that year and rarely split an End or flanker. We just pounded off tackle and ran our special "50 Trap" all year, with the occasional option, in addition to play action and bootleg passing. Passing was very easy in this offense, even for this young age group, and we practiced it relentlessly, becoming very efficient with a high completion percentage.

I will explain the details of the offense in later chapters, but this new found success was incredible. Ron Barto was our Strongside Guard, and he could pull on bootlegs and trap on inside plays as good as I had seen and far better than I had hoped while learning the Offense.

We had beaten Tucker 9-0 in that year's regular season and had to play them again in GYFC Playoff Round One. We had lost to Tucker in '72 and we owed them one. I certainly felt that way myself, as I had made a dumb call at the end of that 1972 loss that cost us the game. However, we had great respect for Tucker, as did Bob Johnson. We all felt that they were the next best overall program in GYFC, behind our own Atlanta Colts.

This Round One game was expected to be a tough one. It was an early Saturday morning the second weekend in November at 10 A.M. It was a bright, clear day with chilly temperatures in the 30's, and the early start and cold weather can sometimes make things a little unpredictable. I always felt that variables like that tend to favor the underdog, so we took great care to be prepared for this important game.

We came out dressed in orange pants and white jerseys, and played extremely well however, and methodically overpowered Tucker, scoring three TD's, but missed all the extra points, winning 18-0. Bob Johnson didn't like missing anything, and let me know that our poor kicking might cost us a game someday, so we worked extra hard on placekicking from that day forward. As with all of Bob's advice, that would prove to be important in several games in the future.

Then, we watched as the Briarcliff Eagles also won in Round One and thus they would be our Bobby Dodd Bowl GYFC Championship Game opponent. They had a very explosive running QB named Tracy something and their team appeared dangerous offensively. In scouting their defense, we noticed they blitzed out of an inside stacked 6-2, filling both A gaps (the gaps between Center and either Guard) with a Guard or LB virtually every down.

This was not a very sound defensive scheme, and seemed very predictable, but we also knew it could wreak havoc in our backfield if any blitzes were successful or if any penetration occurred. It was a classic high risk, high reward, high pressure defense.

Our favorite play, 50 Trap would be a big part of the game plan if Strong Guard Barto could get to the weakside "A" gap quick enough to make his block. The stunts their defense was running made the play even more precise and difficult than normal. Yet if successful, we knew it would gain a lot of yards.

We came out for this 10 AM start on another cool day in our orange pants and navy blue jersey scheme. Strong Guard Ron Barto was able to get to that gap all day, and when FB Preston Coleman cleared the line all day long, he only had Tracy the Briarcliff Safety to beat. He ran for over 230 yards with 50 trap and we won the game and GYFC Championship easily, 26-0. Neil Brewer also had over 100 yards from Tailback in the game and Ken Hemphill came close to 100 as well.

50 Trap is a simple play, but requires precise timing. We had worked hard on it all year, and the timing was so difficult that we almost gave up on it in summer practice. It finally came around and became a prime weapon for us for many years. Timing is crucial in all aspects of Offense and we always spent a lot of time on it in practice from summer all the way throughout the final practices of the year. Our practices were based on six things; football fundamentals (blocking and tackling), toughness (hard hitting), quickness, timing, execution and opponent preparation.

On 50 Trap, very simply, the QB opens quickly counter clockwise and sprints to his left in a shallow arc (it's toward the Offense's right because his back is turned to the line due to the counter clockwise maneuver) holding the ball straight out in his right hand, without bending his arm or elbow. The FB takes a quick jab step to his right, then heads right over center at a slightly angled path, and takes the ball from the QB as they intersect. The TB and HB sprint right with the QB and everything appears like the play is going to the right, but the FB has the ball going straight ahead behind trap blocking.

Coach Doug Perreault and I actually designed that play based on a play we had seen from the 1973 Super Bowl champ Miami Dolphins with QB Bob Griese handing to FB Larry Csonka in a similar fashion. It's a little similar to a draw play, only the ballcarrier hits the line a lot quicker on 50 Trap than on a conventional draw play.

In the line, the Strongside Guard (always Right Guard on this play due to the difficult footwork, timing etc.) pulls across center and blindsides (traps) the first down lineman on the other side of center, or in the case of this blitzing defense, the first gap (aka."A" gap) the other side of center. The Offensive Center blocks the gap to his right that is left open by the trapping, pulling Guard, and the Quickside Guard blocks in or out, linebacker or lineman, depending on the defensive alignment. In the case of this blitzing 6-2 he blocked the away gap to his left as there was no other defender to his inside.

In preparing for this game and this defense, Coach Warren Watson worked very hard all week with the three interior linemen most important to this play, the Center and two Guards on their timing and assignments. We also worked extra time on dummy scrimmage (walk thru and full speed against no defense) and live scrimmage against that defense to perfect the timing and blocking for this play before the game.

Against this particular defense, once Strong Guard Barto hit his man (weakside "A" gap) and Center Richard Chatham picked up his gap (strongside "A" gap), there would be a tiny seam between this cross action blocking, and if properly timed and the blocks are properly executed, the play would break wide open, with no Linebackers there due to the fact they had blitzed themselves out of the play.

The ball carrying fullback is told to hit his seam "right off the pulling guard's behind." FB Coleman timed it perfectly all day, and he was continually into the secondary quickly, leading to over 230 yards in gains from the FB position. One other very important point is that the blocking in this entire offense is designed to pick up stunts and blitzes. In fact, when we designed a trap play, we trapped "first down lineman the other side of center," so with that rule, a blitz into the "A" gap was not a problem, as the trapping Offensive Guard was assigned the gap area, whether it was a Defensive Guard, Tackle or Linebacker that filled it.

Gaining over 400 rushing yards in the Bobby Dodd Bowl game had to be some kind of record. The inside of our line played a near perfect game and that penetration we had been so concerned about never did happen, thus so we were able to exploit their blitzing defensive weaknesses with our running game. Our basic blocking schemes had picked up their blitzes on our other running plays and we had very few negative yardage plays all day.

I always tried to put in something new and unexpected for postseason, and that year for this game we flanked our HB Petey Frye, a very good blocker, and put in a flanker-in-motion crack back toss sweep to the I-Tailback. That was also very effective for Brewer, as there was only a Cornerback for the leading Fullback to pick up once the motion Flanker blocked down on the Defensive End. We used that play in postseason in later years with great success. We usually saved it for that last game as the Flanker in motion would be easily scouted, making the play more predictable and easier to defend.

Next, as back to back defending GYFC champions, the Colt Classic presented another challenger from Charlotte, North Carolina in the Starclaire Cougars. This year's game was a lot easier as we rolled up over 300 yards of offense, as well as a 60 yard Punt Return TD by Guerin. 50 Trap also worked to perfection as FB Preston Coleman had 122 yards in five carries for three TD's, and a 39-0 win culminating the perfect 13-0 season.

With our perfect season finished, I then went with Bob Johnson's 120 lb. team on their bowl trip to Dallas, Texas where the bowl game was played in the old Cotton Bowl on the Texas State Fairgrounds in Dallas. We also had a practice session at the brand new (at that time in 1973) Texas Stadium*, new home of the Dallas Cowboys. That was arranged by Coach Bob Chatham, my Center Richard's and 120 lb. Tackle Robert Jr.'s father. Coach Bob Chatham was also a coach on the 100 lb. Colt team. Bob Chatham had been a NFL player from Ole Miss and was a scout for the Cowboys at the time.

Robert Chatham Jr. actually met the famous Cowboy QB Roger Staubach who told Robert that he would give him a Cowboy #12 jersey if Robert could score a TD in the Colts upcoming bowl game, which would be almost impossible as Robert was a defensive lineman. Robert recovered

---

* While finishing this book in 2010, Texas Stadium was demolished 37 years later, having been replaced by a new $1.5B sliding roof facility, Cowboys Stadium, in nearby Arlington, Texas. How time flies!!

an opponent fumble for a TD in the game the next day, and proudly wore that Cowboy jersey home.

The trip was topped off by a visit to the Cowboys game Sunday afternoon, followed by dinner at Mike Ditka's restaurant where we met Mike Ditka, who was then a Cowboy player, as well as some of the Cowboy executives. That was especially fun for me as I had been a big Cowboys fan since the mid 60's.

On the plane trip home, a couple of things happened that would be significant to our future. First, Jim Wilson stepped down as 100 lb Coach, and Athletic Director Bob Johnson immediately asked me to move up and take that job. Also, Bob asked me who I thought might be the best replacement for the now vacant 80 lb. job. We both agreed that Mac Scoggins deserved that opportunity, and subsequently Bob offered that to Mac, which proved to be a very wise decision. Mac proved that as he would never lose a GYFC regular season game in his five years in GYFC.

Also, Doug Perreault was stepping down as our Defensive Coordinator, and I needed a good replacement for the future defenses. Coach Perreault was a dynamic personality, and a very good coach, from whom I had learned a lot over the years. He knew defense and how to coach it and he would be very hard to replace.

I really had no idea how to replace Coach Perreault, but as luck would have it, my QB's father, Jim Lineberger, had been working with Jim Wilson's 100 lb Colt staff, and he and I talked on the plane trip home from Dallas. It was very evident to me that Jim had a great knowledge of defense like Coach Perreault, and he and I agreed that he would be the perfect replacement to run our defense the next year as we moved up to the 100 lb league.

That was another good break that would be significant for years, as Jim, Warren Watson and I spent many hours over the years together poring over films, reviewing scouting reports and game planning our upcoming opponents.

Colt Safety Richie Guerin scoring on a long punt return for a TD against Northeast at Pleasantdale Park. Guerin had many such TD's in his 4 year Colt career.

Additionally, after the last game, and at our January banquet, I told Richie Guerin and his father that I wanted little Richie to learn to throw and practice his passing during the coming off season. As good as he was at Safety and as a punt returner, he had played no offense in 1973 and I considered that a waste of his great talent. At least, we would be able to groom him as a backup QB and he would be able to play any backfield position in 1974 that injuries might dictate. That would provide valuable depth, which would turn out to be very important at the start of the 1974 season.

*   *   *

1973 80 lb. Atlanta Colts Record, 13-0-0

GYFC Bobby Dodd Bowl Champions
Atlanta Colt Classic Champions

Colts 13 Midway 0
Colts 12 North DeKalb 3
Colts 14 Smyrna 0
Colts 21 Briarcliff 0
Colts 49 Clairmont 0
Colts 44 Roswell 0
Colts 34 Sandy Springs 0
Colts 9 Tucker 0
Colts 32 Glenwood 12
Colts 26 Northeast 0
Colts 26 North Decatur 0

1973 GYFC Playoffs

Round One Chattahoochee Bowl at Pebblebrook High School Smyrna, Georgia

Colts 18 Tucker 0

Round Two GYFC Championship Bobby Dodd Bowl at Forest Park-Kiwanis Stadium
Forest Park, Georgia

Colts 26 Briarcliff 0

1973 Atlanta Colt Classic at Colt Field-Murphy Candler Park, Atlanta, Georgia

Colts 39 Starclaire (Charlotte, N.C.) 0

1973 80 lb. Atlanta Colts Starting Lineups

Offense

Strong End . . . . Phillip Reeves
Strong Tackle . . . Kenny Passarella
Strong Guard . . . . Ron Barto
Center . . . . Richard Chatham
Quick Guard . . . . Tim Hartigan
Quick Tackle . . . Jeff Anderson
Quick End . . . . Jamie Killingsworth
Quarterback . . . . Jeff Lineberger
Fullback . . . . Preston Coleman
Halfback . . . . Petey Frye
Tailback . . . . Neil Brewer

Defense

Left End . . . . Ron Barto
Left Tackle . . . . Mike Stovall
Right Tackle . . . . Scott Carpenter
Right End . . . . Tim Hartigan
Left Outside LB . . . . Petey Frye
Left Inside LB . . . . Chris Whitley
Right Inside LB . . . . Scott Wallace
Right Outside LB. Preston Coleman
Left Cornerback . . . Neil Brewer
Right Cornerback. Jeff Amtower
Safety . . . . Richie Guerin

Coaches: Doug Bennett . . . . Head Coach
Warner Head . . . . Offensive and Defensive Backfield Coach
Warren Watson . . . . Offensive and Defensive Line Coach
Doug Perreault . . . . Defensive Coordinator, Linebacker Coach

1973 80 lb. Atlanta Colts Full Roster

Jeff Currier
Tim Hartigan
Scott Wallace
Russell Ragan
Neil Brewer
Tony Harris
Jeff Amtower
Chris Whitley
Andy Irvin
Wesley Chitwood
Richard Chatham
Kenny Passarella
Jeff Lineberger
Ken Hemphill
Jimmy Awbrey
Jamie Killingsworth

Preston Coleman
Jeff Anderson
Bill Carlson
Scott Rodwin
Mallon Ellenburg
Petey Frye
Scott Carpenter
Mike Stovall
Billy Shaw
Trey White
Ron Barto
Phillip Reeves
Richie Guerin
Steve Noles
Dean Stoll

Cheerleaders

Shawn Amtower
Susan Passarella
Debra Rader
Janet Meadows
Elizabeth Fink
Stacie Reich

Caren Abernathy
Lynda Ragsdale
Kim Perkins
Jeanne Whitley
Laura Hartigan
Susan Frye

120 lb. Atlanta Colt Record 15-0

GYFC Bobby Dodd Bowl Champions
Atlanta Colt Classic Champions
Safari Bowl Champions
Colts 35 North DeKalb 8
Colts 37 Smyrna 12
Colts 14 Briarcliff 7
Colts 38 Clairmont 0
Colts 34 Roswell 0
Colts 31 Sandy Springs 0
Colts 28 Tucker 0
Colts 14 Glenwood 6
Colts 42 Northeast 0
Colts 35 North Decatur 0

GYFC Semi-Final,
The Chattahoochee Bowl, Pebblebrook High School, Smyrna, Georgia

Colts 24 Tucker 0

GYFC Championship, The Bobby Dodd Bowl, Kiwanis Stadium, Forest Park, Georgia

Colts 35 East Point 7

Atlanta Colt Classic, Colt Field, Murphy Candler Park, Atlanta, Georgia

Colts 31 Piscataway, N.J. 15

Safari Bowl, The Cotton Bowl, Texas State Fairgrounds, Dallas, Texas

Colts 28 Arlington 0
Colts 2 Dallas P.A.L. 0

1973 120 lb. Atlanta Colts Complete Roster

Scott Wilder
Ricky Roger
Tony Cushenberry
Eric Cire
Tom Love
Dan Aultman
Greg Sidell
Tony Scoggins
Tony Jackson
Doug Dupuis
Matt Putnal
Wade Doss
Gregg Davis
Roy Beard
Robert Van Gorder
Rich Wampler

Deane Johnson
Charlie Bell
Mike Rummell
Ricky Carter
Tony Sutter
Peter Youtt
Robert Chatham
Pete Zimmerman
John Hardie
Mike Sellers
Mark Grissett
Kevin Schmidt
Frank Baynham
Gerry Romberg
Chip Dickens

Coaching Staff

Bob Johnson Head Coach
Frank Greene
Chuck Willis
George Copelan

Cheerleaders

Diane Hope
Carol Bentley
Lee Barlitt
Lisa Thompson
Carolyn Romberg
Laura Ramsey

Ellen Morrisey
Pam Pillert
Jo Ellen Hough
Cindy Ellis
Susie Willis

1973 100 lb. Atlanta Colts Record 9-3-1

Safari Bowl Champions

Colts 6 North DeKalb 0
Colts 41 Smyrna 0
Colts 16 Briarcliff 0
Colts 35 Clairmont 0
Colts 21 Roswell 0
Colts 21 Sandy Springs 9
Colts 7 Tucker 10
Colts 0 Glenwood 0
Colts 7 Northeast 10
Colts 37 North Decatur 0

Atlanta Colt Classic, Colt Field, Murphy Candler Park, Atlanta, Georgia

Colts 2 Mamaroneck, N.Y. 6

Safari Bowl, The Cotton Bowl, Texas State Fairgrounds, Dallas, Texas

Colts 18 Grand Prairie, Texas 6

Colts 21 New Orleans 6

1973 100 lb. Atlanta Colts Complete Roster

Clay Campbell
Mitch Rushing
David Newby
Mike Youtt
Obi Ingram
Scott Willis
Jeff Dobbs
Roy Thornton
Scott Prosch
John "Bubba" Rushing
Brian Williams
Jamie Swancey
Dave Shillington
Scott Hardy
Marty Connolly
Craig Estep
Gary Newsom

Andy Gastley
Robert Rudder
Reed Barlitt
Tommy "T-Bird" Rose
Trey Garner
Jimmy Allen
Jeff Herring
Bobby Fink
Jim Blake
Steve Quinn
Terry Lane
John Perner
Kevin Companik
Paul Markley
Sammy Long
David NeSmith

Coaching Staff

Jim Wilson Head Coach
Ed Newby
Bob Chatham
Jim Lineberger

Cheerleaders

Susan Perdue
Libby Wampler
Cathy Anderson
Debbie Eschbach
Beth Blake
Nancy Wilson

Melissa Hickson
Jamie Billingsley
Debbie Trense
Jenny Johnson
Lisa Crosby
Kelly Parks

1973 Atlanta Coltettes Drill Team

Cynthia Wilson
Melanie McGuirk
Kiki McClure
Darci McClure
Tracy Husband
Stephanie Davis
Lori Sue Williams
Cindy Wilson
Linda Hancock
Gail Wood
Tracy Matthews
Linda Carpenter
Kay Brock
Dede Yarbrough
Kelly Dempsey

Jean Alexander
Beth Job
Libby Williams
Marci Daugherty
Kelly Skinner
Tina Sutter
Caroline Sherman
Mary Dayton
Pat Fody
Allison Stokes
Suzanne Williams
Lauri McCoy
Kathy Davis
Peggy Fody

Director

Meta Ramsey

CHAPTER 9

1974

Once again in 1974, the ACYA captured two GYFC Bobby Dodd Bowl wins and Championships bringing the record to 11 out of 15 possible at the mid-point of the decade. I will discuss in detail how our 100 lb. Colts were the winners later in this chapter. Bob Johnson's 120 lb. Colts were also victorious.

Bob's 120 lb. team was just about invincible, going 14-0 once again, and they were owners of a 31 game winning streak at the end of 1974. Had it not been for the Jeff Rummell injury in late 1972, I believe this Bob Johnson coached 120 lb. Colt team would have had five straight undefeated seasons, an incredible feat. Even with that costly injury in 1972, Bob's teams were 63-3-1 from 1970-1974, with GYFC Championships in 1970, 1971, 1973, and 1974

This year's team only had three close games, a 7-0 win over always tough Glenwood, and a 17-6 win over Forest Park in regular season. Then in the Bobby Dodd Bowl at Grant Field, East Point put up a good fight before falling to Bob's Colts by a score of 17-7.

The 120 lb. Colts won their two post season Bowl games by 72 points. This team belonged to QB Jimmy Blake. He had been a Running Back on the 1973 100 lb. Colts, but Bob Johnson saw his talent and leadership ability, and did an outstanding job of grooming him as a QB. Bob loved him and he developed into a terrific running QB, a good passer and the team leader.

They had a strong running attack with David Newby and the Rushing brothers, Bubba and Mitch along with Blake's bootlegging and option running from the QB position. Their outstanding line play was led by Phillip Ebinger and John Hardie. They also utilized the outstanding place kicking of Gary Newsom, which included a 30 yard Field Goal by Gary in the Bobby Dodd Bowl.

1974 was Mac Scoggins's first year as a Colt Head Coach and he led his 80 lb. Colt team to a perfect 10-0 regular season, but they dropped the Jim Brazier Bowl GYFC semi-final playoff game to Tucker by the close score of 6-2. They did go on to defeat Charlotte in the Colt Classic ending the year 11-1, outstanding for Mac's first year.

His team was led by QB Alan Lindsay and TB Mike Coveny on offense and Jeff Anderson and Steve Noles on defense.

The overall Varsity record for 1974 was very close to perfect at 38-1-1.

*   *   *

1974 100 lb. Colts, Undefeated Again

Transitioning to the 12 year old/100 lb league was a little intimidating for us as a coaching staff as we entered 1974. We had started out coaching 8 and 9 year old kids in 1970-71, and now all of a sudden in three short years, we're being placed into a greater and more demanding and competitive arena of junior high aged players, with traveling bowl games, tougher competition, more skilled players etc.

We had had two consecutive Championship teams, with one great year with the 13-0 1973 80 lb. Colts after a mediocre one in 1972 where we were very lucky to have won that year's Bobby Dodd Bowl. We all had learned a lot about coaching and the GYFC's fierce competition from Bob Johnson, but I was still not confident we could live up to the 100 lb. Colt team's history of success.

David Johnson had won four straight 100 lb. championships before he retired and rarely lost a game. Jim Wilson had a great first year with one of the absolute best teams in the rich Colt history following David. Then, the next year they followed up with a good, but not championship season his second and last year of 1973. Since both of those previous 100 lb Colt coaches Johnson and Wilson had been very successful in that weight division winning five of the last six championships, I wanted to uphold that tradition, so I was very motivated to be successful.

But, I was unsure and worried about whether or not we could realistically match that tradition. The good news was that almost our entire team was moving up from the 1973 80 lb group so we would stay together and we already knew a lot of what our team would be like. But, could these same kids perform as well at the next level? They had not grown very much and most were undersized. Plus, could we coach at that higher level too?

Continuity is vital in football. The fact that most of our coaches had worked together was important and coaching the same players with the same system can give you a big head start in preseason preparation, and even continuing during the season. Continuity in coaching staff was important to us from 1974 thru 1978 and is also important in every level of football. The two changes we were making were very important ones, first of Defensive Coordinator Jim Lineberger, but at least we already knew Jim, and he knew us and our personnel.

In addition to Jim, I also asked Fred Amtower to join our coaching staff. Warner Head and I had known Fred since 1971 when Jeff Amtower had first played with us on the ACYA Interleague Jets. We knew he would be a great coach with his UGA playing experience and his great personality. He would be of great help coaching the backfield, particularly on the defensive side. Combining Fred's defensive secondary expertise with Watson coaching the line and Lineberger the linebackers and calling the signals, this created an outstanding defensive staff.

The best coaching staffs have little turnover and that continuity generally adds to their ability to be successful. It saves you from having to coach the new coaches on your techniques and strategies, and you don't have to spend any time overseeing them during the year. We were able to have at least some of that continuity throughout the 9 years I was the head coach, which was vitally important to me as Head Coach. Another example of that continuity would be the Mac Scoggins, Charlie Ragan and Pat Eder group who were together all five years of their great run with the Colts from 1974-1978.

In our situation, things worked very smoothly. For example with Warren Watson, he and I knew each other so well, that I would simply give him the practice schedule, showing how much time he would have for his group time on Monday, Wednesday and Thursday and he would know in his own mind what needed to be done each day for the Offensive Line to prepare for that week's game as well as continue to improve the players' fundamental skills. There was never any doubt that our line would be well coached in technique, toughness and assignments. The only time I spent with the offensive line would be to help coach a player in an Oklahoma drill, when all coaches were watching every player in the drill.

Warner Head and I had basically learned our offense together and we were completely in synch on the offensive strategy and how to install and teach each play, and how the backfield action was supposed to work. Warner was excellent with our Quarterbacks and passing game. Fred Amtower was also very good at coaching on the offense, teaching the running back position's fundamentals of running, ball positioning, balance and blocking techniques. I had also learned a lot of this over the last two years watching Bob Johnson's practices.

There were just a couple of variables to the daily practice routine. First variable was the point in the season we were at, and any new plays or modifications to be installed for that week's opponent. We installed our entire offense gradually through the year on Mondays. That enabled us to perfect the offense as we went through it one play or series of plays at a time. Also, by installing new plays on Mondays, we could work on them all week in practice before using them in the intensity of game action.

I also talked with the other coaches routinely during the business day (we all had full time professional jobs, fortunately only Frank Reeves had much travel) as needed to discuss and finalize the practice plans. We would also occasionally meet either after practice or on Sunday afternoon or evening to discuss scouting, game plans etc.

The other variable to the practice routine was the day of the week. We focused on new plays and then fundamentals on Mondays, defense on Wednesdays and offense on Thursdays. We worked on special teams every day during the regular season.

I will go over our practice routines in more detail in Chapter 15, but basically during the season Monday would be to put in any new plays or wrinkles and work the rest of the day on fundamentals. The backfield coaches and I would teach the backs, and the Offensive Line Coach, Watson this particular year, and Jim Lineberger, would teach the linemen.

Wednesday would be defensive day with group work and scrimmage time emphasizing Defense and Thursday was for Offense and Special Teams. This was very routine for us for the last 8 of the 9 years we coached. We worked on punting, punt returning and place kicking in almost every practice of the year in regular season.

The only difference as we planned for the 1974 season was that incoming defensive Coach Lineberger wanted to switch to a 5-2 as our base defense and use the old Doug Perreault 4-4 as a changeup. That was fine with me as Bob Johnson used the 5-2 very effectively, and used a "wide tackle" 6-2 as a changeup. The 6-2 was very similar to our 4-4, and I certainly wanted Jim to coach what he was most comfortable with, and he felt he would be more effective with the 5-2 as the base.

Jim, Bob Johnson and Bob's 120 lb. Colt Defensive Coordinator, Coach Frank Greene, spent a lot of time talking 5-2 defensive strategy over the years which was helpful to all of us. Frank Greene knew it well and sharing his knowledge in "skull" sessions was of immense value. I learned a lot of defense from those three, and also from Doug Cooper in later years. He was also a 5-2 enthusiast, but with a different pass coverage approach.

As we approached the opening game in 1974, we used a similar pre-season practice approach as we had done in the previous year. We were opening with Briarcliff, who I knew would be a good team as they had been our opponent in the 1973 championship game 80 lb. class and they still had that dangerous QB. I started to worry Friday night before the game. We had not played well against North DeKalb in a controlled scrimmage a few days earlier and additionally some of our players had missed some August practice due to an extended Little League baseball playoff season.

Our veteran QB Jeff Lineberger was out with a broken wrist. Richie Guerin had practiced well in his place, and Warner Head had worked hard with him on his ballhandling and play execution fundamentals, but Richie had never played QB in his entire career, except for these last two weeks of preseason practice, and certainly never in a GYFC game.

I recall having worrisome thoughts like: Could Richie perform at QB in a game? Were we properly prepared? How would our new defense work? Had I forgotten to cover some detail? How much tougher is the 100 lb league? Were we tired? We seemed slow to me! Had we worked hard enough? or too hard? I rarely remember worrying as much about a regular season game, even an opener!

Well, we actually played pretty well in the opener, but not great, winning 21-12 over a good Briarcliff team in a very hot and humid game that kicked off at 4 PM on the Saturday of Labor Day weekend. Jim Lineberger had patiently installed the new defense, and I think we were still a little hesitant and unsure of the 5-2 because of the newness and lack of familiarity in game competition. Most of these kids had played in the 4-4 the last two years. The new defense proved to be a good one for many years and Jim did great things with it, with many different players. He knew how to effectively communicate his great knowledge of the stunts, spacing, alignment and techniques so vital to the success of this 5-2 defense. In addition, Jim was an excellent game day signal caller and had a knack of making the right call in a crucial situation.

Guerin played extremely well, scoring one TD on a beautiful option fake and run, and would retain the starting QB job all year, not only executing the offense very well, and improving every week, but becoming a very good passer and a dangerous running threat. His best games would be the most important ones, in postseason. He was small at around 85 lbs, but he was the best running QB we ever had, and his passing was accurate and his arm was just strong enough to be a deep threat.

Like most years, the playoffs were the highlight, but we did stumble once in regular season, tying with the Northeast Mustangs, coached by Jack Moore, 7-7 at Pleasantdale Park in mid-season. They were well prepared for us and Jack seemed to know what we were going to do at all times. We weren't that hard to scout with our basic schemes. We just needed to play harder and quicker, and execute to win, and we did not do it that day. Also, the times we lost or played poorly, we always looked a little slow. We had three other very close games that we won by the score of 7-0 against Tucker, Smyrna and Roswell that year. Thank goodness for that new Lineberger 5-2 defense!

With the perfect season spoiled, we were still undefeated at 9-0-1, and we still had a chance for another GYFC championship. This year the road would not prove quite as easy. Looming ahead were the 100 lb Tucker Lions, out for revenge after three straight losses to us, with Coach Larry Rakestraw's sophisticated passing game. Then, if we could beat Tucker, next would come North DeKalb, our biggest rival of all. They had another high octane passing offense also led by a fabulous quarterback in Ken Escoe, coached by his father, John. They were also big and tough on defense, and they had given us fits in that preseason scrimmage, but we had not met in regular season.

The first round game, now as of 1974 known as The Jim Brazier Bowl, was with Tucker. We had played them and won 7-0 in a very close game early in the regular season at their home field. On defense, they had two very outstanding players whose names I did not know, number 83, an OLB/End and number 85, the MLB. Both had played great against us in the regular season, particularly noticeable was the MLB. He made tackles all over the field, no matter where we ran the ball. Tucker played a Pro style 4-3 Defense, with the two OLB's moved up on the line against our two tight ends, which created a 6 man line, very tight, and hard to run inside against with that great MLB.

We had a small team, very few of our players were anywhere near the weight limit including key linemen like Barto and Passarella. None of our backs were over 90 lbs., including the blocking positions, HB Frye or FB Coleman, and Tucker's team was much larger, particularly that End/OLB, number 83, and that tough MLB, number 85, both playing at or near the weight limit, which was around 105 lbs by the post season play.

Our only outside running game was an outside read on our off tackle plays (26, 84X), or the option out of the Power I. Tucker's 4 deep secondary alignment would make the option play difficult to run, so I did not even include it (the 84B option play) in the offensive game plan. I was very worried about our ability to consistently move the ball against them with our base offense. We did not have the diversity in formations needed to spread them out, or get outside in space and use the superior speed and quickness we had with Guerin, Brewer, Awbrey, Lovelace and Coleman.

John Lovelace, our second HB who played about a third of our offensive snaps, was our largest back at around 100 lbs., and he was very fast, but we did not have that many plays for the HB to carry, as our existing Offense was TB, FB and QB emphasized. John did have a long run for a TD in regular season against Roswell in our 7-0 victory.

I did not think we could slug it out with the bigger Tucker team running mostly inside the tackles for four quarters and come out on top. We needed to take better advantage of our speed and skill.

Our Defense had shut them out in regular season, so I really was not too worried about stopping their Offense, so I expected another low scoring game. Big mistake!

In preparing for this game, as we did often for the postseason, we decided to add some new wrinkles on offense. So, in game planning for this playoff game, Jim Lineberger and I each came up with a vital new play. Mine was an outside running play designed to take advantage of what appeared to be a Tucker defensive vulnerability. The other, an inside running play designed by Jim, was designed to offset a Tucker defensive strength.

The first part of the new strategy was to occasionally move our TB, Neil Brewer to a wingback in a new formation, simply called "Tailback Wing," with the FB and HB lining up in their normal positions, with the usual two Tight Ends. This meant that we were breaking the "I" for the first time ever. I felt we needed something a little different to set up plays that could gain the yardage running inside and outside that would be necessary to win this game. The new formation would also likely make the rest of our entire offense less predictable, thus hopefully making our base offense more effective.

The idea of the formation and play that I designed was to setup a reverse to Tailback Neil Brewer who was a speedy playmaker, from this Wingback position off of our 84 series. Tucker's OLB/Ends played very tight, and we thought we could take advantage of that and get outside of them, particularly to the back side offensive left, away from that number 83 who manned the End to our offensive right. The misdirection would also neutralize that middle linebacker, at least on this one play. I called the play "TB Wing, 84 Reverse." This left side (the offense's left) Defensive End play was the vulnerability we sensed and thought we could take advantage of, that I referred to above.

In preparing for postseason, we always stressed quickness and worked hard on our quickness drills at the end of practice. Against this great Tucker defense, our offense would only work if we were at peak quickness, even using the new plays. Tucker was bigger, we needed to be quicker.

The other thing we decided to do, and Jim Lineberger's new play out of the same new formation, was to use a cross block in the middle, instead of a trap block, to run our FB inside. Number 85, the MLB was so good and well coached, that he had stopped our 50 Traps in the regular season game by quickly moving forward and "filling" the hole before we could get our Quickside Guard on him from the usual side angle. 50 Trap had not worked at all against them in that earlier game due to that MLB, and running the FB inside is very important to our offensive success. Rather than give up running our FB up the middle due to 50 Trap's inability against this defense, we designed the following new play.

This was Jim's new play, and it was called "TB Wing, 50X." The idea was for our Quickside Guard, the big and very tough Mike Youtt, to hit this quick filling MLB head on in the hole, and "quick read" block him, thereby letting the FB read and cut around that block whichever way was easiest, either to his right or his left. It took away some of the effect from Number 85's ability to fill the hole as he had done against our 50 Trap before, as we were now blocking him head-on with this new scheme, as opposed to from the side on 50 Trap. The other difference was that the play started with an 84 fake to the HB and a quick pivot, handoff to the FB after a short jab step, instead of the sprint action handoff on 50 Trap. The 84 fake should distract the MLB and create a little hesitation in his "fill" move, which would help set up the block on him. The fake might also make him lean a little to his left (offensive right) and make the read block a little easier.

Further, on this 50X play, we would Cross Block to the offensive left side Defensive Guard with our Center Chatham, and Cut Block the offensive right side Defensive Guard with our Strong Guard Barto, creating a tight corridor for the FB, Preston Coleman, to squeeze through. These were three very difficult, and each were crucial blocks on this play, which required perfect timing, but our linemen were so good that they executed perfectly the few times we ran the play. Once again, Coach Watson had worked these new blocks and assignments to perfection in practice the week before the game, and they looked as if we had been running them all year.

Barto the Strongside Guard's block was particularly difficult as he had to cut his man, by putting his headgear right into the inside of the right leg very quickly to prevent him from reacting into the hole. But Barto, although smallish at around 90 lbs., was very quick and tenacious and up to the task. Youtt, the Quickside Guard had a difficult head on block, but he was big, quick and plenty tough for his assignment. Additionally, Youtt had the advantage of using an option or "read" block, which meant he could block (or point, as we called it) his man right or left whichever was easier for him. Chatham, the Center, had to be quick to reach his man before allowing penetration that would have disrupted the play. The Center had the most advantageous angle of any of these three crucial blocks.

The play, 50X could be run out of the Power I as well, but using the TB Wing formation would also help disguise the new 84 Reverse, which would have been more predictable if it were the only play out of the new TB Wing formation. I could run anything in our 84 series out of this new formation except the 84B option, which I was not going to use this night anyway, or 84X, which I did continue to use out of the base Power I.

Many teams will tip off their upcoming play by using a single play out of a single formation. If properly scouted, when you see that formation, you know what play is coming. I wanted to avoid that and actually used 50X out of both formations that night.

Our third strategic point going into this game was to attack this very good MLB with different blockers from different directions and angles on our other plays, the new plays as well as the old ones. So, instead of 50 Trap, it was 50X with different backfield action and line blocking. On other plays we would slam the MLB with a Tackle or End, to keep him guessing and looking, instead of instinctively reacting which was what he was so good at. The new 84 Reverse called for the Quickside End to come all the way in and blindside him at MLB. This would pick him off as we expected him to turn and pursue the reverse.

The new play 50X and the variety of blocks and angles we threw at the MLB were the plans to offset that part of the Tucker defensive strength mentioned earlier. We had decided it was best to attack this very good player rather than try and avoid him. He was realistically too good to avoid anyway.

We ran the new 84 Reverse twice that night, and made big plays both times. That play was specially designed for that night against that defense and I don't believe I ever used it again in any subsequent season. It just happened to be the right thing against this particular team and their defensive scheme. Same thing with 50X, we never used it again, but it was very successful against this Tucker defense, whereas I am sure 50 Trap would not have worked near as well this particular night.

This new reverse play also started with an 84 fake, which is a HB dive, and then a handoff to the TB crossing behind the QB from his wing position. The FB would also take a step to his right, his usual move on an 84 series play, he would then reverse pivot and trap/hook (option block) block the backside Defensive End with the reversing TB reading that block.

FB Preston Coleman was able to hook block that End and get TB Brewer outside both times we ran the play that night, which was what we had planned and hoped would happen based on the technique and alignment we had expected that Defensive End to use. The MLB was not a factor on this play due to the misdirection in the backfield and the block on him by our Quickside Ends Chris Whitley and Jamie Killingsworth.

Going into a game like this, with new plays that I'm confident in, I want the ball first. I hate it when teams win the toss and defer to the second half. I thought our new plays would work and I wanted to try them quickly and get the lead and momentum. Often, you will see teams that are running new plays have early success. I had scripted the sequence of plays I wanted to start the game with, and I badly wanted the ball first.

We had decided to go with an all white uniform (except for the orange helmet) for this game. Luckily, we won the toss and received the kickoff. Even though it was very cold, with temperatures in the low 20's, one of the coldest games we ever played, we started hot and drove 59 yards in eight plays and scored a Touchdown, using a combination of the new plays and our basic offense. We were very quick off tackle, outside and inside, everything worked to perfection, even the new reverse.

The series went something like this: On 1st down, as usual, on our first offensive snap of any big game, I often called for an 84K which was an 84 fake, and the QB keeping off tackle behind the Halfback's fake and lead block. I always wanted my QB to get hit the first play of a game to help get rid of jitters and to get the feel of the defense. I also thought that was important due to the extremely cold weather on this particular night.

This night, I called the 84K out of the new TB Wing formation to show that formation to Tucker, and hopefully help setup that new reverse.

Then, on script, we ran 26, our basic Power I off tackle read play. Neil Brewer was very quick to the hole and ran for about 15 yards behind perfect blocking, as HB Petey Frye was able to get a good hook block on that excellent Tucker End, number 83, allowing Neil to make the outside read and scoot around Frye's block for the good yardage. A slam block (he hits the Tackle first and then releases to the "second level" or MLB) by Strong End Phillip Reeves successfully sealed off that dangerous MLB.

1st down again, we run TB Wing, 50X, the new inside play to our FB. Mike Youtt, our Quickside Guard hit their Middle Linebacker so hard on his quick read block that we heard the collision and saw the MLB's head jerk backwards from the sideline, allowing FB Preston Coleman to read the block, and cut left as he cleared the line and gained about 20 more. 1st down again, and we run TB Wing, 84 Reverse, the other new play, and Neil Brewer gained another quick first down, as the FB Coleman was able to hook their backside End as planned, and Chris Whitley had come in from his Quickside End position and hit the MLB from his blind side.

By now, Tucker's MLB had been hit by three different players from three different directions on these three plays, once from each direction by an End, and once from head on by a pulling Guard. This had led to three first downs in our first four plays. Another four plays and we've scored a TD to start the game.

Tucker's number 83, the left End/OLB, was also a great placekicker, and we used our TB Neil Brewer, who was little (about 80 lbs.) and could barely get it over the cross bar, but Neil made his kick and we're ahead 7-0. Then, we kicked off, and Tucker fumbled from scrimmage a couple of plays after the return. We recovered on the Tucker 48 yard line and scored again after five more plays, ending with a 20 yard pass on a 26-2 route from Guerin to Phillip Reeves for the TD. Another wobbly extra point kick by Brewer, and we're up 14-0 before the end of the first quarter.

Then, any thoughts of a runaway ended as things changed bad just as quickly as our fast start had been good. With their great passing attack and a Running Back named Mark Gurley, Tucker fought back to cut it to14-10 at halftime, and in the third quarter took the lead 17-14. They had scored 17 unanswered points! Could we come back? We had not been behind in over two years!

Late in the 3rd quarter, we put together another drive highlighted by the new plays and a key third down bootleg pass for 20 yards from QB Richie Guerin to Chris Whitley. We finally ran it in early in the fourth quarter and led 21-17 after Brewer's third PAT. Tucker's great kicker kicked another long field goal in the fourth quarter, and finished the game driving in our territory as the clock ran out.

We had held on to win 21-20, but what a game! Neil Brewer had barely scratched out our three extra points, but amazingly those kicks would make the difference! Bob Johnson's warning from the previous year was right as usual. Each extra point had been vital. Tucker's super kicker made his two PAT's, plus two long field goals.

I later heard that the fabulous number 83 for Tucker was none other than Kevin Butler, the soon to be famous Redan High QB, and Georgia

Bulldog and Chicago Bear Placekicker. A few years later, another Tucker player that I met who had been on that team confirmed that fact for me, so I believe it to be true.

Whether it was Kevin Butler or not, the kid was a great player as a defensive End and Kicker, as were their MLB, QB, RB's and receivers. This was a great football game at St. Pius X High School stadium, with two great teams, on a very cold night. Too bad someone had to lose!

But, as they say in March Madness we had "survived and advanced," and now it's on to the championship game against the North DeKalb Chargers in the "Bobby Dodd Bowl." This particular year, it was to be played on the Astroturf of Georgia Tech's Grant Field, now also known as Bobby Dodd Stadium after the legendary Tech coach. North DeKalb was our biggest and closest in proximity neighborhood rival, as several of the players on both teams went to the same schools.

We had scrimmaged them in summer practice and it had gotten pretty rough, hard hitting and trash talking, with borderline even late hitting. We knew it would be a grudge match battle. Again, they were a much larger team than we were.

We did only one unique thing for this game. North DeKalb used a defense similar to ours, and their Strong Safety or "Monster" would usually line up shallow in the secondary one of two places, either inside or outside the defensive end on the offense's strong side. We had a choice of two plays that we knew could be very successful against either of those alignments. To take a little advantage of that we put in an A-B option where we would call A-B in the huddle, and run an 84B option if the Monster was inside and an 86A veer if he lined up outside. QB Guerin would call A-B in the huddle and then shout either A or B at the line based on the Monster's alignment. I have since observed that many QB's will key their audible calls by the location of a Safety.

This game was on a bright, sunny day with perfect temperatures in the 50's, kicking off at Noon. Dressed in all white again this week, we kicked off and North DeKalb returned close to mid field, where they made one first down and punted to our 10 yard line where we had a short five or six yard return up to our own 15 yard line.

We started our first drive with an A-B call, and Richie Guerin correctly called the B at the scrimmage line as the Monster was lined up inside. Strong End Phillip Reeves got a perfect hook block on the Monster, Richie read the option properly and pitched to TB Neil Brewer for a quick 12 yard gain. That immediately gained some better field position and some positive momentum, and then we made consistent yards with our base running plays, and arrived at the North DeKalb 17 yard line after about 8 plays, where we stalled with a 4th down and two yards to go after a rare dropped pass on 2nd down that would have taken us inside the 10 yard line had it not been dropped.

There, we stopped and called timeout to talk over what play to call that could gain the necessary two yards to keep this opening drive moving. We were too far out for a Field Goal. As usual, I conferred on this crucial play call with Coaches Warner Head and Warren Watson, and we decided on our reliable play action corner route pass run option to the Strongside.

The play call was 26-2 which had scored a TD the previous week against Tucker. It calls for a fake 26, our base off tackle running play, and two receivers in the pass route. It's a very effective pass play against either a three deep or twin safety "quarters" coverage. North DeKalb had been in 3 deep in this game, and that was what we expected on the 4th and 2.

The 26-2 pass play starts with a 26 running play fake to the Tailback. Leading the play, the Fullback slips through the line and attains about 6 yards depth downfield and squares into the flat. The Strongside Tight End runs a deep corner route, achieving about 25 yards in depth depending on coverage and situation. After the 26 fake, the QB has three options, looking deep first, and then secondly to the FB. The third option is for the QB to keep and run. The QB's read is off the Corner's coverage as the play unfolds.

If the defensive corner stays up and covers the FB, the End will be open deep for a long gain, and if the corner drops back and covers deep, the FB will be open and we can get the first down by throwing to him. The third option is for the QB to keep and run as he is moving toward the outside in a moving pocket. The HB (in this case Petey Frye, an exceptional blocker) has "pass block hook" responsibility against the Defensive End, preventing the end's ability to maintain outside containment. With the TB filling the off tackle hole, all gaps are covered and any blitzing LB should be accounted for, eliminating that threat from breaking up the run option or sacking the QB. The QB keep and run is another way to get the two yards needed for the first down in this situation, and keep the game's opening drive alive deep in enemy territory That third option is an especially inviting alternative with an excellent runner at QB like Richie Guerin.

Calling a pass play in that situation might seem to some like a pretty risky call, but we thought that options two and three hedged the risk sufficiently. Additionally, the play and the ball would be in the hands of

QB Richie Guerin, arguably our best player and I had supreme confidence in him. Richie had a lot of self confidence, as well.

Also, there was one more very important fact that might possibly be overlooked by the casual observer. Despite the recent 2nd down dropped pass which was highly unusual, our passing game was very efficient. We had a very high completion ratio, as we practiced the passing game vigorously and frequently. Our pass receivers had to make one handed catches in some of our practice drills which is a great way to improve concentration and hand eye coordination. Therefore, we dropped very few catchable passes. Also, the repeated practice and timing drills made our passers very accurate. I felt strongly that it would be a well thrown pass and would not be dropped.

On this crucial 4th down play, during the timeout, I told QB Guerin to look for the FB on the short route first as I was most concerned with getting first down yardage. As the play unfolded, Guerin made a perfect fake, but that drew the corner in, and he "jumped on" the short route. Richie saw that, made the proper deep read, and threw the long pass perfectly where it hit wide open End Phillip Reeves right in the stomach about five yards deep in the end zone for the TD. Colts lead 7-0 after the opening 85 yard TD drive, culminated by the 17 yard TD pass and Brewer PAT.

After the ensuing kickoff, the Chargers made another couple of first downs running the basic split veer offense, and on a 3rd down play around mid-field, their QB, a very good player in Ken Escoe, made an errant pitch on an option play, and it was recovered by linebacker Ron Kurtzer who Coach Lineberger had nicknamed "Wild Man." After another short drive, HB John Lovelace went all the way for a long TD run on a 96 sweep.

The Lovelace TD was a weakside sweep called 96 out of the Power I formation. He took it to the end zone from 52 yards, just like he had done in a 7-0 win over Roswell in regular season. The 96 weakside sweep starts with the FB and TB leading the HB around the backside end. It calls for a trap/hook option block by the FB on the End and a read and lead by the TB followed by the ball carrying HB. It is an excellent, low risk, weakside power sweep with all gaps protected by the offensive line.

In this case, FB Preston Coleman trap blocked (blocked out) the End and TB Brewer led Lovelace through the hole created and sealed by the post and read drive blocking (Double Teaming) of Quickside End Chris Whitley and Quickside Tackle Tommy "T-Bird" Rose. Lovelace got into the Charger secondary, and cut back all the way diagonally across the Astroturf field using his blazing speed to take it all the way.

We had another scoring opportunity in the first half, but our drive stalled on fourth down at the North DeKalb five yard line, but we still held the 14-0 lead at halftime. North DeKalb had crossed the 50 only twice in the first half, never getting inside our 40 yard line.

In the 3rd Quarter, we were driving again, and Neil Brewer broke another long run for a 43 yard TD on a play we called "20 Countertrap Outside." On this play, the play starts out like an inside off tackle lead play over the Strong Tackle. Instead, after a couple of his normal off tackle steps, the TB cuts back toward the weakside and the QB, who has his back to the line after making a 180 degree counter clockwise spin, hands to the TB cutting back toward the weakside end. The Strong Guard pulls and has option block responsibility on the backside Defensive End while our End and Tackle on that side execute a post and read drive seal similarly to the 96 play. After blocking down on the Defensive tackle, our End releases onto the defensive corner as a lead blocker.

On this particular play Strong Guard Barto trapped the End, Neil cut inside the trap block as Killingsworth blocked the Corner, made another head fake to get around the Safety, and raced all the way to the End Zone.

That play is difficult for the Tailback, requiring quick footwork and superior cutting ability, but Neil was very good at it, as was Mark Wheaton, our 100 lb. Colt TB two years later.

The rest of the day was all Colts. Jim's defense led by Scott Smith, Ron Barto and Kevin Waxman, had several sacks, fumble recoveries and interceptions for 4 takeaways. Neil Brewer had over 120 yards rushing including the 43 yard TD, and John Lovelace, the big and speedy Halfback had over 90 yards rushing including the 50 yard TD.

So we had won a third straight Bobby Dodd Bowl GYFC Championship, at Coach Dodd's home stadium with Coach Dodd himself in attendance. After three tries, we had not given up a single point in championship game play.

We had two postseason bowl games to go. The Colt Classic, always held the Friday after Thanksgiving on Colt Field, and an away bowl game, The Coral Bowl, to be played in Cape Coral, Florida.

These post season games were fun, and they were intended to be socially interactive as well as good competitive football bowl games. Our away bowl trips were first class and great fun for the players, with some experiencing air travel for the first time. The visiting players would stay in the homes of the home team players, and there would be at least one cocktail party for the parents of both teams.

The parties could get interesting, usually due to the consumption of adult beverages, and there was usually a good bit of boasting and posturing from some of the more vocal parents, on both sides. There is a famous quote from Carroll Rushing, father of Mitch and John "Bubba" Rushing from back at the 1972 Colt Classic cocktail party.

Mr. Rushing was quite a character himself and he came up to me before our game against the Charlotte Bears and said in jest "We're in trouble Coach."

I replied "why is that?"

And he quickly answered "they (the Charlotte parents) can drink more likkah (the way he pronounced liquor) than we can," referring to the previous night's party.

There's another Carroll Rushing story that I cannot print here.

The Colt Classic was pretty uneventful this year of 1974, a methodical19-0 win over a good team from Columbia, Maryland. It was highlighted by a 49 yard punt return for a TD by Guerin, a one yard plunge by HB Petey Frye after a medium length drive and an 18 yard TD pass from Guerin to FB Preston Coleman.

But the Coral Bowl was a little more interesting as the Cape Coral Sharks were also undefeated, and champion of their conference, called the "Peace River League" in Southwest Florida. They had only given up one TD all year. So, as both teams were undefeated and their reigning conference champs, there was a great deal of boasting going on at the parents party the Friday night before the Saturday night game. In fact, I heard that there was a $1,000 bet made on the outcome of the game between two of the more boastful fathers.

The following night, before the game during warm ups, I later heard the two men had gotten together and agreed to "remove one of the 0's" off the $ figure, thus reducing the bet to $100. The game was no contest, with our Colts winning 54-0. It turns out the league the Sharks played in was not nearly the level of competition that the Varsity Colts played in every week in the tough GYFC.

I did not particularly like winning games with that many points and we went to some lengths to try not to run up the score. But our second string players who ran a version of the wishbone, led by QB "Broadway" Phillip Reeves, FB "Roosevelt" Scott Rodwin and HB "Wilbur" Tony Harris wanted to get on the field and do their best, so we let them, and even with conservative play calling, we kept getting in the end zone.

The 1974 team went 13-0-1 and I had coached Richie Guerin 5 years, Preston Coleman 5 years, Jeff Amtower 4 years, and several others three years. These were great kids, hard workers and I would come to really miss them. They had won three GYFC Bobby Dodd Bowl Championships in a row, a truly fantastic and well behaved group of pre-teen students and football players, and excellent representatives of a great football program. I was proud to be associated with this great group of players and coaches. I had a hard time thinking of what the next year might be like without them.

*   *   *

1973 80 LB AND 1974 100 LB Atlanta Colts Key Performers

Richie Guerin, QB and Safety . . . Richie was a natural athlete, the son of a NBA player and coach. He was very fast and had natural instincts as a runner, punt returner and defensive Safety. He was very smart and learned the Quarterback position very well when forced into that by the starter's injury in 1974. He was the natural leader of these teams both years.

Preston Coleman, FB and LB . . . Preston was fast and tough. He was a hard runner, running with a low pad level and good balance. He mastered the 50 trap play early in 1973 and was successful with it for both years, gaining over 230 yards in one Bobby Dodd Bowl game and over 100 in several others. He was an excellent outside linebacker, very smart and a sure tackler. He was a pretty quiet kid, but a very tough hard hitter with good deceptive speed.

Max "Petey" Frye, HB and LB . . . Petey was another very tough kid and he was a very good blocking back. Playing HB, he was the lead blocker on many running plays, particularly our two off tackle plays of 26 and 84X. He was also a good runner and very good at linebacker, playing both inside and outside. He went on to a successful high school career as a Running Back at Peachtree High in their Split Veer Offense.

Ron Barto, OG, DE and LB . . . Ron Barto was an outstanding Offensive Guard. Playing the strongside he was the pulling guard on 50 Trap. He was also an outstanding Defensive End in 1973 and linebacker in 1974. He was a hard hitter and pound for pound one of the best ever, making Pop Warner All American in 1975.

Jeff Lineberger, QB and LB . . . Jeff was an outstanding QB for us in 1973 and the starter going into 1974 when he was injured in preseason. Although he did not regain the starting position due to Guerin's outstanding play, he would likely have been just as good. He was even better on defense as an inside linebacker where he had great instincts and was a hard hitter and sure tackler. Jeff went on to play QB at Chamblee High School.

Kenny Passarella, OT and DT . . . As strongside Tackle on offense, Kenny was the point of attack blocker most of the time and he was very good at that. He had a low center of gravity and thus played with an extremely low pad level which made him that much better. He was also very tough and an outstanding defensive lineman as well.

Neil Brewer, TB and CB . . . Neil was a natural runner. He was quick and fast, had outstanding running instincts and cutting ability. He had many long TD runs and could also run low and make the tough yards inside. He was a good defender and also very instinctive pass defender and he was tough enough to be a sure tackler.

Phillip Reeves, End and LB . . . Phillip was a sure handed receiver and excellent all around athlete. He caught crucial passes in many games, including both playoff games in 1974. He was also an excellent defender and was a very good linebacker at Dunwoody High School.

Jimmy Awbrey, HB . . . Jimmy was small, but lightning fast. He played for us both years as a reserve HB. Had he played a year or two later with some of the offensive changes we made, he would have been even better, as the HB was featured more with some of the new plays. He gets special mention as a SEC Decathlon Champion while running track at Auburn University.

1974 100 lb. Atlanta Colts Record, 13-0-1

GYFC Bobby Dodd Bowl Champions
Atlanta Colt Classic Champions
Coral Bowl Champions

Colts 21 .... Briarcliff 12
Colts 26 .... Midway 7
Colts 7 .... Tucker 0
Colts 7 .... Smyrna 0
Colts 7 .... Northeast 7
Colts 16 .... Forest Park 6
Colts 7 .... Roswell 0
Colts 21 .... Clairmont 0
Colts 38 .... Sandy Springs 0
Colts 35 .... Glenwood 0

GYFC Semi-Final, The Jim Brazier Bowl, St. Pius X High School, Atlanta, Georgia

Colts 21 . . . . Tucker 20

GYFC Championship, The Bobby Dodd Bowl, Grant Field, Atlanta, Georgia

Colts 21 . . . . North DeKalb 0

Atlanta Colt Classic, Colt Field, Murphy Candler Park, Atlanta, Georgia

Colts 19 . . . . Columbia, Md 0

Coral Bowl, Cape Coral, Florida

Colts 54 . . . . Cape Coral 0

1974 100 lb. Atlanta Colts Starting Lineups

OFFENSE

Strong End.................... Phillip Reeves
Strong Tackle................ Kenny Passarella
Strong Guard .... Ron Barto
Center.......................... Richard Chatham
Quick Guard................ Mike Youtt
Quick Tackle................ Tommy "T-Bird" Rose
Quick End .... Chris Whitley
Quarterback................. Richie Guerin
Halfback .... John Lovelace
Fullback .... Preston Coleman
Tailback........................ Neil Brewer

DEFENSE

Left End....................................... Scott Smith
Left Tackle................................... Kevin Waxman
Nose Guard.................................. Mike Youtt
Right Tackle .... Hayes McMath
Right End .... Tim Hartigan
Left Linebacker .... Ron Barto
Right Linebacker.......................... Jeff Lineberger
Strong Safety or "Monster" LB ...... Petey Frye
Left Cornerback .... Neil Brewer
Right Cornerback......................... Jeff Amtower
Safety .... Richie Guerin

Coaches . . . . Doug Bennett, Head Coach
Warren Watson, Offensive and Defensive Line Coach
Jim Lineberger, Defensive Coordinator and Linebacker Coach
Warner Head, Offensive Backfield and Quarterback Coach
Fred Amtower, Defensive Backfield Coach

1974 100 lb. Atlanta Colts Complete Roster

Joey Walker
Bill Carlson
Ron Barto
Mike Youtt
Scott Carpenter
Scott Smith
Kevin Waxman
John Lovelace
Preston Coleman
Vince Vassil
Petey Frye
Jeff Lineberger
Jeff Amtower
Tim Hayes
Tom Archer

Hayes McMath
Kenny Passarella
Richard Chatham
Tommy "T-Bird" Rose
Donnie Rutledge
Chris Whitley
Tim Hartigan
Tommy Wilson
Mike Smalley
Bruce Grant
Phillip Reeves
Richie Guerin
Jimmy Awbrey
Ron Kurtzer
Neil Brewer

Cheerleaders

Shawn Amtower
Melanie McGuirk
Beth Coulter
Debbie Trense
Dee McGowan
Susan Frye

Caren Abernathy
Nancy Love
Debbie Schmitz
Susan Miller
Holly Hansberger

1974 120 lb. Atlanta Colts Record, 14-0

GYFC Champions
Atlanta Colt Classic Champions
Coral Bowl Champions

Colts 21 Briarcliff 0
Colts 40 Midway 0
Colts 28 Sandy Springs 3
Colts 26 Tucker 14
Colts 42 Smyrna 6
Colts 21 Northeast 6
Colts 17 Forest Park 6
Colts 28 Roswell 0
Colts 35 Clairmont 0
Colts 7 Glenwood 0

GYFC Semi-Final, The Jim Brazier Bowl, St. Pius X High School, Atlanta, Georgia

Colts 42 Tucker 17

GYFC Championship, The Bobby Dodd Bowl, Grant Field, Atlanta, Georgia

Colts 17 East Point 7

Atlanta Colt Classic, Colt Field, Murphy Candler Park, Atlanta, Georgia

Colts 34 Fairmont, WV 0

The Coral Bowl, Cape Coral, Florida

Colts 38 Cape Coral 0

1974 120 lb. Atlanta Colts Complete Roster

Jamie Swancey
Andy Hallenberg
Phillip Ebinger
Chip Dickens
John Hardie
Jeff Herring
Marty Connolly
Clay Campbell
Obi Ingram
Jim Blake
Paul Markley
Scott Rogers
Scott Nicholson
John "Bubba" Rushing
Scott Willis

Scott Prosch
Roy Thornton
Ronnie Gaylor
Tom Love
Tony Sutter
Mitch Rushing
David Newby
Doug Sloter
Jeff Booker
Dwayne Chester
Scott Hardy
Robert Rudder
Rich Papineau
Craig Estep
Gary Newsom

Coaching Staff

Bob Johnson Head Coach
Frank Greene
Chuck Willis
George Copelan
Tim Mitchell

Cheeleaders

Julia Bradbury
Pam Brown
Cindy Radtke
Tina Sutter
Wendy Uhlir
Susie Willis

Kelly Parks
Vicki Foley
Karen Wyatt
Beth Doss
Cathy Anderson
Lynn Rushing

1974 80 lb. Atlanta Colts Record 11-1

GYFC Sub Division Champions
Atlanta Colt Classic Champions

Colts 35 Briarcliff 0
Colts 41 Midway 0
Colts 17 Sandy Springs 0
Colts 9 Tucker 0
Colts 21 Smyrna 0
Colts 20 Northeast 0
Colts 14 Forest Park 6
Colts 21 Roswell 7
Colts 25 Clairmont 0
Colts 21 Glenwood 0

GYFC Semi-Final, The Jim Brazier Bowl, St. Pius X High School, Atlanta, Georgia

Colts 2 Tucker 6

Atlanta Colt Classic, Colt Field, Murphy Candler Park, Atlanta, Georgia

Colts 38 Charlotte 0

1974 80 lb. Atlanta Colts Complete Roster

Jim Caudill	Greg Barto
Peter Stephens	James Waring
Ricky Hodges	Neil Gifford
David Killingsworth	Alan Delk
Jeff Currier	Troy Ragan
Jeff Anderson	D. H. Malcom
Mike Rosing	John Cravey
Tom DiFiore	Alan Lindsay
John Murphy	Mike Yancey
Mike Stovall	Steve Noles
Alan Thompson	Marc Douglass
Scott Hardy	Mike Hartigan
Mark Timmons	Mike Coveny
Mallon Ellenburg	Dean Stoll
Scott Young	Mike Gurr
Scott Rodwin	Steve Mahoney
Tommy Rose	

Coaching Staff

Mac Scoggins Head Coach
Charlie Ragan
Bob Chatham
Bill Whitley
Jim Awbrey

Cheerleaders

Jan Ragsdale	Debbie Rader
Jeannie Whitley	Lisa Terry
Kate Lundberg	Kim Barber
Marianne Seidel	Mary Papineau
Laura Ramsey	Susan Perdue
Shannon Scoggins	

1974 Coltettes Drill Team

Diane Mitchell
Laine Beck
Donna McMillan
Julie Perry
Carol Spurlock
Evelyn Davis
Laurie McCoy
Suzanne Williams
Theresa Donahoo
Deborah Clark
Stephanie Davis
Melinda Travis
Jolene Storey
Cindy Wilson
Pam Powell

Jenny Putnal
Sara Kepic
Sheri Lynn Williams
Linda Rhine
Kathy Brown
Kim Lane
Kae Brock
Ann Goode
Sharon Fogarty
Mary Williams
Ashley Howard
Jackie Harlow
Kelly Howard
Joan Alexander
Paula Powell

Director

Jean Davis

CHAPTER 10

. . . . 1975

After winning at least two GYFC Championships every year in the decade from 1970 through 1974, the ACYA only managed one and a half in 1975 with our 100 lb. Colts winning outright and Mac Scoggins's 80 lb. Colts tying for a co-championship.

The 120 lb. team had a subpar 6-3-1 regular season finishing second in their subdivision. They also went 0-2 in the post season bowl games losing close ones in the Colt Classic to the Fort Myers Rebels 21-7 and in the Greater Miami Pop Warner Bowl to Miami K-Land 16-14.

Bob Johnson had lost two of his veteran assistant coaches, Chuck Willis and George Copelan, but replaced them with quality coaches in Bill Whitley, Fred Amtower, Bob Rader, Bob Chatham and Bob Thomas. George Copelan had been an outstanding offensive line coach, as good as Warren Watson, but in a much more charismatic way as he was quite a motivator and character too. I know he was badly missed even though those that replaced him were quality coaches and knew a lot of football.

The same was true with Chuck Willis. He had been with Bob a long time, and replacing a coach who you knew so well was problematic, regardless of how good a coach the replacement is. It just takes coaches a year or so to blend together, run efficient practices, anticipate each other's minds and moves and learn to be cohesive as a staff. Chuck and George were both like that and they knew exactly what Bob wanted and expected of them. Also, all coaches had business careers and taking a lot of time for coaching was a lot easier for some than others, particularly difficult for those that traveled in business.

George and Chuck were both self employed which had allowed for a greater time commitment for each of them.

100 lb. Colt Tailback Mike Coveny leaping over a Central DeKalb, defender for yardage in the 1975 Bobby Dodd Bowl GYFC Championship game in the Colts upset victory over the 11-0 Cardinals.

Mac Scoggins led his 80 lb. team to a second consecutive 10-0 regular season record. This time, they won the first round GYFC playoff 20-6 over East Point, and advanced to the Bobby Dodd Bowl, where they outplayed Tucker, but were held to a scoreless tie. The tie resulted in a co-championship. It was unfortunate that the GYFC had discontinued using the GHSA Penetration Rule as a tie breaker, and thus awarded both teams the co-championship. Recall GHSA Penetration rules had resulted in a Championship tiebreaker for our 1972 80 lb. Colts after a 0-0 tie with Forest Park. Mac's team was not as fortunate.

Mac's team lost the Colt Classic to a tough Palmetto Raider team from Miami in a hard fought 12-7 game. They finished 11-1-1, an outstanding record and a very good team. That would make Mac's record 22-2-1 in his first two years. He would win his next 38 consecutive games.

The overall Varsity record for 1975 was 29-8-2.

* * *

1975 100 lb. Atlanta Colts, The Year of the "Comeback Kids"

Coming in to the 1975 season we were full of confidence as the 100 lb. Colt coaching staff, after winning three straight GYFC championships. We had a brand new team coming up from the previous year's 80 lb. team that had gone 11-1 under Mac Scoggins. It would be our first Colt team without the nucleus of players like Guerin, Coleman, Frye, Brewer, Lineberger, Barto et al. We did have three returning coaches, myself, Warren Watson and Jim Lineberger.

Coach Fred Amtower moved up to assist Bob Johnson with the 120 lb Colt team, but we replaced him with the equally capable Frank Reeves. Frank knew our systems very well, as he had been a close observer the previous three years, as his son Phillip had been a key part of those 1973 and 1974 championship teams. Warner Head was forced to give up coaching due to family and business obligations, but I had learned how to coach the QB position from working with him for the past 5 years, and Frank ably assisted me with the remaining backfield coaching duties. I had similarly learned a great deal from Fred Amtower and Bob Johnson on coaching the other backfield positions.

We had a great nucleus of incoming players from Mac Scoggins's 80 lb. Colt team who had gone 11-1, barely losing out in the 1974 GYFC Brazier Bowl playoff game to Tucker. Veterans like TB Mike Coveny, QB Alan Lindsey, OG Scott Hardy, FB Jeff Anderson HB/TB Tommy Rose, HB Mike Rosing, and many others. We also brought in newcomers who would make great contributions like LB and DL's Ronnie and Donnie Scott and LB Scott Sherretz, a lot of big, talented, fast, hard hitting players.

We were extremely confident in our offensive and defensive systems and strategies, having won three consecutive Bobby Dodd Bowls, and I did not see any reason why we should not repeat as 100 lb GYFC champion. Actually, this group of players was probably more talented and definitely bigger and faster than last year's undefeated championship team. We went through the usual tough summer practices, including two a days for two weeks, and we thought we were right on track with where we needed to be going into the season. Our opening game was with Tucker at home, the same opponent we had barely beaten in the previous year's thrilling playoff game 21-20.

We knew they would be good as they had a nucleus of players left over from that 1974 100 lb. team, and a very good group of new players coming up from the 80 lb. GYFC championship team that had beaten Mac's 80 lb.

Colts, 6-2 in playoff Round One. Our own teams had now beaten Tucker four times in a row in '73 and '74, two in regular season, both at Tucker's home of Fitzgerald Field, and two in playoff games on neutral fields.

Due to having lost four straight to us, I thought surely Tucker would have the same opening game jitters, mistakes, etc associated with playing us in game one that we might have playing them. I always had a great deal of respect for any Tucker team, but at least we had the home field advantage this time, and I fully expected to win this game. We had played three consecutive years of regular season games at Tucker's Fitzgerald Field in a GYFC scheduling quirk.

Well, there were no jitters or mistakes for Tucker. On Colt Field, our famous home game field where we had not lost in three years, they came right in and handed us a humiliating loss, 27-7. It probably should not have been that close. Their Running Backs Mark Gurley, who had played great in last year's 21-20 game, and Steve Bennett (no relation to me) were outstanding as was their QB. In addition, they stopped our Offense pretty cold with their Defense.

What had gone wrong? This was a huge surprise; we had not lost in 31 games, since the regular season in 1972. We were not expecting to lose this game, much less this badly. This just doesn't happen to the Colts! Our previous losses all the way back in 1972 had all been close games, and this was a blowout. David Johnson's 100 lb. teams had never been beaten this badly and neither had Jim Wilson's.

I was shell shocked and I didn't really have an answer, although I did have to try and provide an answer to my Athletic Director, the afore-mentioned Mr. Bob Johnson, who had little tolerance for losing! let alone to Tucker! And on Colt Field! And by 20 points!!

Here's how it went Monday when I saw Bob right before practice: "Doug, son," (I was 27 years old) he said, "We haven't been beaten that bad since that "scallywag" _____ was a coach here." (he was referring to a previous unsuccessful Colt coach from the early years of ACYA whose name I should not reveal here) Well, I knew that this particular coach had a bad record and reputation, and I certainly did not want to be associated or compared with that name in any way. (That's why I did not reveal his name)

After hearing that from Bob, I walked out onto the practice field thinking to myself, "I didn't think I could feel any worse than I did on Saturday after the game, but I do now.

He (Bob Johnson) thinks I'm as bad as _____
(the unnamed coach)." But we had already lost and we couldn't do anything about it. We could only try to make something of the rest of our season and hopefully get our revenge against Tucker in the playoffs.

I looked up to Bob Johnson, and the last thing I wanted to do was let him down, and be compared to someone he had such little respect for. Terms like "scallywag" were the worst names he would ever call anyone. Bob used absolutely no profanity or foul language of any kind. I did hear him refer to someone as a "knucklehead" once.

In reality, Bob was not upset with me, as I look back, that was just a way he used of adding extra motivation for me. He could provide motivation as well as anyone I've ever observed. I already knew from 1972 that I was more motivated by the distaste for losing as much as the joy of winning, particularly after this loss in the season opener. The saying goes, "the lows are lower than the highs are high."

I also did not want to let my coaches, players or their parents down. The Atlanta Colt mantra, as established by Bob Johnson, is all about winning and doing your best, and doing it with class and good sportsmanship, similar to Bear Bryant and Alabama. Like Coach Bryant, Bob Johnson wanted our players to knock the living daylights out of the opponent, then reach down and help them up with a pat on the behind.

I did not want to be associated with anything less. We might lose, but we would not go down without a fight. But this day against Tucker, we did not put up much of a fight. Bob Johnson and the whole ACYA program were watching now to see how we would respond after this devastating season opening loss.

Similar to disgruntled fans and alumni of college teams, I also had to answer to the parents of our current players. There had been some parental unrest and criticism among my team's parents of me back in the 1972 four loss season right up to when the GYFC handed us the championship trophy. I knew it, as some of those parents called me frequently with criticism, suggestions, second guessing etc. and I heard of others, some of which simply thought that my entire coaching staff (mostly myself as head coach) were too young to be in this position of this much responsibility. After all, an Atlanta Colt Head Coach was responsible for leading (and managing) a team of 33 players and their parents, plus 12 cheerleaders and their parents, well over 100 people and a pretty significant management job. Some might think a little too much for a 24 year old.

I actually realized the criticism was justified back then in '72, I was literally in over my head at that time. And I knew I had been very lucky to avoid the great Midway team and squeak out a Bobby Dodd Bowl Penetration win and championship in my first year. Thinking back now, I'm just glad that e-mail and internet message boards weren't around during the middle of that 1972 season. But I had learned so much from Bob Johnson and our teams had done so well the last two years in 1973-74, now with this lopsided loss I don't know what to think!

The GYFC and Colt Classic championships quelled the parental unrest at that time in 1972, and then the years of 1973 and 1974 were relatively criticism free as we were undefeated with one tie in those 27 games.

Now after this opening loss in 1975, I am concerned about that parental unrest possibly recurring, on this team, which would be a major distraction to me. My primary concerns were repairing the damage from this loss and trying to get this team back on track to a playoff run, and hopefully leading to another championship. Now, this group of parents did not know me yet, at least most did not. Why should they be loyal? or patient ?

The only bright spot involved here was that the loss to Tucker had not been a division loss (each season we played 7 GYFC division games and 3 GYFC non-division), so we could still win our subdivision and qualify for post season championship play. That is, assuming we could drastically improve and start playing a whole lot better and win that subdivision. Everybody knows that it is best to have your losses early in the season, especially if you can learn from them and use the knowledge you gain as a springboard to improvement. Most coaches say that you learn more about your team after a loss than after a win. Many also theorize that your team makes its greatest improvement between games one and two in a given season.

In any sport, you can't look too far ahead, and after a start like this one, all you can do is work on one practice at a time and one game at a time, stressing continuous improvement by individuals and continually attempting to blend them together as a team. I knew that we had a very good group of players that were talented and championship worthy. So, we went back to work, doing the only things we knew how to do, working hard on fundamentals, making no changes to our practice routine. But I also felt deep down inside that once again, we needed to make some pretty significant changes to our Offense.

I didn't want to throw out what had worked so well in the past two years. After all, our new (two year old) Offense had produced two championships in a row, in two tries, with a cumulative two year record of 26-0-1 prior to this loss to Tucker. Bob Johnson, and now Mac Scoggins were both very successfully using almost exclusively the Leonard Jones Power I. But I decided to add some new wrinkles to the Offense and expand on things that were already part of the Offense.

I admitted to myself and recognized that Tucker had just stopped us pretty cold in the recent 27-7 loss, as Northeast had also done the previous year in the 7-7 tie. There had been a total of four games in 1974 in which we had only scored seven points, although we managed to win all with 7-0 scores except the tie with Northeast. Those wins were due to the outstanding play of the Lineberger Defense. Jim Lineberger was clearly holding up his end with outstanding defensive coaching, so it was up to me to design ways to make the Offense perform better and score more points.

As I mentioned before also, I had been thinking that we probably needed to be able to spread out an opposing defense on occasion for strategic purposes, especially in this 100 lb. division with more mature players capable of doing more advanced things on both offense and defense. We needed to get our speedy playmakers in open space more of the time and in more different ways.

Those opposing GYFC teams were able to stop us now because they knew our base offense. We weren't hard to scout. Our offense was simple, focusing on the "I" Tailback, and unless we were absolutely superior, we could have a hard time moving the ball, making first downs and scoring points. I knew Bob Johnson's staff could coach a team to be that good in the base Power I Offense, they basically had done it every year since 1970, but I was not sure that we could. I was not confident that we could rely on the brute strength of the Power I and beat really good defenses. I wanted, and felt that my team needed, more versatility.

Furthermore, being held to 7 points is boring and nerve racking, with every game being close. Football is hard work, but it also needs to be fun. Scoring a mere 7 points is neither fun nor exciting for the players or fans. Winning is the ultimate goal, and scoring only 7 points of Offense keeps every opponent in the game against you, within one play of a tie or loss. I wanted to add excitement and fun by creating a more wide open offensive strategy, but without completely abandoning the conservative principles, blocking rules etc. that we held near and dear, and without scrapping the basic offense we already had and starting over.

As I mentioned earlier, the Leonard Jones offense used at North Springs High School incorporated the Fullback and Tailback lined up in the I, but the primary formation also included a Split Veer Halfback lined up directly behind the strong side (usually right, but occasionally left) Guard, creating a "Power" I. Our base formation was Power I Right, but we also used a Power I Left, (we, as taught by coaches Johnson and Jones, called it "L Left").

We already successfully ran a few "Veer" plays in the Leonard Jones Offense featuring the HB that we called our 84 and 86 series out of that Power I, so I knew how The Veer plays fundamentally worked, as I had also learned from coaches Jones and Johnson. The Jones-Johnson play numbering referred to these plays as the 14 and 16 series.

I had also been watching many pure Split Veer college and high school teams over the recent years in the early and mid '70's, and they were very exciting to watch, lots of long runs, options, counter options, and it used formations that were easy to pass out of. It was made popular by the high powered University of Houston in the late '60's coached by Bill Yeoman, and the Offense had spread throughout the NCAA. In fact, my favorite college team, the Georgia Bulldogs coached by Vince Dooley, who was one of my coaching heroes, were using it at the time. Bulldog future head coach Ray Goff was their Quarterback, and he was a great option runner. This offense takes advantage of some natural creases in normal defensive alignments similar to the wishbone, just in different points of the defense. It looked like a fun offense to coach.

The Veer was similar to the triple option wishbone being used by powerhouses Texas, Oklahoma and Alabama, but it employed two backs behind the Quarterback in the backfield instead of three. Therefore, it was better for passing and spreading defenses. It was a high risk offense* with "reading" handoffs and a lot of option pitches, but I knew the risks could be offset by not reading, but pre-determining the handoffs instead. I also felt pretty sure that we could master the option pitches if we practiced them in the same fashion we practiced our passing game. Also, we already had two option plays in our Power I package that we consistently practiced and executed pretty well.

So, I decided to blend more of the basic two back Split Veer Offense into our attack. It fit nicely into schemes we were already using, so it was easy to build off of, pretty simple, and we could use the same blocking rules

---

* The Offense was so high risk that Vince Dooley abandoned it after 1977, his only losing season out of 25 at UGA, due to the costly turnovers his team committed that year.

etc. that we already had in place. We had a good quarterback for it, and Alan Lindsay learned and directed it well all year. But in order to do this, we would need to get out of the Power I some of the time and add new formations.

We would start by always leaving the HB behind the Strongside Guard as we already were doing in our base Power I, and then also move either the TB or FB behind the Weakside Guard, creating a "twin" or divided backfield. The third back (either TB or FB, whichever was not in the "twin") would always be positioned outside, either in a wing, slot or flanker position. If I wanted two tight ends, I would either wing or flank the third back, and if I wanted a Split End, I would slot the third back.

We could also do a pro set, Tight End and Flanker or Wingback on one side, Split End on the other, with the twin backs. Also two split ends, with a slot or flanker either side. If I were coaching it today, I would further incorporate more motion into these various sets to further confuse opponents as well as to set up blocking angles and pass routes. That would work similarly to what today is known as the "H" Back. In fact, we did add motion to one play two years later in 1977 that assisted us in winning a crucial game.

The intention in this new strategy was to give our opponents more different looks, and move our playmakers around lining them up in different places to better utilize their skills and talent. Our backfield players were usually versatile with all three starters being good runners, receivers and blockers, so they would be pretty easily interchangeable.

We were already occasionally flanking or slotting the HB and leaving the TB and FB in the I, so this new strategy fit with that as well, and the play calling and numbering was simple. A single two digit number like 26 meant it was a Power I formation play. To use any different formation, we would call the formation first, then the number, as simple as FB Slot, 90 Countertrap, or TB Flank, 84A, plays we were already using, out of new formations. The name of the formation tells every player where to line up. No formation call before the play number simply means the play is from the base Power I Right formation. A Power I left play is called "L Left" and then the number, and any other formation to the left would be called something like "L left, TB Flank, 86A.'

In fact, now we could run some of the same plays out of several different formations, to either side, creating more of a "multiple" offense. I had learned from Bob Johnson how to move an opposing defensive alignment around with change in formations, and the one time in the past we had broken the I formation, in the previous year's playoff game with Tucker, we had been very successful with it. So why not add more and do it more often?

I believe this was instrumental in turning the 1975 season around as well as to diversify our offensive attack for the years to come. With split backs we could run either way, weak side or strong side, behind a Tight End, Wing or Slot. We could pass to Tight Ends, Split Ends, Flankers or either of the "twin" Backs. We could trap, bootleg and do everything else in the Leonard Jones system. We could still run our I formation lead option attack as well. We would not be near as predictable as we had been when we always lined up in the Power I formation.

100 lb. Colt Halfback Mike Rosing sprints through a large hole in the Central DeKalb defense in the 1975 Bobby Dodd Bowl. This play was a "90 Countertrap" especially designed to take advantage of the speedy Rosing's running ability. Key blocks were thrown by Guards Scott Hardy and Mike Donahue, Center Chris Doty and Tackle Scott Carpenter

The first new play I put in, I called 90 Counter trap, a HB Trap with the same blocking as 50 Trap, with the ball carrier coming into the hole from a different angle and position, and the QB using different footwork on the handoff. It could be run from the Power I or any split veer formation, slot or pro-set, with split or tight ends. It could also be run from the weak side and be called 20 Counter trap or 40 Counter trap with the TB or FB carrying from the weak side twin back position.

It was similar to a counter play that was fundamental to the veer offense the colleges were using at the time. But I made subtle changes in the running angles and blocking, so I could say I made it up, but in reality, I actually copied the basic play and made the slight changes to adapt to our blocking system and the capability of our age group player.

That particular play was an instant success, and what fun and a challenge it was to be able to put in this new system in addition to the tried and true usual I formation plays without confusing the players with new numbering, language etc. I tinkered with it for years, and most of it worked famously!

Another key point I learned from Bob Johnson, Leonard Jones, and other successful coaches that I had read about. It's usually not WHAT you run that matters, it's HOW WELL you run it and how hard you practice it.

Bob Johnson used to say "you can slice a pie a lot of different ways, but it always tastes good if it has the right ingredients." The ingredients to "good tasting" offensive football are blocking, running, passing, receiving, timing and execution. We stayed with our same practice routines as we put in these new formations and plays and repeated them until perfected before we would use anything new in a real game.

In the 1975 season, we continued adding new split veer formations and plays a little at a time after the opener and improved consistently. We won the next four games, scoring an average of over 30 points per game, setting up a big mid-season showdown at Glenwood, at Exchange Park in south DeKalb County. The Glenwood Panther team was the feeder program for the mighty SouthWest DeKalb High School Panthers and wore the same blue and gold colors as SWD.

We were in the same subdivision with Glenwood, so the winner would have the inside track to be subdivision champion, and qualify for the playoffs, thus making this game the key to our season. We had to have this one if we were to have any chance of settling that score with Tucker. The loser of this game would need a lot of help and some luck to recover and win the subdivision. In the event of a tie for first place in the subdivision, the first tiebreaker was the regular season game head to head winner. So this game was vital, particularly in view of our first game loss.

Glenwood's record was a perfect 5-0, and we were 4-1, winners of four in a row after the opening loss to Tucker. The game was at Glenwood. In what was becoming a big game tradition, we were in the all white uniform for this big regular season intra-subdivision game. We had a game plan I was very confident in. As usual, I wanted to win the toss and get off to a fast start. We were very confident that most of our offensive package would work against the Glenwood defensive alignment. The blocking angles were set up almost perfectly. I had scouted Glenwood myself, and it looked pretty easy to run the I formation plays and also easy to trap. We had put in a new counter option play out of a slot formation that I was anxious to try in game conditions.

With no disrespect to Glenwood, a good program with good players and coaches, but this one turned out to be easy! We were hungry to prove ourselves and fired up because of the game's importance. We won the toss and scored a TD on a quick drive in a few plays. We kicked off and held Glenwood to three and out on the next series, forcing a punt. On the next play after the punt, our speedy HB Mike Rosing ran a long 90 Countertrap for a TD behind perfect blocking from about 60 yards out for a quick 14-0 lead.

We kicked off again, Glenwood fumbled on the return, we recovered, and we scored quickly again and it's 21-0 in the first quarter. We scored twice more in the second quarter and led 34-0 at halftime. Bob Johnson used to kid about making the scoreboard "light up like a pinball machine," and that's what this first half felt like. It seemed like every time we looked up, the scoreboard was blinking additional points on our side. We wound up with an easy 40-0 victory with our subs playing the entire second half.

We continued on a high scoring roll and won the rest of our games pretty easily, continued averaging over 30 per game, and therefore another subdivision championship. We only had one close game, which was a 10-6 win over Northeast. We never scored many points against Northeast, with the exception of a 26-0 win by our 1973 80 lb. team. Northeast always had very good coaches and players and they always got up to play us.

But one strange thing happened in the GYFC in that 1975 season. The mighty Tucker Lions who had beaten us so badly in game one were beaten out as champs of their subdivision, and thus eliminated from the GYFC playoffs by a team I knew nothing about prior to this season, the Central DeKalb Cardinals, coached by Joe Cunningham and Bill Eakin.

Central DeKalb, based at Norman Park in Clarkston, Georgia had gone 10-0, in regular season and had beaten that great Tucker team that had handled us so easily in game one. I knew very little about Central DeKalb, as we had never played them, but I knew they must be very good if they had beaten that great Tucker team. In watching their first round playoff game, one thing about this team jumped out, and that was their Tailback Tracy Soles was the best and fastest back in our league and he was dominant. He was so good in fact that he would later play college football for the great Pat Dye and Auburn University.

To get the opportunity to play this outstanding undefeated team, we had to play a first round playoff game, aka "The Jim Brazier Bowl" against the North DeKalb Chargers, who were good, as they had been our opponent in last year's GYFC championship game. But we were really good by now, too, and we beat them 18-6, setting up the 100 lb Bobby Dodd Bowl at Kiwanis Stadium in Forest Park between the 10-1 Atlanta Colts and the 11-0 Central DeKalb Cardinals.

We noticed a few things about CD beside Soles in our scouting. Their offensive line played a little high and did not appear to have a very quick takeoff, so we emphasized playing low, fast and hard on defense while maintaining gap control and correct defensive spacing in order to keep Soles from breaking loose. They had one very good receiver, a tall tight end, but otherwise, their QB was small and their passing attack was limited and not too much cause for concern against our very good secondary. Soles had been the key to all of their wins.

So the answer to this game was obvious, we had to stop Tracy Soles to have any chance to win the game. We also noticed something in our scouting about their special teams play that we thought might possibly become an important factor as well.

In defensive practice sessions, we told our Defensive Ends to not let Soles by them whether he had the ball or not, Central DeKalb liked to screen or swing pass to him after he had cleared containment, and that was usually deadly to their opposition. And we told our interior defense to attack and hold their gaps, and reminded everyone to keep proper spacing on stunts and blitzes. The plan was to clog the middle, protecting the inside gaps with the down linemen and linebackers, and have our Ends and Corners protect the flanks. The Safeties were to play their normal pass first and inside-out technique.

During the game, the speedy and elusive Soles got loose twice, once on a punt return and once from scrimmage, and both times Neil Gifford, our smallest player but a very good, feisty Defensive Cornerback was able to barely trip him up.

In addition to their dangerous Offense, Central DeKalb's Defense had been very good, in fact they had only given up two TD's all year, and a total of 14 points, but we felt that if we were patient and made the proper adjustments once into the game, our running game could make consistent yards with Coveny, Rose, Anderson and Rosing.

I actually liked the way we matched up with our offense against their defensive alignment, and thought it presented some pretty advantageous blocking angles for us. I also thought their defensive line played a little high like their offensive line. That should allow our line to eventually win that important battle upfront with our quick attacking, low charging offensive linemen. In addition to playing quick with good low technique and pad level, this year's line was big with all of our starters playing near the weight limit. The Tackles were Steve Noles and Mike Gurr, the Guards were Scott Hardy and Mike Donohue and the Center, Chris Doty. The Ends were Scott Rodwin and Andy Curl. By this 12th game under the watchful eye of Warren Watson, they were an outstanding unit.

One of the advantages of taking MARTA buses to this championship game, as opposed to car pooling which the other GYFC teams did, was that we could hold a meeting during the 60 minute bus trip from Murphy Candler Park to Kiwanis Stadium and remind the players of all of the important points in the game plan. Each of our coaches would sit and rotate by the different players with their key responsibilities on the bus and go over the strategic points that might make the difference in being Champion or Runner-up. I would also move from player to player on the bus talking to them and re-emphasizing to many of them about their specific role in the game plan, and any new or different assignments they might have for this big game. Even in 12 year old football, a player's keys and responsibilities can vary from game to game as you prepare to attack and defend your opponent. You cannot remind them too many times about these changes, especially with the Bobby Dodd Bowl/GYFC championship at stake.

The offensive game plan against Central DeKalb was to start conservatively, play for field position, and avoid mistakes, nothing special or new. We had an outstanding kicking game, because Scott Young was an excellent kicker and we worked on special teams every day in practice. The only new play we had put in for this game was actually a trick play on Special Teams.

It was a cold and cloudy day, in fact it actually snowed that night after the game, which is rare for North Georgia in mid-November. The game kicked off at noon, with temperatures in the 40's and dropping. Once again, we wore the white jerseys and white pants, trimmed in colt orange and navy blue. The first quarter was one of feeling each other out, playing conservatively and we were basically exchanging punts and trying to get that superior field position. The key play in this game would come early in the second quarter.

Our Offense had worked the ball up to about mid-field, where we were confronted with 4th down and about 5 to go. There, I called for a fake punt, with a screen pass, which was the trick play we had put in specially just for this game, simply calling the play "red punt." We called the fake for two reasons; first, Soles had just about broken the previous punt for a long TD and I was not anxious to kick to him again.

Secondly, the thing I mentioned about CD's special teams was that their front line defenders did not penetrate very deep on a punt and they seemed more concerned about setting up a return for Soles than making sure the ball got punted, or watching for a possible fake punt. So, I felt confident that our fake could be successful. But I also figured it would only work one time in this game.

Knowing that, I wanted to save the fake punt and use it when it would likely help us the most, and now, relatively early in the game, and after playing conservatively in the first quarter, just might be that time. The fact that we were at mid-field also made it less risky for field position just in case it did not work.

Scott Young was our Punter, PlaceKicker and a very good Defensive End. He was tall, smart, very mature for his age and the perfect one to pull off a fake punt. He executed it perfectly as designed, stepping forward and holding the ball as if to punt, and then after his second step, he raised up and dumped the little screen pass off to Scott Rodwin, our best pass receiver, who was very fast, and also was the usual personal protector on the Punt Team.

The CD defenders had already turned their backs and were retreating to set up the punt return! Sprinting wide to his right behind a wall of blockers, the speedy Rodwin easily made the vital first down, plus additional key yardage, down to about the CD 20 yard line.

This was the break we needed! The momentum went to us and the first down kept the drive alive, ultimately leading to a TD by TB Mike Coveny on a short run a few plays later, as we took a 7-0 lead in the second quarter after the Scott Young PAT.

On the ensuing kickoff, one of the Scott twins, Donnie or Ronnie, made one of the hardest hits I've ever seen (or heard) against the CD return man, loudly hitting him square in the numbers and knocking him straight backwards, sending "oohs and ahhhs" through the stadium. That hit put an exclamation point on the 7-0 lead and made the famous pronouncement "here come the Colts!" It remained 7-0 at the half, but our defense pretty much dominated the rest of the way.

At halftime, we made one adjustment to our running game, tightening the running path on the 50 Trap fullback play. The CD defensive lineman we were trapping was playing very tight, and that required a slight realignment to the Fullback's running lane. After that, the 50 Trap play worked much better in the second half, and it keyed a resurgence in our running game, which allowed us to move the ball much more consistently on the ground in the 3rd and 4th Quarters, dominating time of possession in the second half

Scott Young kicked a field goal that pretty much clinched the game in the 3rd Quarter for a 10-0 lead, and QB Alan Lindsey hit Strongside End Rodwin on our favorite 26-2 play action pass for another TD in the 4th quarter. Alan threw that pass from a full sprint running to his right after the 26 play fake and the ball hit Rodwin's outstretched hands on the dead run as he crossed the goal line. It was a perfectly timed throw and catch. CD never mounted a serious scoring threat as we took the 17-0 upset victory over the previously undefeated Cardinal team.

This Central DeKalb team was a great one, and Tracy Soles was probably the most dangerous individual we ever faced, but our Colt team was determined to atone for our opening game loss to Tucker, and the GYFC title did just that.

Jim Lineberger's 5-2 Defense led by DT Steve Noles, DB Neil Gifford, LB Scott Sherretz, and the Scott twins, Donnie and Ronnie, and the stunts and blitzes Jim called, kept our linemen and linebackers running free in CD's backfield all day with QB sacks and tackles for losses. This may have been our best defensive effort ever.

We had great pride in our team and program and our Captains handed AD Bob Johnson another Bobby Dodd Bowl trophy for the Colt Field trophy case. I got the big bear hug from Bob that always made me so proud and we had won four straight Bobby Dodd Bowl Championships for this proud program. We remained unscored on in Bobby Dodd Bowl championship game competition as the defenses led by Doug Perreault (the first two in 80 lb.) and now the two 100 lb. shutouts led by Jim Lineberger, were dominant every year.

We then immediately had to prepare to play two tough post season bowl games, the first being the annual Colt Classic the day after Thanksgiving against the famous Ft. Myers, Florida Rebels. I had heard Bob Johnson speak of this program many times and he had great respect for them. They always gave the Colts a tough game.

I knew they would be a tough opponent, but at this time, we were playing really well, scoring a lot of points and playing terrific defense. In fact, we had given up only 26 points and scored over 300 since that opening game loss to Tucker. That loss was probably one of the best things that ever happened to us as it gave us the ultimate rude awakening, causing the retooling of the Offense for the future, and leading to a great stretch of 12 wins in a row in the 1975 season.

We won the Colt Classic over Ft. Myers, 30-0 in a game that was actually pretty close for a while, in fact 10-0 at halftime. In the second half, we broke away as Mike Coveny had a 65 yard punt return, and our other backs, Tommy Rose and Mike Rosing both ran for TD's.

The Punt Return TD against Ft. Myers, the fake punt against Central DeKalb and the three vital PAT's against Tucker the previous year are perfect illustrations of why special teams play is so important and how the outcome of a game can often be determined in the kicking game !

We then went to Miami, at Florida International University Stadium, where we were defeated by the Tamiami Colts, 14-0 in a game where we had one TD called back by a penalty and ended the game on the Tamiami 5 yard line. They were a very good team, from the same age, but a higher weight class, and we played well and fought hard in this tough loss.

We ended the 1975 season 12-2, as GYFC champs once again, another great year, and there was no doubt that the 12 game stretch was some of the best football we ever played, and losing to this fine Tamiami team did nothing to diminish the season or make me think otherwise. Coming back to win that Bobby Dodd Bowl over undefeated Central DeKalb after losing so badly in our opening game made this season one of our proudest moments.

1975 100 lb Colts Key Performers:

QB Alan Lindsey . . . . Alan was not a tough kid at all, he did not like to hit or be hit, and he did not like the contact drills in practice but bravely hung in there for them and did every one when called on. What he was, was a very good performer at QB. He made good option reads, and ran the ball well when he the read made him keep it. He passed very accurately and had the length to throw it deep, and he threw the TD pass against Central DeKalb on the dead run, a perfect strike. He rarely made mistakes and was an outstanding QB by the end of 1975.

TB Mike Coveny . . . . Mike was big and strong and fast. He was hard to bring down with a single tackler and he had particularly strong thighs and upper body, you had to hit him low, but he had excellent balance as well and home run speed, the complete Tailback. He was a very successful high school player at Marist, a very smart young man and also played Ivy League Football at Princeton University.

ST Steve Noles . . . . Steve was a complete player, smart, aggressive and talented. He loved to play the game and was a big leader on the team. He played part of the year with his wrist in a splint due to a fracture, a true competitor. At strongside Tackle, the job requires strength, intelligence and quickness, all of which Steve possessed. He was also a very good defensive player.

LB and DL Ronnie and Donnie Scott . . . . Identical twins and great players both. They played Defensive line and Linebacker and were ferocious hitters. In the Central DeKalb Bobby Dodd Bowl, one of the twins, not sure which, made a huge hit on the kickoff returner after our first touchdown, sending the "oohs and ahs" through the stadium and also sending the clear message "Here Come the Colts !" It was probably one of the most memorable tackles I've ever seen in football.

SE Scott Rodwin . . . . Another complete player who had played as a 10 year old substitute on our 1973 80 lb team. Scott had matured, he was smart, sure handed and a very good blocker which our Strong End had to be, with Cross Block and Read Drive blocking responsibilities. In that position, he would be the primary pass receiver on many passing plays scoring numerous TD's including the clincher in the Bobby Dodd Bowl.

SG Scott Hardy . . . . Scott was our strongside Guard. In that position, he had to pull and trap, and pull and lead bootlegs. He was quick, strong and tough, a prototypical Colt Strong Guard.

CB Neil Gifford . . . . One of the smallest, but smartest and toughest players on the team. He made two TD saving tackles against Central DeKalb and played a good and consistent Cornerback all year.

DE and Kicker Scott Young . . . . Scott had kicked the field goal against us for North DeKalb in 1973, so when he joined us, we knew we had a great kicker. He was tall and strong with a strong kicking leg. He was a serious kicker so he had very good technique and consistency with his place kicks. He punted out of brute strength and became very good at that as well, improving his technique as the year progressed. He also was a very good football player, and played a good Defensive End for us and was instrumental in the containment of the dangerous Central DeKalb Tailback Soles.

HB Mike Rosing . . . . At the Halfback position, Mike was the point of attack blocker on our base off tackle running play 26, and the fill and double team blocker on our power play 84X. He was very fast and was the reason I designed the 90 Countertrap play, with which he had great success running the ball for several touchdowns.

FB Jeff Anderson . . . . Jeff was a starting weakside Tackle as a 10 year old on our 1973 team, one of only three 10 year old starters on that team. A very bright kid, he matured the following year, his second on the 80 lb team, and came up in 1975 as a complete player. At the Fullback position, the FB is the point of attack blocker on the I formation plays. Intelligence and quickness are also required because the FB has to read the point of attack linemen to determine where to lead the play. The FB then has to be tough enough to take on linebackers with head on blocking. Jeff was a very successful QB in high school and went on to play in college at Furman University as well.

1975 100 lb. Atlanta Colts Record 12-2-0

GYFC Champions
Atlanta Colt Classic Champions

Colts 7 Tucker 27
Colts 42 Briarcliff 7
Colts 21 East Point 0
Colts 26 Midway 7
Colts 42 Stone Mountain 0
Colts 40 Glenwood 0
Colts 35 DeKalb
Yellow Jackets 0
Colts 28 North DeKalb 0
Colts 10 Northeast 6
Colts 28 Roswell 0

GYFC Playoffs

Round One Jim Brazier Bowl, Kiwanis Stadium, Forest Park, Georgia

Colts 18 North DeKalb 6

Bobby Dodd Bowl, Kiwanis Stadium, Forest Park, Georgia

Colts 17 Central DeKalb 0

Atlanta Colt Classic, Colt Field at Murphy Candler Park, Atlanta, Georgia

Colts 30 Ft. Myers, Florida 0

Greater Miami Pop Warner Bowl,

Florida International University Stadium, Miami, Florida

Colts 0 Tamiami 14

1975 100 lb. Atlanta Colts Starting Lineups

Offense

Strong End.................... Scott Rodwin
Strong Tackle................ Steve Noles
Strong Guard .... Scott Hardy
Center.......................... Mike Doty
Quick Guard................ Mike Donahue
Quick Tackle............... Mike Gurr
Quick End .... Andy Curl
Quarterback.................. Alan Lindsay
Halfback .... Mike Rosing
Fullback .... Jeff Anderson
Tailback....................... Mike Coveny

Defense

Left End....................... Mike Smalley
Left Tackle.................... Steve Noles
Nose Guard.................. Donnie Scott
Right Tackle................. Ronnie Scott
Right End .... Scott Young
Left Linebacker .... Scott Sherretz
Right Linebacker.......... Jeff Anderson
Strong Safety, or
"Monster" LB............... Mike Coveny
Left Cornerback........... Steve Mahoney
Right Cornerback......... Neil Gifford
Safety .... Barry Newsom

Coaches . . . . Doug Bennett, Head Coach
Warren Watson Offensive and Defensive Line Coach
Jim Lineberger, Defensive Coordinator and Linebacker Coach
Frank Reeves, Offensive and Defensive Backfield Coach

1975 100 lb. Atlanta Colts Complete Roster

Barry Newsom	Troy Ragan
Ricky Hodges	Mike Rosing
Scott Rodwin	Jeff Anderson
Mike Smalley	Cy Johnson
Don Scott	Jeff Currier
John McMath	Marc Douglass
Scott Sherretz	Mark Harper
Bob Bell	Tom Rose
Ron Scott	Alan Lindsay
Mike Miller	Mike Gurr
Andy Curl	Neal Gifford
Steve Mahoney	Mike Coveny
Steve Noles	Mike Donahue
Scott Young	Scott Carpenter
Scott Hardy	Chris Doty
Mark Timmons	

Cheerleaders

Debbie Rutledge	Allison Hintze
Marianne Seidel	Lisa Kynoch
Cindy Booker	Jane Foster
Allyson Bailey	Lisa White
Katie Reily	Cindy Edwards
Susan Passarella	Jill Reeves

1975 120 lb. Atlanta Colts Record, 6-5-1

Colts 7 Tucker 13
Colts 14 Briarcliff 7
Colts 6 East Point 0
Colts 49 Midway 0
Colts 14 Stone Mountain 0
Colts 7 Glenwood 0
Colts 7 DeKalb Yellow
Jackets 7
Colts 0 North DeKalb 9
Colts 35 Northeast 6
Colts 7 Roswell 13

Atlanta Colt Classic, Colt Field, Murphy Candler Park, Atlanta, Georgia

Colts 7 Ft. Myers 21

Greater Miami Pop Warner Bowl, Florida International University, Miami, Florida

Colts 14 Miami K-Land 16

1975 120 lb. Atlanta Colts Complete Roster

John Lovelace
Kevin Waxman
Chuck Googe
Tommy "T-Bird" Rose
Phillip Ebinger
Mark Heller
Ken Hemphill
Chris Whitley
Petey Frye
Kenny Passarella
Tim Stowe
Neal Brasfield
Mike Youtt
Jamie Killingsworth
Tim Hayes
Jeff Amtower

Robert Rader
Phillip Reeves
Hayes McMath
Scott Smith
Donnie Rutledge
Barry White
Tom Wilson
Roland Sorel
Tom Archer
Richie Guerin
Ron Barto
David Farmer
Jeff Lineberger
Preston Coleman
Richard Chatham
Neil Brewer

Coaching Staff

Bob Johnson Head Coach
Frank Greene
Bill Whitley
Bob Chatham
Fred Amtower
Bob Rader
Bob Thomas

Cheerleaders

Shawn Amtower
Jamie Billingsley
Debbie Trense
Lori Perkins
Susan Miller
Judy Robinson

Lynn Haeberle
Cindy Radtke
Debbie Schmitz
Jenny Johnson
Kim Perkins
Susan Frye

1975 80 lb. Atlanta Colts Record, 11-1-1
GYFC Co-Champions

Colts 10 Tucker 0
Colts 26 Briarcliff 0
Colts 21 East Point 0
Colts 40 Midway 0
Colts 20 Stone Mountain 12
Colts 20 Glenwood 0
Colts 27 DeKalb Yellow
Jackets 0
Colts 27 North DeKalb 0
Colts 18 Northeast 0
Colts 28 Roswell 0

GYFC Semi-Final, The Jim Brazier Bowl, Kiwanis Stadium, Forest Park, Georgia

Colts 20 East Point 6

GYFC Championship, The Bobby Dodd Bowl, Kiwanis Stadium, Forest Park, Georgia

Colts 0 Tucker 0 Tie Results in Co-Championship

Atlanta Colt Classic, Colt Field, Murphy Candler Park, Atlanta, Georgia

Colts 7 Palmetto 12

1975 80 lb. Atlanta Colts Complete Roster

Mark Wheaton	Chris Yancey
Mike Hartigan	Greg Thomas
Jed Dodd	Robbie Conley
John Cascone	Mike Yancey
Tom DiFiore	Paul Stuker
Drew Williams	Alan Thompson
Jim Caudill	Scott Robbins
Daryl Sloter	Greg Barto
Mike Ahern	Craig Coleman
Richard NeSmith	Frank Coulter
Roger Rubinson	Peter Stephens
Chuck Trense	Brent Carpenter
Randy Walters	Wade McKinney
James Waring	Don West
Scott Miller	D.H. Malcolm
Guy Thacker	

Coaching Staff

Mac Scoggins Head Coach
Charlie Ragan
Pat Eder
Alton Conway
Bob Carpenter

Cheerleaders

Anne Miller	Mary Papineau
Susan Hope	Pam Brown
Debbie Rader	Judy Schmitz
Amy Arrowsmith	Jeannie Whitley
Kim Barber	Tona Munday
Robyn Barto	Shannon Scoggins
1975 Coltettes	Drill Team
Laine Beck	Jenny Putnall
Diann Mitchell	Linda Rhine
Melinda Travis	Kim lane

Laura Patchen
Evelyn Davis
Sue Kirkland
Paula Powell
Sherri Williams
Julie Bolton
Kerry Holder
Donna Presnall
Stacie Reigh
Lisa Paracsi

Donna McMillan
Lisa Cox
Pam Powell
Terri Goldman
Julie Perry
Kathy Brown
Cara Robbins
Michelle Heslin
Sloan Usher
Vickie McMullan

Director

Jean Davis

Instructors

Kathy Davis
Stephanie Davis

CHAPTER 11

1976, The Final Year for "Coach" Bob

VARSITY COLT SUMMARY, 1976

The ACYA program got back to more of its winning ways in 1976, placing all three weight class teams in the Bobby Dodd Bowl, and taking home two of the three championship trophies and banners. The overall Varsity record for 1976 was 35-5-1.

100 lb. Colt Tailback Mark Wheaton dives into the End Zone for a TD against Tucker in the 1976 Bobby Dodd Bowl.

Our 100 lb. team and Mac Scoggins's 80 lb team were Bobby Dodd Bowl GYFC Championship winners and Bob Johnson's final 120 lb. entry fell to Central DeKalb in a close, hard fought 14-7 defeat.

Just like our 100 lb. team, the 80 pounders played North DeKalb in the first round Brazier Bowl, winning 20-0. And just like our 100 lb. team, the 80 pounders played Tucker in the Bobby Dodd Bowl, winning 14-7 after falling behind 7-0. Mac's team was awarded the Pop Warner National Championship for their perfect 13-0 record after they defeated Eastchester, New York in the rainy Colt Classic, 17-0. This was Mac's third consecutive 10-0 regular season and this time they took it all the way to 13-0.

Mac's team was led all year by his fabulous Quarterback, Frank Coulter and the fine play of running backs Drew Williams, Keith Tyson and Greg Barto. Coach Charlie Ragan's defense was led by Guy Thacker, John Cascone and Craig Coleman.

Bob Johnson once again had to rebuild his coaching staff adding ACYA veteran Buddy Ragsdale and newcomer Jay Williams. Buddy was a good offensive coach and Jay was a defensive secondary specialist. With those additions, the 120 lb. Colts had a good 9-1 regular season and also played North DeKalb in the first round GYFC playoffs which oddly matched our Colts and North DeKalb in all three weight classes. The ACYA won all three with the 120 pounders winning theirs by a score of 28-14.

Then the 120 pounders ran into a very good Central DeKalb team in the Bobby Dodd Bowl and fell 14-7 in Bob Johnson's last ever Bobby Dodd Bowl game. They also beat a very good Eastchester, New York team in the Colt Classic by the exciting score of 28-14 in quagmire conditions. Then, in Bob's final game as Colt Head Coach, they lost to an outstanding Clearwater team by the same score as my 100 pounders, 22-14.

Bob's final team finished 11-3 a good record by most measures, but disappointing to Bob. He had been very sick the last part of the year and missed parts of the Bobby Dodd Bowl and the Clearwater Bowl game, and finally decided he could coach no longer. This was a sad time for the ACYA and youth football everywhere as this legendary coach was finally forced by health to retire at the young age of 41.

Fortunately, Bob would live almost 28 more years, which was a testament to his strength and fortitude along with that of his wife Meredith, his three children and his team of Physicians. Although he was not able to coach football, he did have many healthy times, developed an interest in saltwater sport fishing and continued a successful business career.

Like Dr. Wells said, he was one of a kind.

*   *   *

1976 100 lb. Atlanta Colts

After winning four GYFC Championships in a row in two weight classes, our 100 lb. coaching staff eagerly anticipated another new group of players coming up from Mac Scoggins's 80 lb team. His players were always very well coached and they already knew most of our blocking schemes, terminology and many of our basic plays which gave us a big early season practice teaching head start.

This was another good group led by QB Mike Yancey, LB D.H. Malcolm, lineman Chuck Trense and TB Mark Wheaton. Mark had fought for the starting TB position most of the previous year on the 80 lb. Colts, shared it for a few games and then won it for keeps toward the end of the year. However, Mark was small, only about 80 lbs, preparing to play in the big time 100 lb league, but he had a very good birthday and played all year at 13 years old, as he turned 13 shortly after the August 1st 12 year old cutoff date. The whole team turned out to be a little undersized, but they were mature, quick and tough for the most part, similar to our 1974 100 lb. team in size.

It was also a bit of a "cast of characters" with Wade McKinney, Steve Oxford, Jimmy Costlow, Jamie Perner and the "enforcer," FB and LB Jimmy Caudill, being among the somewhat unique players. But they were good fundamental football players, every one, even if some of their personalities were a little unusual.

Caudill was a swimmer and had a build like a little weightlifter. He also had a large head, and had to wear an oversized headgear. Most of all he was all business, very mature for his age, very intense and a brutal hitter. He was a two way starter at Fullback and Inside Linebacker and would turn out to be a valuable asset to toughen our other players in practice. Everyone on our team knew that no one else in GYFC would hit them harder in a game than Jimmy Caudill would in practice.

We did our usual August preparations, avoiding preseason scrimmages with opponents as we did not like to show our stuff to opponents any more than we had to. We started the regular season at Tucker, and that game ended in a 6-6 tie. Having lost our kicker Scott Young, we did not have an accomplished kicker, so we used Mike Yancey our QB, who became very consistent over the next two years as a kicker and punter, but we missed this season opening extra point attempt.

As mentioned before and emphasized by Bob Johnson, every PAT is vital and missing this one cost us the win. The same thing also cost Tucker a potential win, so the missed kicks on both teams led to this unusual score and tie game.

In that game with Tucker, we had a lot of good holes opened by our line, but our timing was a little off, and we looked very slow, so we didn't feel too bad about it. I knew we could fix the timing with more practice and repetition. I also knew that we would become quicker every week as we emphasized quickness in every practice.

Timing is a vital part of offensive football and we worked on it almost every day in practice. By repeating each play over and over until perfection in practice, this led to better execution in running as well as passing Offensive plays. As the year progressed, repeated running of each play in practice continually improves the timing and coordination between the backfield and offensive line.

In retrospect, this opening game tie was with Tucker, on their home field and we didn't lose to them. After that 1975 opening game humiliating loss on Colt Field, a tie was somewhat of a welcomed relief. It sure beat losing like last year !

We had a good regular season with a couple of memorable games. The first was against North DeKalb, coached by John Ramsey, at Colt Field. Once again, in a very intense game fueled by the heated neighborhood rivalry, and now with former ACYA President John Ramsey on the Charger sidelines, giving his team extra motivation, this was a barnburner of a youth football game.

North DeKalb scored first early in the game, a rare occasion against us, so we were behind 7-0 from the start. On our first possession, trailing 7-0, we ran an 84B option, and the pitch to Mark Wheaton was a little high, and a ND blitzing LB hit Mark with his headgear right under the chin as he reached up for the high pitch. Mark never knew what hit him, and North DeKalb recovered the errant pitch deep in our territory, and quickly drove it in for a 14-0 lead.

Mark was woozy after that hit and it took him several minutes on the bench to recover, but he eventually did recover and re-entered the game around the mid-point of the second quarter. We immediately got a drive going and the key play in the drive was 84X. It was working well to both sides with Wheaton's determined running behind the powerful cross blocking of Strong End Jimmy Costlow, HalfBack D.H. Malcolm, Strong Tackle Chuck Trense and FB Jimmy Caudill. The key play in the drive was an "L Left" 84X run by Mark for about 40 yards off the left side ending deep in Charger territory. Mark finally scored a TD over the right side on that same play and I immediately thought we could completely change the momentum in this game, and let North DeKalb know that we intended to WIN this game by going for a two point conversion right here in the second quarter.

Without hesitation or calling timeout, I looked at Coach Watson and said "84X." He nodded agreement by crossing his arms in front of him, indicating an "X," so we quickly called on another 84X for the two point try. It was working so well, another three yard gain shouldn't be too much, and I didn't want to call timeout and give North DeKalb time to talk about defensive strategy. They obviously could have called their own timeout but chose not to.

84X works like this: in our base offense language, anything starting with 84 means that the play starts with the HB diving between the strongside guard and tackle. 84A is a handoff to him behind "veer" blocking. 84B is a fake to the HB and an option play with the QB keeping or pitching to the TB running wide. 84X is a fake to the HB and an off tackle handoff to the TB, just like our basic 26 off tackle play, so it's a fake 84A, 26 run, but we just called it 84X. The other difference is the line blocking.

We put the "X" in the terminology for two reasons, first the backfield action is sort of like a scissors play and second, the point of attack blocking is a cross block or what we called an "X" block between the strongside End and Tackle. The End blocks down on the Defensive Tackle through his usual read drive inside gap responsibility. The HB also hits the tackle "inside out" through his gap as the 84 fake takes place, covering both gaps and creating a double team on the Tackle. Our strongside Offensive Tackle goes behind the down blocking End looping outside and reads the Defensive End, blocking him down (in) or out, whichever way the DE chooses to play, or as we called it a "trap (or) hook" option block.

The FB leads the TB on the play and they read the Offensive Tackle's option block on Defensive End and take the play inside or outside whichever the read calls for. If the End closes down to the tackle hole, we hook block him to the inside and the TB runs wide, and if the end plays wide, we trap him out and the TB carries to the inside or off tackle. It is a great power play and tough for a defense to penetrate as all the gaps are well protected, plus the reads are easy for the Backs. It was called 14X in the Leonard Jones terminology.

Mark Wheaton easily dived into the end zone for this two point conversion with more than a yard to spare, and now we are only down 14-8. I confidently expected to win the game 15-14 in the second half. But

North DeKalb had something else in mind, and with a couple of minutes to go in the first half, they threw a little screen pass to their left side from about their own 30 yard line. Mike Ahern, our Right Defensive End, somehow diagnosed the play perfectly, intercepted the pass, and ran it in untouched for the tying touchdown. Yancey's important PAT kick put us ahead 15-14 late in the second quarter, giving us the lead at the halftime break. There's the significance of the kicking game showing up again.

I believe the two point conversion can be a game changer when used at the right time. Many coaches and TV commentators call it "chasing points" and don't think it should be used until late in the game. I strongly disagree, particularly at this youth league level of football competition. I knew I could win the game right there with the two pointer and I was right! Even though we were still behind 14-8, that single point making it 8 instead of 7 made it seem to North DeKalb like they were already tied, even though they were still ahead by 6! Also, in a game that matters, why would you ever be satisfied being tied? I want to know as soon, and as early in the game as possible how many points I need to WIN!

We did the same thing twice in the following year in situations that were just as critical with the exact same results. We just used different plays that were appropriate for the existing conditions in those games. I will describe those situations and the plays we used for two point conversions in later chapters.

In this situation, the 84X call was a play on momentum. Another piece of Bob Johnson strategic advice was always "if something is working, keep using it until the other team stops it." I tried to rely on Bob Johnson advice whenever I could, so that's exactly the reason we called that 84X play at that time.

In this game, we went ahead and scored again in the second half defeating North DeKalb 22-14 in a very exciting game. I think Mark Wheaton still remembers that hit under his chin, and I'm sure his dad Henry Wheaton does.

We lost a game in mid-season in which we played very poorly to the DeKalb Yellow Jackets from south DeKalb County on their field by the score of 15-7. They were a proud program that had been in GYFC a long time with a successful history. Their coach was so excited to beat the Colts that he sprinted to midfield for the postgame handshake and jumped into my arms. I congratulated him and was happy for him that he was so proud, but I told my team that I was not happy with our effort, and we should NOT have lost that game.

Our other memorable game that year was against Northeast at their field on Halloween night. It rained all day and night, but the field remained in pretty good shape, and we scored 14 points, which I thought was very good given the sloppy conditions and tough opponent in an away game. This Northeast team had a good passer, and in scouting them, it appeared that he only liked to throw to one receiver, number 7, a tall very athletic player, and they moved him around all over the field.

So we decided on a defensive plan to shadow number 7 man to man with Mike Yancey, and play a rotating zone for the rest of coverage. They did not appear to be much of a threat to move the ball on the ground against our front 7. The defense worked great, and we held them to one TD, winning the game 14-7, and Mike harassed that great receiver all night. Mike was a great competitor, although quiet, but he always gave his best, which was always very good on both offense and defense. As stated before, all of our games with Northeast were close. They were well coached by Jack Moore and staff, and a very good home field team. I was very proud of that victory at rainy Pleasantdale Park on a foggy, spooky Halloween night. Any win against Northeast was a good win.

We finished the regular season 8-1-1, winning our subdivision and meeting the rival North DeKalb in the first playoff round. This time it wasn't as difficult as that regular season game, and we won a pretty uneventful game, 21-0. The highlight was a 60 yard TD pass from Yancey to Jimmy Costlow late in the 2nd Quarter. Yancey to Costlow was probably the best pass-catch duo I ever coached.

This particular play was a straight fly or "take off" pattern, using Costlow's superior speed and athletic ability. He and Yancey worked very hard on their timing in practice and Mike hit him in full stride this time with a perfectly thrown pass just over the outstretched arms of the North DeKalb defender, and Jimmy took it all the way to the end zone outracing the North DeKalb secondary easily. Costlow was probably the most athletically talented and gifted player on our team, as he played near the 100 lb. weight limit all year.

In the second half, it was all Colts led by Yancey's 19 yard TD run on a bootleg play, and another 55 yard TD run by Mark Wheaton on a 26 base off tackle play.

Tucker won the other semi-final game, so in the Bobby Dodd Bowl, we squared off against our other old nemesis the Tucker Lions, with Larry Rakestraw's passing game to defend. I considered this quite a challenge in view of our recent history of tough games with them. I expected no difference in this one with the GYFC championship on the line. Recall we had tied 6-6 in the season opener, and lost in the 1975 opener by that embarrassing score of 27-7. We had not beaten a Tucker team in two years since the 21-20 squeaker in the 1974 GYFC Brazier Bowl.

Going into this year's Bobby Dodd Bowl we were rolling pretty well offensively with a very talented group of offensive players led by Yancey, Wheaton and Costlow, and very good on defense led by Malcolm, Trense and Caudill as well. Therefore, the only thing we added was a little pre-snap shift on our 26 and 84X plays to disguise our strong side until the last second before snapping the ball.

To do this, we lined up with the TB in normal position but with the FB and HB behind the Guards in an inverted wishbone look. Then right before the snap, the QB would raise a heel which would indicate which side he wanted to become strong (it was pre-called in the huddle). The backfield would then shift into L left or right and we would run either 26 or 84X toward that strong side before the defense could re-align. We did that almost every year thereafter for the Bobby Dodd Bowl and gained an early advantage every year.

For this GYFC championship game, it was a mild day with intermittent light rain and drizzle. Dressed in the traditional solid white uniforms, we received the kickoff and started with an immediate drive deep into Tucker territory which was halted by a rare fumble, probably caused by a slippery ball combined with a hard hitting Tucker defense. But, starting with that first drive, and even after that first turnover, our Offense dominated all the way, winning the game 28-14.

To score 28 points on this Tucker defense on a drizzly day was impressive and a testimony to our great offensive players. We ran, passed, trapped, optioned, everything worked for over 300 yards of total offense. We had two rushing TD's by Wheaton, and one by Halfback D.H. Malcolm. The fourth TD came on a pass from Yancey to Left End Don West. Our offensive line played a near perfect game, led by Guards Pete Stephens and Mike Ahern, and Tackles Chuck Trense and Paul Restuccia. The line was anchored by Center Brent Carpenter.

In scouting the Tucker Offense in preparation for this game, we noticed that their left end was rarely in their pass routes, so we ran a lot of corner blitz from that side with Mike Yancey coming off the right defensive corner and Mike Ahern, Right Defensive End, dropping off and covering the area vacated by the blitzing cornerback Yancey. In today's football terminology, they call that a "zone blitz." That worked well too and Mike harassed their QB all day.

Tucker's last TD was late, after we led 28-7, and naturally Coach Rakestraw found our defensive weak point and passed for a TD to that End who was usually never in the route, as the End slipped behind our zone coverage. Despite giving up that late TD, this was our most lopsided win ever against Tucker, at least since the 18-0 win back in '73. Plus, going undefeated against them in 1976 including taking the GYFC championship game sort of made up for that opening day loss in 1975.

After securing the 5th GYFC Bobby Dodd Bowl in a row, we had two more bowl games, the usual day after Thanksgiving Colt Classic, this year against Eastchester, New York and a trip to Clearwater, Florida.

The 1976 Colt Classic game, with a U.S. Bi-Centenniel celebration theme, was played in heavy rain conditions, but we executed very well on Offense, scoring twice in the first Quarter on runs by Yancey and Wheaton. Wheaton added another in the second half and went over 100 for the game, and was in the 1,200 total rushing yard range for the year. We won this game 21-0. Having the rainy game against Northeast earlier in regular season probably helped prepare us for these adverse conditions in the Bobby Dodd Bowl and even worse conditions in the Colt Classic.

In addition, I always liked to practice on rainy days as much as possible during the season, absent lightning, to prepare for rainy games like these three in 1976. We usually played well in those adverse weather conditions, I believe due to the willingness to routinely practice in them.

The away bowl game was against the Clearwater, Florida Tornado, a famous program who played on the high school field of the same name, the Clearwater High School Tornado. Like Tamiami, the previous year's away bowl opponent, Clearwater played in a league whose 12 year old weight limit was slightly higher than ours by about 10 lbs. That weight disadvantage had made a big difference against big and strong Tamiami, but the difference in Clearwater wasn't the size, it was the *SPEED*. They were fast, in fact blindingly fast and we had our hands full in this game immediately.

In Youth Football in Florida in those days, an extra point kick was twenty yards as the goalpost was on the end zone end line instead of the goal line, where it was located in GYFC, making a PAT kick 20 yards as opposed to the 10 yards in GYFC. But, because of the difficulty of a 20 yard kick, and to encourage young players to start place kicking at an early age, by rule a successful PAT kick was worth two points.

Clearwater scored twice in the first half, made both PAT kicks, and led 16-0 at halftime. We were shocked and surprised to be down that far, but we had had some success on offense in the first half and actually felt that we could move the ball and get back in the game in the third Quarter.

We received the second half kickoff and staged a valiant comeback, scoring twice in the third quarter on Yancey TD passes to Costlow, but missed one of the 20 yard PAT's, tightening it to 16-14. Then, late in the 4th Quarter, Clearwater is driving and we can't stop them.

I turned to Jim Lineberger and said in jest "if we let them score, maybe they'll miss the PAT, and we can get the ball back, score a TD, kick a PAT, and tie the game at 22." **

Although not deliberate on our part, that's what happened. They scored quickly, but missed the PAT, and led 22-14 late in the fourth quarter. There are just a couple of minutes left, but we can score a TD, make the two point kick, and get out with a tie, a pretty good outcome against this high caliber, larger, very speedy opponent in this intersectional game.

We received the final kickoff with a pretty good return, and started passing the ball down the field, running the "two minute drill." We're passing to the sidelines, going out of bounds, throwing incomplete passes to stop the clock, making first downs and stopping the clock, but we finally ran out of timeouts. We were using a combination of the 26-2 play action passes, and the 28 series of short rollout passing to a combination of routes to our Ends and slot back out of our TB Slot formation. Mark Wheaton was a very good receiver from the slot position, particularly when paired with the dangerous Jimmy Costlow on the Split end side in a slot formation. Quickside Ends Hal Moore and Don West also had key receptions.

We got all the way down to the Clearwater 10 yard line, and the clock finally runs out, we're inside the 10 yard line, we have first down, but no time and a 22-14 loss to this great Clearwater team. I couldn't be too unhappy about this season. We had lost this intersectional bowl game, but to an outstanding team, finishing 11-2-1, and we had won yet another GYFC championship, our 5th in a row.

** In the 2010 UGA-Georgia Tech game, Tech Coach Paul Johnson did exactly that. Trailing by 1 point with time running out and no way to stop the clock, Tech deliberately allowed UGA to score and go up by 8. Tech got the ball back with a minute to play and had a chance to tie and send the game into overtime, but failed to score and UGA held on for the 8 point win. It was hailed in the media the next day as a brilliant move and UGA Coach Mark Richt admitted that Coach Johnson of Georgia Tech had outfoxed him on that play.

Bob Johnson's 120 lb team lost to Clearwater that night also by the identical 22-14 score, and after the game, Bob gathered everyone into the hotel's restaurant and announced he would be retiring from coaching due to his health. It was just too hard for him to continue. In fact, he almost missed this game due to illness. This legendary man, who had taught so many of us such valuable lessons, such a great coach and leader who had started this great program to serve the youth of North Atlanta has coached his last game.

One other thing, by the way, he tells me that he wants me to be the next coach of the team he loved so much, his team, Bob Johnson's team, the 120 lb Atlanta Colts.

I immediately thought two things. First, "what an honor" and second, "I cannot possibly do this."

* * *

1976 100 lb. Atlanta Colts Record, 11-2-1

GYFC Champions
Atlanta Colt Classic Champions

Colts 6 Tucker 6
Colts 34 Briarcliff 0
Colts 21 East Point 0
Colts 28 Midway 15
Colts 34 Stone Mountain 0
Colts 22 Glenwood 0
Colts 22 North DeKalb 14
Colts 7 DeKalb
Yellow Jackets 15
Colts 14 Northeast 6
Colts 49 Roswell 0

GYFC Semi-Final, The Jim Brazier Bowl, St. Pius X High School, Atlanta, Georgia

Colts 21 North DeKalb 0

GYFC Championship, The Bobby Dodd Bowl, Kiwanis Stadium, Forest Park, Georgia

Colts 28 Tucker 14

Atlanta Colt Classic, Colt Field, Murphy Candler Park, Atlanta, Georgia

Colts 21 Eastchester, N.Y. 0

Clearwater Pop Warner Bowl, Clearwater High School Stadium, Clearwater, Florida

Colts 14 Clearwater, Fla 22

1976 100 lb. Atlanta Colts Starting Lineups

OFFENSE

Strong End	Jimmy Costlow
Strong Tackle	Chuck Trense
Strong Guard	Peter Stephens
Center	Brent Carpenter
Quick Guard	Dutch Minor
Quick Tackle	Paul Restuccia
Quick End	Jamie Perner
Quarterback	Mike Yancey
Halfback	D.H. Malcolm
Fullback	Jimmy Caudill
Tailback	Mark Wheaton

DEFENSE

Left End	Jimmy Costlow
Left tackle	Joel Farmer
Nose Guard	Steve Oxford
Right Tackle	Chuck Trense
Right End	Mike Ahern
Left Linebacker	Jimmy Caudill
Right Linebacker	Dutch Minor
Strong Safety or "Monster"	LB D.H. Malcolm
Left Cornerback	Roger Rubinson
Right Cornerback	Mike Yancey
Safety	Mark Wheaton

Coaches Doug Bennett, Head Coach
Warren Watson, Offensive and Defensive Line Coach
Jim Lineberger, Defensive Coordinator and Linebacker Coach
Frank Reeves, Offensive Backfield Coach
Fred Amtower, Defensive backfield Coach

1976 100 lb. Atlanta Colts Complete Roster

Peter Stephens	Mike Hartigan
Mark Wheaton	D.H. Malcolm
Mark Rudder	Mike Ahern
Brent Carpenter	Greg Edwards
Roger Rubinson	Steve Oxford
Chuck Trense	Dutch Minor
Mike Yancey	Greg Carlisle
Jimmy Caudill	Dale Barlitt
Mark Gurr	Greg Thomas
Hal Moore	Joel Farmer
John McMath	Paul Restuccia
Jamie Perner	Jamie Waring
Wade McKinney	John Rideout
Jimmy Costlow	Don West

Cheerleaders

Debbie Rutledge	Jill Reeves
Shawn Amtower	Mary Papineau
Allison Hintze	Jeannie Whitley
Tona Munday	Anna Marie Googe
Kim Barber	Amy Arrowsmith
Sandy Smith	Pam Brown

1976 120 lb. Colts Record, 11-3

GYFC Runner-up
Colt Classic Champions

Colts 27 Tucker 7
Colts 30 Briarcliff 7
Colts 0 East Point 17
Colts 43 Midway 0
Colts 49 Stone Mountain 0
Colts 27 Glenwood 0
Colts 41 North DeKalb 0
Colts 42 Roswell 3

GYFC Semi-Final, The Jim Brazier Bowl, St. Pius X High School, Atlanta, Georgia

Colts 28 North DeKalb 14

GYFC Championship, The Bobby Dodd Bowl, Kiwanis Stadium, Forest Park, Georgia

Colts 7 Central DeKalb 14

Atlanta Colt Classic, Colt Field, Murphy Candler Park, Atlanta, Georgia

Colts 28 Eastchester, NY 14

Clearwater Pop Warner Bowl, Clearwater high School, Clearwater, Florida

Colts 14 Clearwater 22

1976 120 lb. Atlanta Colts Complete Roster

Mallon Ellenburg
Ron Scott
Larry Joiner
Mike Gurr
Mike Youtt
Steve Noles
Andy Curl
Mike Rosing
Charlie Conway
Paul Messer
Rob Shuler
Bob Bell
Jay D'Meza
Alan Lindsey

Tommy Rose
Don Scott
David Farmer
Jeff Anderson
Jeff Currier
Chris Doty
Mike Viggiano
Mark Cooley
Scott Howard
Mike Coveny
John Hunt
Cy Johnson
Barry Newsom

Coaching Staff

Bob Johnson Head Coach
Jay Williams
Bob Thomas
Buddy Ragsdale
Bill Schmitz

Cheerleaders

Jan Ragsdale
Kelly Wiggins
Beth Harvey
Jane Biven
Susie Willis
Susan Passarella

Marianne Seidel
Laura Hartigan
Cindy Booker
Angela Ray
Linda Ragsdale
Emily Reilly

1976 80 lb. Atlanta Colts Record, 13-0

GYFC Champions
Atlanta Colt Classic Champions
Pop Warner National Champions

Colts 13 Tucker 0
Colts 35 Briarcliff 7
Colts 21 East Point 0
Colts 13 Midway 6
Colts 48 Stone Mountain 0
Colts 7 Glenwood 0
Colts 28 DeKalb
Yellow Jackets 0
Colts 14 North DeKalb 3
Colts 20 Northeast 0
Colts 34 Roswell 0

GYFC Semi-Finals, The Jim Brazier Bowl, St. Pius X High School, Atlanta, Georgia

Colts 20 North DeKalb 0

GYFC Championship, The Bobby Dodd Bowl, Kiwanis Stadium, Forest Park, Georgia

Colts 14 Tucker 7

Atlanta Colt Classic, Colt Field, Murphy Candler Park, Atlanta, Georgia

Colts 17 Eastchester, NY 0

1976 80 lb. Atlanta Colts Complete Roster

Daryl Sloter	Tony Hargis
Mark Fredo	Chris Sheffield
Jeff Craven	Craig Coleman
Jim Storey	Lee Cawthon
Scott Miller	Richie Locklear
Adam Furth	Greg Barto
Chris Yancey	Steve Forsberg
James Reinstein	Gregg Webb
David Rose	Sean McDonald
Scott Robbins	Keith Tyson
John Cascone	Frank Coulter
Guy Thacker	Drew Williams
Tom Haeberle	Frank Doherty
Richie NeSmith	Roger Shadburn
Robert Harry	Ken Harmon

Coaching Staff

Mac Scoggins Head Coach
Charlie Ragan
Pat Eder
Alton Conway
Bob Carpenter

Cheerleaders

Deidre Compamik	Jan Jones
Robyn Barto	Denise Doherty
Lisa Sandusky	Kristin Scmmitz
Karen Newlin	Jennifer Moore
Anne Miller	Nancy Papineau
Stacey Jackson	Shannon Scoggins

1976 Coltettes Drill Team

Julie Owens   Lynn Guerrant
Ann McKenzie   Kim Lane
Teresa Pike   Kathy Brown
Donna West   Nangela Edwards
Lori Chastain   Holly West
Stacie Reich   Kim Stoll
Suzie Redman   Helen West
Diana McGuirk

Director

"Pete" Chastain

CHAPTER 12

1977, John Ramsey Returns

VARSITY COLT SUMMARY, 1977

For the first time since 1971, and the second time in GYFC history, the Atlanta Colts swept all three weight classes and took home the Bobby Dodd Bowl conference championship trophies and banners.

In addition to our 120 lb. victory, John Ramsey led his 80 lb. Colts to victory and a perfect 14-0 season, ending with a Pop Warner National Championship. They had a close win over Briarcliff 14-13 in the GYFC Brazier Bowl, and over Glenwood 14-6 in the Bobby Dodd Bowl championship game.

In post season, they handled Winston-Salem 17-0 in the Colt Classic, and then in the first ever 80 lb. away bowl game, they defeated Savannah by the score of 31-14 in Savannah, Georgia ending the year at a perfect 14-0.

The team was led all year offensively by QB Jeff Radtke, and running backs Craig Goldberg, Derek D'Alonzo and Scott Mischnick. Their defense was led by Chris Sheffield, Jim Ferguson and Tommy Thomas.

Mac Scoggins had a second consecutive National Championship, this time in the 100 lb. division with basically the same group of kids that had won it in the 80 lb. class the previous year. The one significant player they added was Tailback Brian Jager. They had a perfect 14-0 record, and did not have a close game all year. It was Mac's fourth consecutive undefeated regular season and second consecutive undefeated, untied GYFC and Pop Warner National Champion.

The team was led by QB Frank Coulter and super running back Brian Jager. Jager was outstanding and may have been the best Colt player ever, at running back or any other position. He was a once in a lifetime player, fast and powerful, like a 100 lb. version of Herschel Walker. With two great players in Jager and Coulter, and a fine supporting cast, their offense scored well over 400 points and averaged over 30 points per game.

Their defense, coached by Charlie Ragan, only allowed 25 points all year and had great players at every position. This team was one of the absolute best in Colt history, rivaling the finest the Johnson brothers or Jim Wilson had produced earlier in the decade.

That made the overall Varsity record 41-1 for 1977, with two Pop Warner National Championships, the best ever. Although Bob Johnson was not a coach this year, he was present for most of it, and this wonderful year was a direct result of his leadership and mentoring of the entire program, and each of the three winning varsity coaches were products of his ACYA "Minor Leagues" Interleague program.

*   *   *

1977 120 lb. Colts

Since we accepted the challenge of following Bob Johnson and staff as 120 lb coaches, now we have to go up against the "big boys," of GYFC, high school 8th and 9th grade players with veteran coaches like Virgil Sorrels and Jerome Roberts among others. Central DeKalb had moved their best coaching duo in Eakin and Cunningham to this level in 1976 and they had won the conference championship. Almost every program generally put their best, most experienced coaching staff at the 120 lb. level, so that was what we were going to be up against. Bob Johnson had always competed in this class, and had usually dominated the league more often than not since 1970.

Many of the programs in GYFC had their 120 lb. team play all of its home games in the prime time slot of 8 PM Saturday nights. Bob Johnson has asked me to lead his former team, so I have the unenviable task of following this great legend of youth football coaching in this very tough and competitive league.

Once again I wonder, "can I do this?" How in the world will I ever take the place of this giant, this legend, my personal hero and friend? This is like following Bear Bryant. I'm just a little kids' football coach and the 120 lb league is too much like high school! Will my Offense work at this higher level? Who would be the new ACYA Athletic Director? Who would be the leader of this program that I loved so much and had so much time invested in?

In a few short days, we learned that John Ramsey might be returning to ACYA as Athletic Director. It quickly became official. I would be the 120 lb Coach, Mac Scoggins would move to 100 lb level and John Ramsey would head the 80 lb team, in addition to being the new A.D. I liked and respected John, and felt this was the right thing to do.

Nobody understood the ACYA better than John Ramsey and he had only been gone two years and had been a leader in ACYA for many years before leaving to be a varsity level coach at rival North DeKalb.

I would miss Bob Johnson very much, but he would still be accessible to me for advice, counsel and friendship. That would never change. Also, I was happy with John Ramsey as the new A.D., as I knew the program needed strong leadership which John Ramsey was without a doubt, capable of providing. I also knew he was a good football coach, having taken his North DeKalb teams to the GYFC playoffs both of his years there.

So, once again, I moved up in age/weight classification and now I'm Head Coach of the ACYA flagship team, the 120 lb Colts, entering my 6th year of varsity coaching at the age of 29 (The same age Bob Johnson was when he founded the ACYA). The good news is I have Mike Yancey, Mark Wheaton, Jimmy Costlow, Pete Stephens, Chuck Trense, Mike Ahern and Dutch Minor along with a fine supporting cast of players that will have a good head start, as they will have played together for the third year, the second under our staff. Also, our entire Coaching Staff would make the move, that's myself, Warren Watson in our 5th year together, Jim Lineberger in his 4th, Fred Amtower and Frank Reeves, each in their 3rd year with our staff as Colt Coaches.

With that group together, you don't have to train or even watch any new coaches. Everybody knows their job, everybody knows everybody else's job, and we would all know most of our key personnel.

We did suffer two crucial losses from last year's team in HB/LB D.H. Malcolm and FB/LB Jimmy Caudill. But, one crucial replacement came to us from arch rival North DeKalb in Billy Daugherty, a solid 120 lb, fast, tough and talented player who was a perfect fit for the HalfBack position. He had been the best player on last year's North DeKalb Charger team. He was a good friend and classmate of Mike Yancey and Mike convinced him to play his last GYFC year with us.

Although GYFC rules precluded the recruitment of rival players, this in no way violated even the spirit of any rules. It was simply two friends wanting to be on the same team, and Billy and Mike lived in the same neighborhood, so there was no geographic boundary issue either. North DeKalb granted his release and he became a valuable Colt player. I never spoke with him until after the release was granted, but I still remember the happy look on his face when he showed up for the registration day of that 1977 season.

We replaced FB Jim Caudill by moving Mike Ahern from his previous year's Guard position into the backfield as FullBack. Mike was a talented athlete if you recall the interception he returned for a TD in last year's regular season game against North DeKalb from his Defensive End position. Mike actually turned out to be a better runner at FB than Caudill had been, in addition to being very good at blocking, the primary job of our FB. Dutch Minor moved into the starting Guard position vacated by moving Ahern into the backfield.

In addition to those two moves, the GYFC made a rule change in 1977, allowing 14 year olds to play from a birth date of January 1, 1963 or later, as opposed to the previous birthday rule which would have been August 1, 1963 or later. That extra seven months brought some very good players into eligibility for us. Troy Ragan would be a valuable two way starting lineman and Co-Captain, Charlie Conway would be our starting Center and Barry Newsom, the third of the famous Joel and Adele Newsom family, and one of Gary's younger brothers, would be our Free Safety. He had played for us in 1975 on our 100 lb. team.

Jimmy Caudill moved away due to his father's business transfer, and we would play against his team from Winston-Salem, North Carolina in the post season Colt Classic.

Our regular season went about like usual, we lost one game, 15-14, once again to an underdog team, this time from Clairmont. We seemed to slip up once a year to an inferior opponent, an annoying habit, but we never really lost a crucial division game. That season, the most memorable regular season game was late in the year with the Central DeKalb Cardinals on Colt Field. As usual, they were coached by Bill Eakin and Joe Cunningham, two of GYFC's best.

As in the past, we weren't in the same subdivision with CD this year, so the game wasn't crucial from that standpoint, but I thought they were the best team in the league, and a loss to us would likely knock them out of the playoffs in their own division.

I DID NOT want to play this CD team in the playoffs, they were too good and dangerous, so I wanted to win this regular season game at all cost. A tie with us in this game would not hurt either of our playoff chances, but a late season loss would likely ruin CD's playoff hopes. On the other hand, a loss in this game would not hurt us in our subdivision race as we had a two game lead, so we could play to win at all cost.

CD was defending 120 lb GYFC champs, as they had defeated Bob Johnson's Colt team in Bob's last GYFC game in the Bobby Dodd Bowl in 1976 as previously reported.

CD played very good defense with an unusual alignment. They had held Bob's team to seven points last year in the Bobby Dodd Bowl. I considered them to be the best defensive team and coaches in GYFC and I wanted to get a very good and detailed film on them in case we did have to play them again. We filmed every game, in those days using Super 8mm movie cameras, usually from a high sideline angle.

But I decided to have two camera angles to film this game, one from the high sideline, the usual angle, then I also had a second camera on top of the Colt Corral building, an end zone view. That way, I would have a film angle to see their spacing and alignment on defense, in case we did have to play them again. That could possibly provide more valuable scouting information against this tough opponent if we did have to see them in the post season GYFC playoffs.

Simple things like where the defensive linemen lined up opposite their offensive opponent, either head up, inside or outside shoulder, gap alignment etc. are vital pieces of information which you cannot always see from a sideline angle, even from a high place like the Colt Field press box. These things were very important to me in preparing an offensive game plan against a defense as good as Central DeKalb's. Our Offense was designed to take advantage of blocking angles, and I always wanted to know ahead of time where those angles might be, if at all possible.

The game went as tight as expected, and CD scored first in the first half, and led at halftime 7-0. I told the team at the halftime meeting that we were going to score in the second half, go for two, and win the game 8-7. I even showed the team a new play, actually a familiar play, a variation of our reliable 86A, but out of a new formation that I made up right there at halftime. In large part, it relied on "Influencing" one CD defender, the Left Defensive End (to our offensive right).

We had never run the play out of this new formation before, or practiced it, so using it was a bit of a risk and contrary to my usual policy of practicing a play frequently before game use. But I thought the new part was simple enough and that our players were smart enough that we could run it successfully without practice. From what I had seen and Frank Reeves had told me of CD's defensive alignment against a WingBack in the first half, it made me think this particular play and formation would work against them with the addition of the Influence strategy.

Mark Wheaton was the only player with a new assignment, and that was simply to go in motion after a signal from QB Yancey and then Yancey had to time the snap of the ball properly. Everything else on the play was the same as the play always ran.

What I didn't say at halftime was HOW we were going to get that Touchdown. Well, we got it, on a fumble recovery in CD territory, and a TD pass from Yancey to Costlow, off of our bootleg series. It was a spectacular catch by Costlow who went up high and outfought the CD defender in a "jump ball" type play. The play for the two point PAT was simple, but again, a little different, just different enough to cause enough hesitation in the CD defense to get that necessary three yards, and the hard earned two points that came with it. We called it immediately without calling timeout to talk it over.

Here's the play that I told the team about at halftime: the formation is Fullback Wing, Tailback Strong Motion, 86A, a simple wide veer handoff, outside the defensive Tackle, leaving the Defensive End unblocked. It would require perfect execution and timing against this great Central DeKalb defense to get the vital three yards for the two point PAT.

The Tailback and Halfback line up behind the Offensive Guards in normal twins or Split Veer formation. The Fullback lines up a yard outside the strongside (right) Tight End, in the backfield as a WingBack. I assume here that the Defensive End will likely adjust a little to the outside which is what he had done in the first half against a Wingback. That's what we want him to do, as we want to "influence" him away from the off tackle hole and run the play into that hole which is just to the inside of his usual position. The inside linebackers may adjust a little in that direction too, but we expect to seal them enough with our double team and second level blocking to keep them from stopping the play which is run at a "veer" angle "inside out" toward the outside.

Also, and to influence the Defensive End to loosen his position further, we send the Tailback in motion to the strongside right, toward and just beyond the Wingback's position. Now, the Defensive End has two players just outside of him. We wanted to create hesitation and doubt in his mind as to where the play might run. Protecting the outside is his primary responsibility. Off tackle to his inside is his secondary responsibility, and we wanted to influence him to neglect that part of his assignment.

The ball is snapped as the man in motion (TB) is barely past the WB's position, and we run the 86A Veer handoff to the HB behind a double team by the strongside End and Tackle on the Defensive Tackle, leaving the End unblocked. The End is preoccupied, or influenced, by his concern about these two potential blockers outside of his position of responsibility.

There are six important strategic aspects to the play. The first two are the Wingback's positioning and the Tailback in motion, creating the influence. The third key to this play is that the play hits the hole very quickly, a difficult assignment for QB Yancey, but one he was quite capable of, the fourth is a slam or scrape block off of his double team by our Strong End Costlow, allowing him to hit the Tackle first and slide off and seal second level inside linebacker pursuit. Chuck Trense was good enough at Strong Tackle to keep his man inside by himself and allow Costlow to slide off on that "second level" linebacker pursuit. The fifth strategic point was that we had the ball placed on the left hash mark (the Offense has the option of either hash mark or the middle on a two point PAT attempt), leaving a wide right field, adding additional pressure on the CD End, knowing he had a wide field to defend.

The sixth and final point is that our HB is Billy Dougherty, a big, strong and quick runner, very hard for one defender to tackle solo. By the time Billy hit the hole on this play, the Defensive End saw what was happening, tried to adjust to the play, but Billy was by him, through his attempted arm tackle. The double team and scrape by Costlow had sealed off the inside pursuit, and Billy dived into the End Zone for the needed two points, Colts take the lead and the victory, 8-7.

The play had worked just as we had hoped! Their End was so influenced by the WingBack and TailBack in motion as potential double team blockers, and Billy Dougherty was so quick and strong that we had sneaked that one by them.

The best example I have seen that I can cite of "Influence" Blocking occurred in the 1967 NFL Championship Game between the Dallas Cowboys and Green Bay Packers, aka "The Ice Bowl" played in 13 below 0 degree temperatures in Green Bay.

Bob Lilly was an All Pro Defensive Tackle on the right side of the Dallas 4-3 "Doomsday" Defense. He was famous not only for his quickness and strength, but also for his ability to read keys and diagnose an Offensive play. He was known to follow a pulling guard (reading that as a key), realizing that the guard would usually lead him to the hole where the running play would go.

Knowing that from scouting, Vince Lombardi, and the Green Bay offensive coaches created a simple running play that called for pulling the Left Guard to the left side like a sweep, influencing Lilly to follow the Guard, and then sending a Running Back on a simple straight handoff into the hole vacated by Lilly. I will never forget seeing the gaping hole in the Dallas defensive line, and no one had to block Lilly as he ran himself right out of the hole chasing that Guard. It worked great for the Packers and the play made a long gain for a first down in a crucial situation, in a low scoring game eventually won by Green Bay on the last play of the game.

The play was very simple, yet deceptive as it took advantage of the aggressiveness of a great Defensive Tackle like Bob Lilly tricking him into running away from the hole.

It would likely only work one time in a game and the wily Lombardi saved it for a crucial time.

Back to our game. 86A is a very good play, very reliable in short yardage situations. It is one of those plays that requires a lot of practice time due to its precise timing. It is hard for the QB to get to the handoff before the HB gets to the hole. We practiced it a lot every day, and I learned to be patient and repetitious from, who else but Bob Johnson. He insisted on perfect execution and got it by repeating plays over and over in practice. Our two players involved in this play, Yancey and Dougherty worked hard in practice on their timing, as did Yancey and Wheaton when the play went to the other side.

Defensive Ends are usually coached to close to the inside when a Tight end on their side blocks down to the inside as we did on 86A. But by adding the Wingback and Tailback in Motion, both to the outside, the doubt was created and the CD End failed to close down in time to stop the 3 yard gain for the two point PAT.

We also had a weakside version of this play called FB Slot, 36A. That would be the same play to the TB from split veer formation and the double team is on the weakside Defensive Tackle, leaving the End on that side unblocked. More on that play will come later.

As I had hoped, Central DeKalb would not make the playoffs due to that loss. After the game at midfield Coach Eakin asked me two things; first why did we go for two in that situation, and second, why we used two film angles with the second camera in the end zone?

I truthfully let him know that both answers were due to the great respect we had for his team. He also said "I can't believe you ran a simple dive play for the two points in that crucial situation." He was right, it was a simple dive play, but in reality, it was the design of the play, the combination of formation, motion, influence and veer technique that made it successful. The best, most important plays don't have to be fancy, they just have to be planned and executed properly. That's more of the Bob Johnson/Leonard Jones theory.

Also, and always, against a quality opponent, the more information you have to use in your preparation, the better your chances of success.

The truth is that I wanted to win every game, and not tie. The only way I would not have gone for two in that situation was if a tie would have had a positive effect on our playoff chances, or if a loss would have hurt them. In this particular year, we had the subdivision already locked up, so a tie or loss would not have hurt us. What's the difference in 8-1-1 or 8-2? To me, none as long as we are subdivision champs. I liked 9-1 a lot better, and that's what going for two got us. Just as important that particular year was avoiding playing Central DeKalb in the playoffs, as I repeat that I thought they were the best in the 120 lb. league that year.

So, now on to the GYFC playoffs where we face Forest Park in the first round, with Glenwood, coached by the great veteran Virgil Sorrels, a Bob Johnson nemesis, but friendly rival, expected to be our likely opponent for the championship. No disrespect to Forest Park, but I was pretty sure we could beat them pretty easily. However, we had never faced a Virgil Sorrels team, and of course, he had never faced us. I KNEW they would be a test just because of watching Virgil's teams compete against Bob Johnson's over the past years.

I had watched Virgil's teams play against Bob Johnson's Colt teams several times over those years, and they were always very good. They were quick and fast, hit hard and played clean, fundamentally very good football. Virgil had better success against Bob than anyone else in the GYFC after C.K. Braswell of Midway retired. I knew Virgil would have their entire coaching staff scouting us in our first round game against Forest Park, and I didn't want to show them any more of our offense than we had to in that game. Films of our games were not accessible to Glenwood due to GYFC rules as we had not played them during the season.

So, our game plan against Forest Park was to pass more than usual and run all split veer formation plays, thereby not showing Virgil and his scouts any of our bread and butter I formation at all. We would try to beat Forest Park with passing and a running game with inside and outside Veers, traps, and options. Then we would use our whole offensive package the following week against Glenwood, with the Power I that Glenwood's scouts had not seen, as our base offense.

I actually wanted Virgil and the Glenwood scouts to view us as a passing team and spend most of their practice time preparing for a passing attack, while I knew full well that the only way we could beat Glenwood was with our complete diversified ground attack, mixing in play action passes at the appropriate times. The passing attack we used against Forest Park would be all drop back and rollout passing, no play action, no Power I.

I'm a big believer in scouting and preparation. I want all the information I can get about my upcoming opponent, and at the same time, I wanted to reveal as little as I could to opposing scouts, thus the diversionary tactics that we used here.

From scouting them myself, I did not think Forest Park could score against Jim Lineberger's defense in 8 quarters, much less 4. I was right. That defense was playing very well, led by LB's Trense and Minor, linemen

Ragan and Oxford and the secondary anchored by veterans Roger Rubinson and Barry Newsom.

We did beat Forest Park a pretty easy 14-0, with a lot more passing than normal. I think we passed about 15 times, a very high number in 14 year old football, using no I formation or play action passes. We stayed in the various "Twins" or Split Veer formations all day and ran and passed exclusively from that. QB Yancey and our receivers (particularly Ends Mike Viggiano, Don West and Jimmy Costlow) had a great time with all of that passing. That victory set up the highly anticipated match with Glenwood who had a great running back in Alfred McKerson and a QB named Kevin Anthony.

Wearing our traditional Bobby Dodd Bowl all white uniform for the fifth straight year, our game with Glenwood went about as expected, back and forth, very tough and hard hitting, and we managed a 7-6 lead going into the 4th Quarter. We started a drive early in the 4th Quarter and got down to about the Glenwood 25 yard line, facing a crucial 3rd down and about 5. I pulled out a little used play at that time, FB Slot 36A that I described before.

This call was a weakside veer to TB Mark Wheaton, a simple wide dive handoff behind the double team of the Weakside End and Tackle, leaving the Weakside Defensive End unblocked. Remember, the strategy of the veer is to leave a lineman unblocked and seal off the rest of the defense's pursuit, whether to the weakside or the strongside. The unblocked lineman usually has outside leverage responsibility, and the play would be running to his inside, as close to the double team as possible. The back is told to run "right off the read drive (Double teamer) man's behind."

Leaving an End on either side unblocked was usually successful for us. Quickness by the QB is also required to execute this play properly. The running back is told to hit his hole full speed which makes it difficult for the QB to reach him in time. As I said above, we practiced these simple handoffs repeatedly in drills during offensive practice time. Mike Yancey was very quick with the ball, and he was perfect after having run these plays for two years

We rarely ran it to the weak side, but it was part of our package and we had prepared to use it in this game because we felt that Glenwood would adjust and load up to stop our strongside running game once they saw and got hurt by the Power I in the early stages of the game. We also felt they would rotate their secondary toward the slot formation, as most defenses would do, and this created a chance to get the ball to Mark Wheaton in open space, a huge advantage for us and one of the primary reasons I had designed the additions to the Offense back in 1975 with new formations like this FB Slot.

The outside veer had worked to perfection on the strong side against Central DeKalb for the important two point PAT. This one to the weak side worked as designed too, for the first down and more and as Mark Wheaton hit about the 15 yard line, he made a nice cut back to the inside of the Safety who slightly over ran him, and sprinted into the End Zone for a TD, holding the ball high after he crossed the goal line, a Mark Wheaton trademark TD celebration.

The effective strategy on that play comes from running away from the slot formation. That particular formation keeps a Tight End to the weak side, allowing the offensive line to make the double team block, while usually requiring the defense to overload toward the slot side where the extra man is lined up. That gives the Offense a man advantage because you do not use a blocker on the End, there is no outside linebacker, and the secondary has rotated toward the Slot formation. If your back can split the Corner and Free Safety, he can go a very long way, which is what Mark was able to do.

Back in the 1960's and 70's when good college teams used the Veer Offense, you would see a lot of long runs that started with simple dive handoffs. Colt TB Mark Wheaton was very hard to tackle by a single defender as he was very quick and could cut without slowing down. Although he was a classic I formation Tailback most of the time, he could run veer dive plays and inside trap plays just as well. Although small, playing in the 120 lb. league at under 100 lbs., he was just that good, and a natural as a running back. This particular veer dive play against Glenwood scored from about 20 yards, but Mark likely could have taken it 80 yards if necessary. He never got caught from behind.

Now I decide it's time for another surprise two point conversion try. Why, we're ahead by seven and an almost automatic, routine PAT kick makes it eight? The reason I told myself was that at this point, late in the game, a 9 point lead (they would call that a two possession lead in today's TV Announcer lingo) is insurmountable, assuring a win, and I wanted that assurance. Plus, Glenwood was down after the TD, and not expecting to have to defend another scrimmage play. The element of surprise would also be in our favor if we moved quickly.

Again, without calling timeout, the try was simple, our favorite strong side play action pass, 26-2. The difference, I believe after seeing it on film was that Yancey and Costlow improvised the pass route, with Costlow cutting back to the middle of the end zone instead of going to the corner. Mike completed the pass, we had our two point conversion and the Colts led by nine and go on to win 15-6, a 6th Bobby Dodd Bowl in a row and first try in the 120 lb class!

I never asked Mike or Jimmy Costlow about the improvised pass route, but I did see them nod and communicate before the play, and I believe that signal was the changed pass route. They were smart kids and had played together two consecutive years and had collaborated to complete many passes in 28 games together.

So, in our first year in GYFC's ultimate big league of 120 lb. football, we had done it after all, winning a 6th straight GYFC championship Bobby Dodd Bowl. Bob Johnson himself was there to see it, and I was never more proud than to shake his hand after taking his former team, the 120 lb. Colts to another championship.

Now, two bowl games, first at home against Jimmy Caudill's Winston-Salem, North Carolina team in the Colt Classic. We handled them pretty easily, winning 21-0 and unfortunately Jimmy Caudill suffered a broken collarbone trying to chase down Mark Wheaton on a punt return. Someone, I believe Costlow, blindsided him right in front of our sideline.

Whoever made the block, no one was happy to see Jimmy Caudill get hurt as he had been a good friend and team mate the prior year, but I think deep inside some of our guys thought it was ironic that he was injured after having dealt out so much punishment in practice to them last year. As I had said about his performance in the previous season, he was our "enforcer" and hardest hitter.

Our other hardest hitter was Steve Oxford, or "Ox", our Nose Guard, on this year's team as well as the previous year's 1976 100 lb. team. There was one funny incident in practice that I remember about those two that occurred back in the '76 season. One of our fiercest contact drills in practice is "Oklahoma," a drill matching two blockers, an offensive lineman and lead blocking back, against two defenders, a defensive lineman and linebacker, with the fifth participant a ball carrier. We usually ran that drill in practice at least two days in every week.

The Oklahoma drill allows you to work on several things. It matches an offensive lineman against a defensive lineman, so you are working blocking technique with the offensive player while another coach works on defensive line technique against him. Same thing with a blocking back against a linebacker, where both players had a running start and there were some very hard and violent full speed collisions. The other helpful aspect of this drill in our Leonard Jones" Lead Option" offensive attack was that the running backs also practiced reading the offensive lineman's quick read block.

In the Oklahoma drill on the practice day I'm now talking about, Ox was running Fullback and Caudill was the Linebacker which made them go "head to head" and provided for some very hard hitting. As in many other drills, we had them going several times in a row. Repetition as I said before, always makes you better. That's the way Bob Johnson ran practice, as I recall watching Billy Todd sporting that ugly eye contusion, but remaining in that 1971 Oklahoma drill.

In this particular drill in 1976 at the 100 lb. level, Ox was slightly bigger than Caudill and finally got the best of him, successfully drive blocking him to the ground and landing on top of him, the perfect "pancake" block. So then, after that result, I took Ox out, left Caudill in, and asked another player, who I will call Player X, to go against the agitated Jimmy Caudill. After being beaten and knocked down, the angry and frustrated Caudill would not have come out of the drill if I had told him to anyway.

There was some stalling going on, and Player X was the one delaying things. I did not like wasting valuable practice time, so I said to him "son, get in there. What are you waiting on ?" Player X took his mouthpiece out, looked up at me and then pointed his trembling finger at Caudill, who was red faced and scowling with anger like an angry bull in a bullfight, after being knocked down by Ox. Player X, pointing at Caudill in fear, said "Steven made him mad!"

Everyone broke up laughing, and a little humor like that always helped everyone's spirits in the middle of a grueling practice.

Another word about the Oklahoma drill. It was very useful, particularly as we taught our linemen how to execute the quick read block, and the backs to read that block and prepare for the violent collisions that would occur when the lead blockers encountered the opposing linebackers filling the holes.

We used it every Monday and some Wednesdays and Thursdays. On this team, Billy Dougherty, our halfback was very good at it, as were FB Mike Ahern, OT and LB Chuck Trense, Caudill, Oxford and many others on both sides of the ball. It was an excellent teaching drill and worked offense and defense at the same time. It also required all five of our coaches to participate and coach the five players in the drill.

The 1977 away bowl game was the Louisiana Classic, played in New Orleans. Our opponent was actually an all star team, and that does not work against a well organized team like ours. They were unable to do anything at all with their Offense. They did have a lot of talented players and they played decent defense, but we methodically scored three TD's and won easily 21-0, ending the year 13-1-0.

KEY PLAYERS FROM 1976 100 lb. and 1977 120 lb. ATLANTA COLTS

Mike Yancey, QB and DB . . . . Mike came to us as a QB and he had played that position for Mac Scoggins on the 1975 80 lb team. He was smart and tough, average size for his age, and with an accurate passing arm. He was an excellent Defensive Back and tough and quick enough that we played him in man coverage on occasion when our opponent had a very good receiver. We also put in a corner blitz package for him. He went on to a successful high school football career and was a very good baseball player for Georgia Tech's powerhouse teams in the 1980's.

Mark Wheaton, TB and Safety . . . . Mark was very small for his age. He played 120 lb league at well under 100 lbs. But he was very fast, quick, tough and a very instinctive breakaway runner. He scored many touchdowns from TB and had over 2,000 yards in his two years with us. He played a very good cornerback and free safety and led the team in interceptions both years. He went on to be an outstanding high school basketball player, as he was too light to play football in high school.

Chuck Trense, OT, DT and LB . . . . Chuck was underage for his weight division, playing in the 100 lb, 12 year old league at 11, and the 13-14 year old 120 lb league at 12. So he was big for his age and also could run fast. He was our Strongside Tackle on offense both years, and played Defensive Tackle on the 100 lb Team. As a DT, he was so fast and aggressive, he covered the field like a linebacker. The next year, with Jimmy Caudill moving away, we moved Chuck to Linebacker, where he also excelled. Chuck was one of our fastest players and he went on to play Running Back at Marist High School.

Pete Stephens, OG . . . . Pete was our Strongside Guard, where the primary job is to protect the "A" gap, and be a trapping guard. Trapping was a very important part of our Offense, and we needed someone quick and tough at that position. He was very good at that. Pete also went on to be an outstanding Running Back in high school.

Dutch Minor, OG and LB . . . . Dutch played both ways for us for two years, taking almost every snap for 28 games. He was also very tough and very fast. Like Trense and Stephens, his speed allowed him to play Running Back in high school.

Jimmy Costlow, OE and DE . . . . Another two way player, Jimmy was our leading pass receiver and a consistent TD maker. He may have been the best pure athlete on the team as he had great natural ability, and good size. He had very quick feet and was hard to block defensively, where he defended our left defensive flank where most teams based their primary attack.

Mike Ahern, all purpose . . . . Mike played Defensive End and Offensive Guard his first year on 100 lb., and Fullback and Linebacker the next. He actually played two years at FB/LB on the 120 lb team, having one of those good birthdays and playing again in 1978. He was big, tough and instinctive, and consistently made big plays

Roger Rubinson, Defensive Halfback . . . Roger was a great kid, a little quiet. He played a very good secondary for us for both years. He was small, but quick and determined, pound for pound an outstanding player

D.H. Malcom, 1976, Billy Dougherty, 1977, HB/LB . . . . These two played the same positions each for one year. They were similar performers although different shapes. Malcom was short and stocky, Dougherty, tall and lean, but both were outstanding blockers, runners and tacklers.

Mark Rudder, all purpose . . . . This kid deserves special mention. He never played a lot for us, as he was very small for his age. He was very determined and gave maximum effort at all times, and he had the respect of our entire team. Although he never started for us, he went on to a terrific high school and college career as a wide receiver, proving to everyone that lack of size can be overcome by talent, heart, effort and determination. Mark had all of those qualities.

1977 120 lb. Atlanta Colts Record, 13-1-0

GYFC Champions
Atlanta Colt Classic Champions
Louisiana Classic Champions

Colts 20 Midway 0
Colts 14 Clairmont 15
Colts 24 DeKalb Yellow Jackets. 0
Colts 21 Briarcliff 0
Colts 14 Northeast 6
Colts 24 Sandy Springs 15
Colts 16 Forest Park 7
Colts 8 Central DeKalb 7
Colts 33 Stone Mountain 0

GYFC Playoffs, Round One Jim Brazier Bowl at Kiwanis Stadium, Forest Park, Georgia

Colts 14 Forest Park 0

GYFC Championship, The Bobby Dodd Bowl at Kiwanis Stadium, Forest park, Georgia

Colts 15 Glenwood 6

Atlanta Colt Classic, Colt Field at Murphy Candler Park, Atlanta, Georgia

Colts 21 Winston-Salem, N.C. 0

Louisiana Classic, New Orleans, Louisiana

Colts 21 Louisiana Cavaliers 0

1977 120 lb. Atlanta Colts Starting Lineups

Offense

Strong End..............................Jimmy Costlow
Strong tackle ....Chuck Trense
Strong Guard ....Peter Stephens
Center....................................Charlie Conway
Quick Guard...........................Dutch Minor
Quick Tackle ....Troy Ragan
Quick End ....Mike Viggiano
Quarterback ....Mike Yancey
Halfback ....Billy Daugherty
Fullback ....Mike Ahern
Tailback..................................Mark Wheaton

Defense

Left End...................................Jimmy Costlow
Left Tackle...............................Joe Whitley
Nose Guard..............................Steve Oxford
Right Tackle ....Troy Ragan
Right End ....David Natsch
Left Inside Linebacker..............Chuck Trense
Right Inside Linebacker...........Mike Ahern
Strong Safety or "Monster"......LB Billy Daugherty
Left Cornerback ....Mark Wheaton
Right Cornerback.....................Roger Rubinson
Safety Barry Newsom

Coaches:

Head Coach Doug Bennett
Offensive Line Coach Warren Watson
Defensive Coordinator Jim Lineberger
Offensive Backfield
Coach Frank Reeves
Defensive Backfield
Coach Fred Amtower

1977 120 lb. Atlanta Colts Complete Roster

Billy Daugherty	Mike Ahern
Jimmy Costlow	Steve Oxford
David Natsch	Mike Yancey
Don West	Chuck Trense
Vince Apruzesse	Dutch Minor
Tim Geiger	Charlie Conway
Jimmy Hunt	Mark Spiezio
Mark McGlaughlin	John Harry
Mike Viggiano	Joe Whitley
Mark Rudder	Greg Edwards
Roger Rubinson	Joe McGuirk
Mark Wheaton	Peter Stephens
Mark Gurr	Barry Newsom
John McMath	Troy Ragan
Hal Moore	

Cheeleaders

Katy Reiley	Donna Presnall
Lisa Paracsi	Dena Miles
Shari Noren	Kim Toole
Judy Schmitz	Kim Fry
Jeannie Whitley	Shelley Wheaton
Debbie Rutledge	Jill Reeves

1977 100 lb. Atlanta Colts Record, 14-0

Pop Warner National Champions
GYFC Champions
Atlanta Colt Classic Champions
Louisiana Classic Champions

Colts 42 Midway 7
Colts 34 Clairmont 0
Colts 45 DeKalb
Yellow Jackets 0
Colts 41 Briarcliff 0
Colts 40 Northeast 0
Colts 36 Sandy Springs 0
Colts 48 Forest Park 0
Colts 28 Central DeKalb 6
Colts 28 Stone Mountain 0

GYFC Semi Final, The Jim Brazier Bowl, Kiwanis Stadium, Forest Park, Georgia

Colts 21 Central DeKalb 6

GYFC Championship, The Bobby Dodd Bowl, Kiwanis Stadium, Forest Park, Georgia

Colts 27 Glenwood 6

Atlanta Colt Classic, Colt Field, Murphy Candler Park, Atlanta, Georgia

Colts 40 Winston-Salem 0

Louisiana Classic, New Orleans, Louisiana

Colts 20 N.O.R.D. Raiders 0

1977 100 lb. Atlanta Colts Complete Roster

Robert Harry
James Reinstein
Jeff Morris
Glenn Gandy
Kevin Minor
David Rose
Scott Miller
Steve Squire
Bobby Humphrey
Steve Forsberg
Roger Shadburn
Jeff Craven
Guy Thacker
John Cascone
Richie NeSmith
Keith Killingsworth

Tony Hargis
Troy Sadowski
Brian Jager
Brad Billingsley
Lee Cawthon
Franklin Coulter
Doug Miles
Adam Furth
Marc Fredo
Frank Doherty
Dean Farber
Gary Humphrey
Keith Tyson
Greg Barto
Drew Williams
Chris Yancey

Coaching Staff

Mac Scoggins Head Coach
Charlie Ragan
Pat Eder
Alton Conway
Bob Carpenter

Cheerleaders

Deidre Companik
Tracie Wiggins
Maureen Egan
Sharon Spivey
Ann Miller
Dina Williamson

Tracie Jensen
Toni Eder
Kristin Schmitz
Laura Ramsey
Nancy Papineau
Debbie West

1977 80 lb. Atlanta Colts Record, 14-0

Pop Warner National Champions
GYFC Champions
Atlanta Colt Classic Champions
Geechee Bowl Champions

Colts 19 Midway 0
Colts 14 Clairmont 6
Colts 28 DeKalb
Yellow Jackets 0
Colts 14 Briarcliff 0
Colts 24 Northeast 0
Colts 24 Sandy Springs 0
Colts 14 Forest Park 6
Colts 35 Central DeKalb 0
Colts 56 Stone Mountain 0

GYFC Semi-Final, The Jim Brazier Bowl, Kiwanis Stadium, Forest Park, Georgia

Colts 14 Briarcliff 13

GYFC Championship, The Bobby Dodd Bowl, Kiwanis Stadium, Forest park, Georgia

Colts 14 Glenwood 6

Atlanta Colt Classic, Colt Field, Murphy Candler Park, Atlanta, Georgia

Colts 17 Winston-Salem 0

Geechee Bowl, Savannah State College, Savannah, Georgia

Colts 31 Savannah 14

1977 80 lb. Atlanta Colts Complete Roster

Chris Sheffield	David Myrick
Robert McEachern	Sean McDonald
Jay Montgomery	Richie Combs
Ken Harmon	Jeff Radtke
Stephen Chessin	Gregg Routt
Tommy Thomas	John Duncan
Jim Ferguson	Billy Schmitz
Todd Simmons	Derek D'Alonzo
Scott Mischnick	Mike Dion
Jeff Scott	Mark Sherretz
Stacy Campbell	Jimmy Hargis
Craig Wudi	Jay Wesevich
Jeff Mitchell	Freddie Rosenthal
John Wischmeyer	Charles Shaw
Dan Gastley	Craig Goldberg
Ricky Mitnitsky	A.J. Paracsi
Richie Locklear	

Coaching Staff

John Ramsey Head Coach
Jay Williams
Buddy Ragsdale
Tom Hartley
Bill Schmitz

Cheerleaders

Lisa Schmitz	Laura Lee Wall
Brittany Harmon	Wendy Croft
Penny Presnall	Lisa Sandusky
Jan Ragsdale	Denise Doherty
Robyn Barto	Teri Eder
Sheial Hartigan	Linda Kurtzer

1977 Coltettes Drill Team

Lisa Larson   Julie Bodenheimer
Kem Halsell   Karen Wilhelm
Lori Dueker   Stephanie Gainer
Karen Bryant   Lisa Lilly
Sherry Dolan   Sheila Crook
Vanessa Lane   Laura Flack
Rene Wischmeyer   Diana McGuirk
Debbie LeShane   Lynn Britt
Andrea Daney   Holly Parker
Donna West   Kim Lane
Barbara Parker   Suzie Crowder
Lynne Larson   Kelly Musselman
Liz Newsom   Mellie Klinger
Kitty Klinger   Kristie Hightower
Alicia Wilfong

CHAPTER 13

1978, The Year of the "Goose"

Varsity Colt Summary, 1978

We had two of our three Colt teams make the Bobby Dodd Bowl in 1978, but for the first time since 1966, we had no winners and thus no GYFC championships.

My 120 lb. team suffered a last second loss to Midway and Mac Scoggins, who had his fifth consecutive perfect 10-0 regular season, also took his team to the Bobby Dodd Bowl. They easily beat Smyrna in the Brazier Bowl first round game by the score of 42-6, but in the championship game, they were shut out by Glenwood 10-0.

They were victorious in the Holiday Bowl game in Pensacola over Brentwood 19-6, but lost the Colt Classic to Clearwater, 7-6. They finished 12-2, an excellent record and that ended Mac's career as a Colt Head Coach. His varsity Colt record was 61-4-1, two National Championships, Two GYFC Championships, One GYFC Co-Championship, One GYFC 2nd Place and one GYFC 3rd Place in 5 years, an amazing record for a truly great football coach.

His final team was led by QB Todd Rampley and had very good running backs in Derek D'Alonzo and Ken Harmon. They also had very good line play with Chris Sheffield, John Zagarella and Ward Murphy leading the way.

The 80 lb. team was John Ramsey's second and last. They had a 7-3 regular season. And won both post season games for a 9-3 overall record.

The overall record for the 1978 varsity was 31-9.

* * *

1978 120 lb. Atlanta Colts, Year of "The Goose"

Coming into the 1978 season, our 120 lb. Colt coaching staff had higher than usual expectations. We had our entire coaching staff coming back, and Mac Scoggins had had possibly the greatest ever 100 lb. team in 1977, undefeated GYFC and Pop Warner National Champs. They had a very good quarterback in left handed Franklin Coulter, and one of the best ever Colt running backs in Brian Jager. They had scored over 400 points, and averaged over 30 points per game.

Jager became an outstanding player at Dunwoody High School and then in college as well. Coulter was small, in fact reminded me of Bob Johnson's 1971 QB, and one of Bob's all time favorite players named Mike Killeen, small, but a slick ball handler, field general and good passer. Franklin also became a successful QB at Chamblee High as a Senior.

I expected Franklin to be very good for us as well. He appeared to be able to do anything that I expected or needed of a Quarterback in our offensive system. Jager had had an incredible season for Mac's 100 lb. team, possibly the best and most productive ever for a running back, playing for any Colt team or anyone else in GYFC that I had seen to date, including Tracy Soles of Central DeKalb. If they had kept statistics, I would have little doubt that Brian Jager may have had the most yards and Touchdowns in 1977 of any running back that ever wore the Colt uniform, in any weight class in the entire history of this storied program. He was a once in a lifetime type performer, a 100 lb. Herschel Walker.

About that time, the ACYA was beginning to shrink in size, due to the aging of the neighborhoods and the beginning development of farther out metro areas like Roswell and Alpharetta. At the 13-14 year old and 120 lb. level, we had had continuous recruiting battles with the high school 8th grade and JV teams at Marist, Chamblee, Peachtree and Dunwoody high schools that seemed to be getting more intense. There weren't as many kids that wanted to play serious football.

Soccer was becoming popular with younger kids. It was easier, not very rough and every player gets to touch the ball. Bob Johnson joked that the rising popularity of soccer was due to a "communist plot" to undermine the youth of America. Or . . . . was he really joking?

In their effort to get the players into their football programs, some of the less successful high school coaches would threaten the kids that they might never get a chance to play football on the school's varsity team if they played with us once they entered the high school, even as young as

8th grade. There were no middle schools in the 1970's. This threat was not true, just a bluff, as we had many players play out their eligibility with us and become high school stars. It was just an unethical ploy by the high school coaches to try and intimidate the kids in the battle for the numbers. The more successful high school coaches were less of a problem as they recognized that GYFC was a good experience for upcoming players.

We lost these two great players to their high school 8th grade teams, Coulter to Chamblee and Jager to Dunwoody. I'm not sure why that happened to these two players, but these were crucial losses. However, out of something bad came something very good. I received a call in early summer from Al Humphrey, father of upcoming player Bobby. The call had to do with a co-worker of Al's who had a son that might want to play for us and he was a quarterback.

The co-worker of Al's was Rus Anthony and his son was Kevin, nicknamed "Goose." He was the QB that we had faced for Glenwood in the previous season's Bobby Dodd Bowl and he had another year of GYFC eligibility remaining. The GYFC had very strict recruiting and tampering rules to discourage players from changing programs and to encourage players to stay in their own geographic area. There were no formal borders, but there were implied informal borders. But even in those days heavy metro Atlanta traffic prohibited families from driving too far for four times a week activities, which included three practices a week at rush hour, and a weekend game somewhere in the metro area on Saturday. Therefore, not many players traveled very far to play in GYFC since the 16 programs were well spaced throughout the metro Atlanta area. There were very few youth football programs of any consequence in metro Atlanta that were not in GYFC. A player who wanted to change from one GYFC program to another in consecutive years was required to obtain a written release from the program he was leaving to be eligible in the coming year for his new team.

So I told Al that the Anthonys would be welcome to join ACYA, but they would have to comply with GYFC rules and obtain a release from Glenwood before I could talk to them. We were always very careful to obey GYFC rules regarding recruiting, practice hours, exchanging films, etc. I thought all of the GYFC rules were reasonable and fair, and evenly applied and enforced.

Virgil Sorrels graciously granted the release, as I would have. No coach would really want a player that wanted to be elsewhere, certainly not a 14 year old kid. Plus, the Anthonys were moving residency into farther north DeKalb County, so the move made the release easier to justify for all concerned.

So, I met the Anthonys and they were a terrific family, and fit right into our program, becoming some of my closest friendships in the program. Rus was a great guy and we talked frequently, and in fact we remained good friends for many years, and I even joined them for one of Kevin's UNC games in Chapel Hill a few years later. Kevin's mother Lorelei was equally nice and gracious, and invited me to their home for dinner occasionally over the years.

Kevin, or "Goose," had grown substantially and was about the size of Mike Yancey, with similar physical characteristics and ability. At about age 14, Kevin was starting to grow rapidly and eventually wound up matching his father at about 6'3" in height. He was also smart, in fact very smart and we quickly figured out he could play anywhere on the field, and with his experience at QB, it was obvious he would be a very good QB in our system. He also was our starting Free Safety and was outstanding on defense as well.

So, we never missed Coulter at QB. We will never know, but I doubt that he would have been good enough to beat out Anthony.

Kevin Anthony went on to be an all-state player at QB for the famous Weyman Creel at Lakeside High School. In college, he became a starting QB at the University of North Carolina. Smart coaches like Weyman Creel certainly did not mind their future varsity players playing in the GYFC while in 8th or 9th grade. Coach Creel, for one, realized they would receive good coaching either place, and actually a longer season and more competitive environment and very good experience in the highly competitive GYFC.

The loss of Jager was a little more difficult to replace, as he was a once in a lifetime type running back. We tried a few different players and we finally settled on Keith Tyson, similar in height to Mark Wheaton, a little stronger and stockier, not quite as fast. Keith turned out to be a very good tailback, in fact outstanding at the end of the year, and although we missed a player like Jager, we never really noticed it because of Keith's outstanding play.

In addition, the rest of our backfield was experienced and outstanding, with Greg Edwards at Halfback and Mike Ahern at Fullback. These two were big, tough and quick. They had experience in the difficult requirements of reading our linemen's blocks and lead blocking linebackers that our Offense required from their two years with us on the previous two Colt teams of 1976 and 1977. Ahern would be a two way starter all three years he played for us.

Central DeKalb was our key opponent in regular season. In an unusual circumstance, they were in our subdivision after realignment for the first time ever in this particular year. The conference realigned every two years in an attempt to maintain the best and fairest competitive balance. So, this year Central DeKalb appeared to be the biggest obstacle to us in order to win the subdivision. They were always so well coached and consistently among the best teams in the league.

This season, we squeaked by them early in the year on their field, 7-3 on a Goose Anthony weakside option keeper for a TD from about 50 yards. The rest of our regular season was up and down, with close losses to North DeKalb who had a speedy running back named Mario Williams and were coached by a fiery, competitive newcomer named Paul Zarynoff, and Northeast, coached by the wily veteran Jerome Roberts, again playing with less than optimal consistency on offense. We just seemed a little out of synch all year, but I knew we had quality players in the line and backfield and I honestly felt all year that we had great offensive potential. That win over Central DeKalb kept us in the driver's seat to be subdivision champs all year despite the two losses to North DeKalb and Northeast, our first losses ever to either of those two competitors.

Toward the end of regular season, we were 6 and 2, with an unusually dangerous Smyrna team coming in to Colt Field, coached by Charles Cook. They were undefeated at 8-0, played very good basic offense and defense and had very good skilled players on both sides of the ball. I always expected that of Charles Cook's teams, he was a good coach and a first class individual.

Being a home game, I was optimistic and pretty confident, but I thought we might be a slight underdog to this undefeated team. We had practiced hard, and had a typical regular season game plan. The only thing special or new in the plan, was some stuff we had seen LSU use in a TV game that we wanted to try. I've always been a "closet" LSU fan due to the Louisiana side of my family, and Coach Charles McClendon was a pretty innovative coach at the time. By this 9th game, we expected to be ready and close to peak performance capability and I expected good results with the LSU package to supplement our base offense.

Our usual regular season strategy was to work hard all year, gradually adjust our strategy to best fit our personnel, and try to peak the team at the end of the year for playoff time. We were undefeated at home for almost four full years, since the 1975 opening day loss to Tucker. We knew Smyrna was good, but we had no idea they were as much better than we were as the results showed. They pounded us 24-0. It was not a very close game at all, quite reminiscent of the 1975 home loss to Tucker. Nothing worked, not even LSU!

This was devastating. Sure, we had lost a couple of close games on the road this season to two very good teams, but never expected to be blown out by Smyrna. This was as big of a surprise as that 1975 loss to Tucker. But this was worse, because this time we did not have the rest of the year to catch up and improve, we only had one week left in the season. Plus, now we're behind CD in the subdivision because of this late season loss. We're now facing the possibility of missing the playoffs altogether for the first time ever in seven years.

But, we still had a chance to win our subdivision. We had to beat Tucker in game 10 and Central DeKalb needed to lose their game 10. So, in week 10, we did beat Tucker 17-0 in an afternoon game, and played much better, led by Anthony and Tyson. Keith had continually improved all year to become a very good Tailback. Now, if only CD loses later that night, we are in the playoffs and have a chance to earn a 7th straight GYFC championship.

It was classic good news, bad news. The good news was that Central DeKalb lost, and we were subdivision champs. The bad news is we have to play Smyrna again, just two weeks after losing to them 24-0.

How could we possibly beat this team that had just overwhelmed us on our own home field? Well, rather than be pessimistic, we decided to do what we always did, and that was a lengthy film review and planning session with our coaching staff Sunday afternoon and into the night at Jim Lineberger's house to go over the film from our regular season game that was only one week old. At least as bad as it was, we would not expect Smyrna to make any drastic changes. Why would they change anything after cruising past us so easily just one week ago?

It turned out that it was really fortunate that we had played them so recently. GYFC did not allow the exchange of game films, unless your own team had participated in the game that you were watching. So, we had a good, recent film to break down of our week 9 game, and we broke it down play by play and position by position.

One particular thing immediately and obviously jumped off the film. That was that their offensive guards came off the ball very quickly and tied up the two inside linebackers of our 5-2 front. Consequently our linebackers had not made a play all night in that loss! As soon as I saw that on film, I commented to Jim Lineberger, "we have to cover their guards with down linemen." Jim agreed, but we both knew that we needed to cover their offensive tackles too.

I only knew of two ways to do that, either a pro 4-3, or a split 6-2, and we decided on the 6. The 4-3 required use of a Middle Linebacker and I do not like Middle Linebacker defenses, I think they put too much emphasis on one player, and if he is out or has a bad game, you're in serious trouble. Additionally, I felt the 6-2 eight man front was a better run defense than the 4-3 seven man front and Smyrna was much more of a run threat than pass threat. Also, they ran a balanced offense, so there was not a "strong" side to favor or even cheat to.

So we took Greg Edwards and Keith Killingsworth and put them on the ground as Defensive Guards. Their job was to neutralize Smyrna's quick hitting Offensive Guards, which should allow our Linebackers, Mike Ahern and Guy Thacker to pursue unimpeded and free of that Offensive Guard blocking. Instead of a 4 deep secondary that we usually played (even though our Strong Safety often played close to the line like a third linebacker), we went to 3 deep, a true eight man front.

Also, this would likely initially confuse Smyrna's Offensive line blockers as we had not shown the 6 man line all year and it would catch them by surprise with no likely practice preparation for it. In fact, we had never used it at all before and never did again after this game. This was another situation where we used one bit of strategy that fit in one game. We had not used it before, and never used it again.

One other key point that we noticed on film was that their quarterback was their deep snapper on their kicking teams. So, we decided we would give him a little extra punishment since he would be vulnerable in that position. So, when Smyrna punted, we told Greg Edwards, one of our hardest hitters, to line up a good yard back of the line in a three point stance and blast the QB snapper as soon as he released the ball.

That might be effective, but only if we could stop their offense and make them punt! We emphasized to Greg to keep his head up in this situation, and not to lead with the crown of his helmet, which would have been illegal "spearing," a 15 yard penalty, a dirty play, and possible ejection.

We always emphasized clean, hard hitting, but we wanted no part of dirty play. I even told the officials in the pre-game conference of this plan so they would be watching for it, and make sure the play remained legal and not an illegal helmet hit. I would always inform the officials in pre-game conference of special plans so as not to catch them off guard. In this case, Greg, a kid as tough as any, was also a very nice and well behaved young man, and he had no desire to play dirty either, yet he was anxious to put a hard hit on the Smyrna QB/Deep Snapper.

The other thing we took out of the week 9 film was that we were too slow, so as usual we worked extra hard on our quickness in practice the week before the game. It's hard to improve your running speed, but you can improve your quickness, with simple repetition. Also, Smyrna did nothing fancy or unusual, they should not be too hard to defend or run against if we could just play better, ... and quicker!

It was a typical November night game, played at St. Pius X High School Stadium frequent site of Round One GYFC Playoffs, also known as the Jim Brazier Bowl. There were 6 semi-final games, two in each of the three weight classes, starting at 10 A.M. and ours was the sixth of the day. This one was colder than usual, down in the low 30's by the 8 PM kickoff.

We lost the toss. In this case, that was just as well, I was not particularly interested in getting the ball first in this game anyway. We had nothing new except the 6-2 defense, and I actually wanted to see it in action first. We had not seen any obvious points to attack in the Smyrna defense, therefore our plan was to just conservatively use our base offense in its entirety. No more LSU in this plan.

So we had just concentrated all week in practice on offensive precision and quickness. Plus, in reality, you can gain offensive momentum by defensive and punting excellence if you are patient, and I was prepared to play it close as long as I had to and take advantage of the excellent punting and place kicking of Bobby Humphrey.

I just wanted to win, and 3-0 would have been just fine. Our offensive plan was simple, just use our Colt Offense, all of it, and use it better and certainly, more importantly, quicker. We expected and hoped to grind it out, keep it close, and play for a low scoring game, and thus hoped to win in a close one. We did not expect to score a lot of points in this game.

Our Place Kicker as well as Punter, Bobby Humphrey, was a very good and accurate straight on place kicker. All of the other kickers I have mentioned in previous years were soccer style kickers. Bobby was a true traditional kicker, and the best we ever had with the possible exception of Scott Young in 1975. We were confident Bobby would make a crucial field goal if that were necessary in this playoff game. He was also a very good Offensive Guard.

We kicked off to start the game and held Smyrna to a short return up to about their own 35 yard line. Then the new defense held on the first three downs. We felt we were probably most vulnerable on wide plays, as the End stood alone as outside containment defender in the new defensive scheme we employed on this night. Our ends were good ones, hard hitting Randy Smith and Mike Stewart, a smart player, not as quick as Randy, but always in the right place. In 1978, anytime we heard a loud collision in practice or a game, we knew it was likely that Randy Smith was involved.

Smyrna's first two plays were inside and off tackle with minimal gains. They looked to run inside first, as that is where they had hurt us two weeks ago with that excellent Offensive Guard blocking that we had seen on the film. We had taken that away with the new 6-2 alignment, as we now had four defenders in the middle as opposed to three in the defensive scheme we had used in that regular season game just two short weeks earlier. The third down and 6 play was a bootleg by their QB, who was fast and a very good runner. We held our breath as the play began, but it was perfectly defended by our Left End Stewart, the tough, lanky kid from Louisiana, for no gain. 4th and 6 on the first possession. So far, so good!

On the ensuing punt, Greg Edwards hit the Smyrna QB/deep snapper so hard that the snapper literally did a reverse head over heels somersault. That sent the famous message "here come the Colts." The Umpire, the official who lines up right behind the defensive line on all plays, gave a little wave indicating "clean hit," but now Smyrna knew we were prepared and that we had come to seriously compete, and I think it fired up the rest of our team with that same message.

As a result, their QB was shaky after that and realized he was going to be punished on every punt the rest of the night. That result was the exact purpose of having Greg hit him, not to injure, but to harass, hit hard and legally intimidate one of their key performers.

We got the ball after the punt and made a few yards, but were playing very cautiously to avoid mistakes. Our philosophy in this game, like the Central DeKalb Bobby Dodd Bowl of 1975, was to play conservatively early "not to lose" on a mistake, and get more aggressive as conditions and field position permitted and as the game progressed. Also, by being more conservative early, a more aggressive play might surprise the opponent when it actually was called. We generally used that attitude in a game where we were the underdog or where we expected a very close game.

We had one chance in the first quarter, in Smyrna territory, QB Goose Anthony threw a perfect 26-2 pass, our favorite and most reliable pass play again this year, to Strong End Glenn Gandy, who had slipped behind the secondary, wide open for a big gain, and possibly a long TD. But the usually reliable and sure handed Glenn dropped it. I kept that one in memory for later.

We probed both sides of the Smyrna defense most of the first half, and found some success with our Veer series, alternating between a Pro Set and the FB Slot and TB Slot formations. The inside traps, the 20 Countertrap to TB Tyson and 90 Countertrap to HB Edwards were being very effective. The Power I was not working as well, but we were making consistent yardage, and had several first downs. There was one scoring opportunity, a missed field goal from long range that just fell short right in the middle of the crossbar.

We held superior field position the entire first half due to booming punts by Bobby Humphrey and excellent play by our Defense holding Smyrna without a first down. It was a 0-0 tie at halftime. At halftime, I felt that we were playing very well, and expected a good chance to pull off this upset. Coach Lineberger had mixed in some of the 5-2 defense to cause further confusion to the Smyrna Offense, but we knew that we were certainly not out of the woods or confident of victory. We just knew that we were playing well, especially on defense as Jim's defensive play calling seemed to have Smyrna completely mystified and off balance, just like he had done to Central DeKalb in that 1975 Bobby Dodd Bowl upset.

We received the second half kickoff and gained one first down. But then we stalled and punted, again deep into Smyrna territory downing the ball around the 10 yard line. Smyrna made one first down on a QB scramble, but from there, we got the first big break of the game, a diving pass interception by our left cornerback Fred Mozzo, on the Smyrna 40 yard line. From there, TB Keith Tyson broke free on the very first play for about 30 yards on the weakside Veer, the play called "FB Slot, 36A," down to about the Smyrna 10, where we sputtered on first and second down bringing up 3rd and goal from the 8 yard line.

There, on the third down, I called for a little used play, a play that I really liked, but that we rarely used. It was called "FB Slot, 90-2 Quick." It's a fake 90 Countertrap, a running play that was working well that night for consistent yardage. Then right after the fake, without dropping back, the QB stands straight up, looks to his left and throws a quick pass to the Left or "Quickside" Tight End.

To make this play work, the QB and End both look at the defensive secondary coverage before the snap to find a seam or soft spot in the defensive secondary. The idea is that they will hopefully see the same point where the pass route needs to be run and where the ball needs to be thrown. The slot formation should cause at least a little shift in the Smyrna 3 deep secondary alignment to create the seam we want by moving the safety toward the slot. Because the play 90 Countertrap, had been making yardage that night when we had run it, a fake of that play should momentarily freeze the Smyrna linebackers and Safety.

If the Safety does not move over toward the slot as expected, we can audible to change the receiver to the Slot back, and pass to the right. But that did not happen here, as the three deep Safety did adjust toward the slot. There was a little seam to our offensive left as expected.

If it works properly, the Receiver is between the Quarterback and defensive Cornerback, with a clear passing lane, with the Receiver using his body to shield the Cornerback. The Corner should have no chance to knock down or intercept a well thrown and accurate short pass without committing pass interference. The Safety should not be in position to make a play as the combination of formation and play action should keep him just far enough away.

The pass needs to be low and hard, nose down and low ("downhill") because you cannot risk a tipped ball or deflection in this scoring situation. An incomplete pass has to hit the ground immediately. I wanted to be sure and to come away with at least three points and the lead in this potentially low scoring game, especially in the second half. Who knows, three points has won games before, and that might be enough on this cold night in a contest of good defensive teams. We were pretty sure of at least a field goal from that close range with the reliable Bobby Humphrey kicking, while our Defense was completely shutting Smyrna down. I was also confident that QB Goose Anthony would throw a good, low pass to the right place and I felt an interception was a very low risk with a QB as smart as Goose.

On this occasion, both of our players read the secondary the same, which was the End going basically straight ahead out of his stance at a slight angle into the secondary just inside where the corner had lined up in his position, a little to the outside, but well inside the Safety. Although the seam was very tight, Goose drilled the ball into Lee Cawthon's midsection about 5 yards deep in the end zone. The Smyrna Safety and Corner hit Lee (I nicknamed him "Lee Roy") so hard you could see his mouthpiece come flying out of his mouth, but he held the ball and our Colts took the lead 7-0 after the Humphrey PAT.

Our Defense continued to hold Smyrna scoreless and in the Fourth Quarter, we were moving the ball consistently with our running game, as Tyson was now slashing the Smyrna defense with his running from the twin back position, going over 100 yards for the game. Both sides of our line were now dominating with John McMath, Richie NeSmith, James Reinstein, Bobby Humphrey and Mark Gurr clearing the way for Tyson and Greg Edwards from both of the twin back positions. The trap plays and outside veer plays were working to both sides.

Once again in Smyrna territory and on a 3rd down and short yardage, I remembered how Glenn Gandy had gotten behind the Smyrna secondary earlier in the game on a play action 26-2 pass that he had unfortunately dropped.

I thought this might be a good time to give him another chance and sure enough, Goose Anthony threw another perfect strike. This time, Glenn hauled it in on the dead run and he scored from about 30 yards. After another Humphrey PAT, Colts now lead 14-0.

In the next series, after another defensive stop, we're moving the ball around mid-field, where we have Ken Duncan, a speedy reserve fullback in the game. There, I called another of my favorite plays, right out of the Veer Playbook. The college Offenses called this one the "Counter Option."

In our terminology, we called this one Tailback Slot, 48. It's another fake 90 Countertrap, with a lead option to the strong (slot) side. It works like this: starting with a fake 90 Countertrap to the halfback into the strong side "A" gap, the FB, lined up in usual split veer twin back formation behind the weakside guard on the left side of our backfield, arcs around to his right, toward the slot formation side as the 90 CT fake is taking place and attains about a six yard, 45 degree angle to the QB in option pitch position.

After faking to the HB, the QB tracks laterally down the line, with the FB trailing at the 6 yard, 45 degree angle, and the QB option reads the Defensive End. Ideally, we want that End to play the QB, and the QB to option pitch to the FB. If the End plays the pitch man, the QB keeps which is ok for us, as we will gain some good yards with a good running QB like Kevin Anthony, who had made a long TD run earlier in the year on an option play. But that is not as likely to make the big outside yardage as the pitch to the option back might do.

The blocking is play side gap protection in the line. That is a controlled charge by the linemen, making sure that there is no penetration by the defense. Each lineman is assigned the gap toward the play side, and has to pick up any defensive player going into that gap with the faking HB adding extra protection and gap coverage.

The Split End, from his position about 8 yards outside his Tackle, counts off (locates) the second defensive back from the outside, in this case, a single "free" Safety in the Smyrna 3 deep secondary, and judges the proper angle to block him or "pick him off" as the Safety pursues the ballcarrier, whether it be QB or FB. The widest, or first defensive secondary man, usually the Cornerback, is picked up in lead block position by the TB from his Slotback position.

The Slotback is lined up halfway between the Split End and Tackle, leads the play wide as a lead blocker for the ballcarrier. The Slotback's first move is to slide down the line of scrimmage as the backfield fake is taking place, attempting to attain a head up position on the Corner, while setting up the timing of the block. His goal is to block the outside leg of that Corner, just ahead of the ballcarrier, which would allow the ballcarrier to continue running wide.

This simulates sort of a cross blocking action against the defensive secondary. That crossing action gives both blockers good angles to execute their blocking assignments. One of the benefits our offense allowed was to always give our blockers advantageous angles and in this case, an option play gave us the advantage in numbers.

In this game against Smyrna, the play was executed perfectly. Again there was a good fake of 90 Countertrap, which had been continuing to make good yardage. The FB Duncan had good spacing and angle as he arched behind the fake, and the QB Anthony made the correct track toward the outside, where the Defensive End came at him quick and hard, quickly forcing the option pitch which Goose made perfectly, hitting Duncan in full stride.

The Split End Gandy, was in the correct position and cut the Safety to the ground as the Safety pursued the ball, and the Slotback Tyson, leading the ballcarrier with perfect timing, also had a good lead block on the Corner's outside leg and cut him down as well. That left no standing defender in sight, and I looked up to see Ken Duncan sprinting down the sideline into the end zone untouched for a 21-0 lead after Bobby Humphrey's third perfect PAT.

Tailback Slot, 48 (or the same play is FB Slot, 28, if you want the TB to carry and the FB in the Slot, recall the FB and TB are interchangeable in the "twin" position) is a beautiful play to watch unfold if executed perfectly which is what happened on this night. It requires perfect timing and spacing, which both require the repetition and patience that we used in our offensive practice sessions. This whole night went that way, and we won 21-0, avenging that loss from just two weeks earlier and placing us in a 7th in a row Bobby Dodd Bowl.

Looking back and reviewing this playoff game against the very talented Smyrna team, the Veer portion of our Offense had saved us on this night. The outside dive handoffs, 36A and 86A had made consistent yards, and the one weakside 36AVeer by Tyson had led to the first score, which came on a Veer series play action pass, 90-2 Quick. The other most successful plays that night had been the inside traps out of the twin formation as well, and the third TD had been from the Veer series counter option after a fake of a trap play, TB Slot 48. In summary, two of the three TD's came from the Veer Offense in this crucial game, with the other TD coming on a 26-2 pass play (our "old reliable") out of our base Power I series.

After beating undefeated Smyrna, in what was a stunning upset, I shook hands at mid-field with Charles Cook, who is a true gentleman, and I really did not know what to say. I was almost apologetic to ruin his perfect season. But he understood that this was just our night and that we had played a near perfect game, so he graciously congratulated us.

On this night, the Smyrna QB was so upset that he would not talk to me when I tried to console him after the game.

I took note of the Smyrna QB's behavior, and thought that I want my players (and myself) to be more gracious should we ever lose a big game like this. Fortunately, to date that had not yet happened to us in seven years, but we had one big one left in the GYFC in 1978, another Bobby Dodd Bowl at Kiwanis Stadium with the 10-1 Midway Mighty Mites against our now suddenly dangerous and potent 8-3 Atlanta Colts.

Midway was a proud program and had had great success in the GYFC in the 60's and early 70's. As I mentioned before, Coach C.K. Braswell was a great rival of Bob Johnson's and had driven Bob to make those significant changes to his tactics in 1969.

This Midway team was coached by Jerry Gulledge, a name that I recognized to have been an outstanding player at Avondale High School, a perennial high school football power in DeKalb County and the state of Georgia in the 50's, 60's and 70's. His team was loaded with talent, and had a very fast running back, named "Pee Wee" Dorsey.

He was not little as that nickname might indicate. He was tall and lanky with *blazing speed*, reminding me of a Clearwater Tornado type player.

Once again, we felt to stop Dorsey would be hard, but if successful, would likely lead to victory for us and Bobby Dodd Bowl championship number 7 in a row, no doubt a GYFC record.

On another cool and overcast mid-November day in our traditional white pants and jerseys, things went as I expected, tight and tough, very similar to the '77 game against Glenwood, and about half way through Quarter number 4, we have a 17-14 lead, and we're driving in Midway territory for the game clinching score. We're running right at them with strong side plays, 26, 84X and 86A, with Tyson and Greg Edwards gaining consistent yardage behind our strong side line of James Reinstein, Bobby Humphrey, Mark Gurr and Glenn Gandy, along with FB Mike Ahern's lead blocking. In this situation, I had no intention of trying a field goal, as I did not think a 6 point lead was much better against this Midway team than the three we already had.

With about three minutes to go, at about the Midway 30 yard line, we had about 3ʳᵈ and 5 and I thought back to last year's game with Glenwood and decided I would do the same thing I had done last year in the similar situation. That was FB Slot, 36A, the weakside veer that Mark Wheaton had taken in for the clinching score from similar distance and that Keith Tyson had been very successful with against Smyrna, having made the long gain leading to the first TD in the previous week's upset win.

The situation was also similar to last year's Bobby Dodd Bowl in that we were hurting them badly to the strong side and they might not be expecting a weakside run. Keith Tyson might be able to take it a long way, for a first down and possibly more.

I sent the play in and as we run it, I see some confusion on our weakside and all of a sudden, a Midway player streaking toward our end zone, and he had the ball! He took it all the way for a score, and Midway is suddenly ahead 21-17.

We had fumbled the handoff exchange and the Midway End had picked up the rolling ball and took it in for a 70 + yard TD. One of the dangers in running that play is we have no one there to catch a defender like that, but that probably would not have mattered as this Midway kid was faster than anyone we had anyway.

I had outsmarted myself, and no doubt was greedy trying to make a big play, where I should have been conservative and continued to hammer the strong side that had been working so well. I should have used the Bob Johnson strategy of stay with what's working until they stop it!

We still had a couple of minutes left, but could not muster a drive fast enough to make the yardage necessary to drive all the way for another TD. We had to pass and the speedy Midway secondary was there to knock away the passes. Play action is not deceptive in a situation like this when you have to pass. When the last 4th down pass fell to the ground, I knew we had finally lost a playoff game, a Bobby Dodd Bowl, in our 7th try.

I called my last timeout and called Captain Kevin Anthony to the sideline and told him to go back to the defensive huddle and tell our players, "no helmet throwing, no crying, let's accept this defeat with our heads high, and congratulate the winners like men and good sports."

I wanted to show the GYFC that the Colts are more than just about winning, that we could accept a loss graciously. That did not mean we liked it, but that we could accept it. Even Vince Dooley and Bear Bryant lost a few games. Even Bob Johnson lost a few games. No one hated losing worse than Bob, but he was always gracious the rare times it occurred. I wanted our team to make him proud of his Colt program in this situation too. Bob was more about good character and integrity than winning games, they go hand in hand.

That is exactly what our team did and I was just as proud of this group as if they had won for this display of true sportsmanlike behavior. Plus, we had fought hard and played valiantly and had been within one play of another championship. Jerry Gulledge came running over to mid-field and I congratulated him and his team. They had played just as well as we had and deserved the win. They had taken advantage of our one mistake and made the big play that counted.

So, now we're 8-4 and GYFC runner-up. We have no time to feel sorry for ourselves. We have a Colt Classic coming up against the always dangerous Clearwater Tornado and a trip to Pensacola, Florida that would turn out to be very exciting and a fun conclusion to this up and down season. Depending on how we might respond to this devastating loss, our season is going to leave us with a record of 8-6, 9-5 or 10-4.

No doubt in my mind, the goal now is to go 10-4 and at least have double digit wins for 1978, then re-load for next year. This team had made a great comeback and played two very good playoff games just coming up one play short of the championship. They were playing at their best when it counted, at the end of the year, and I wanted to make sure that they had a good conclusion to their final Colt experience.

This year, it was unusual as we traveled on Thanksgiving for our Bowl trip, to Pensacola, Florida to play a team called Brentwood. These bowl games were unpredictable as we had no idea of the quality of our opposition. However, they do usually play very good football at all youth levels in Florida, so we knew most Florida opponents were good teams. The Cape Coral team in 1974 had been the one exception.

This particular team was a very good one and we found ourselves in a shootout. Our offense was working smoothly and we managed two TD's in the first half. The PAT rules had changed to allow one point for a successful kick.

But Brentwood, behind a sensational passing tandem of QB and receiver also scored twice and they were making yards passing almost at will. It was 14-14 at halftime. We made some alignment adjustments in our pass coverage at halftime and went out in the 3rd Quarter expecting more scoring and excitement.

We stopped their first sequences of passes with our Corners wider and Linebackers and Safeties deeper in the new defensive secondary alignment. That must have discouraged them because after that, they stopped passing! In the meantime, our offense found something in the middle of the line and we started gashing their defense with inside runs, primarily by TB Keith Tyson out of the I formation. Keith wound up with well over 100 yards in the game and was named the game's MVP.

We had a long sustained drive for the only TD in the second half, and wound up dominating the clock and winning the game 21-14, and it was a tough and exciting game, one of the most fun we ever had.

We came home to greet the Clearwater Tornado the following weekend and managed to defeat them 14-6, avenging the loss of 1976 and squaring the rivalry with them at 1-1.

The key to Clearwater was big and fast African-American running backs with blazing speed.

That had been the advantage we could not overcome when they had beaten us at the 100 lb. level in 1976. Since then, in two years, we had faced many backs like that in GYFC, some previously mentioned here in Alfred McKerson of Glenwood in 1977, two players from Smyrna and Pee Wee Dorsey of Midway this current year and the fastest of all, Mario Williams of North DeKalb this year as well.

Having experienced all of those speedy running backs in GYFC, we had learned how to defend and at least slow these players down and Clearwater could not surprise us with all that speed this year, as they had done two years before.

So, our 1978 team wound up 10-4, with two Bowl wins against very good teams, a GYFC second place and within one play of the GYFC Championship, not as good as usual, but not too bad.

As I think back about this year of 1978, I realize how really good the GYFC 120 lb. competition had become. The league was full of good coaches, Jerome Roberts at Northeast, Paul Zarynoff at North DeKalb, Bill Eakin and Joe Cunningham at Central DeKalb, Jerry Gulledge at Midway, Charles Cook at Smyrna, Virgil Sorrells at Glenwood and on and on. On top of that many brought with them the addition of the aforementioned type running backs, very similar to what occurred in the SouthEastern Conference in the 70's as well.

In further retrospect, this year's 120 lb. Colt team proved that it was as good as any of them, as it had a good combination of passing, running, kicking, defense and toughness and I liked them very much. They had come within one play of the GYFC championship. The offense had sputtered in mid-year, but when the chips were down in games 10 thru 14, we had moved the ball consistently and scored a lot of points against undoubtedly the best competition we had ever faced, both in regular season and in post season.

This team was indeed worthy to represent Bob Johnson and the ACYA as well as any that I ever coached. I know that we all would like to have that one play against Midway back, I certainly would make a different play call if I could, but that's the way the ball bounced on that particular day, creating a tough loss and valuable lesson, but not diminishing the excellence of this proud group of football players in my eyes.

As I watch football now and see how college and NFL fans clamor and complain about their favorite team's occasional losses, and always blame their coach, I can look back at this season and that one game, and realize that a single bounce can make such a huge difference, and sometimes the other team, who has worked as hard as you, wants to win just as bad as you do, and who has players and coaches as good as yours, comes out ahead.

At that point, you can take solace in the facts that you fought hard, played clean and gave your best. That was always good enough for Bob Johnson, and it's certainly good enough for me as retired Colt Coach and Georgia Bulldog and Atlanta Falcon fan.

1978 120 lb. Atlanta Colts Key Performers

Kevin Anthony, QB . . . . I have said a lot about Kevin in the previous pages of this chapter, but you can sum him up with one word and that's leader. He came to the program his last year, so he was new to the Colts, but he already knew the GYFC and what it was about. He immediately commanded the respect of everyone on our team. Regarding his playing skills, he became a starter at the University of North Carolina so he obviously was talented, but he was a very hard worker and an eager listener, and he produced big time results in the big games for us.

Mike Ahern, FB and LB . . . . Mike was a three year starter for us and played at the weight limit his last year in 1978. He was also very smart and tough and converted from Offensive Guard and Defensive End his first year into starting FB and LB his last two.

Greg Edwards, HB and LB . . . Greg had patiently waited for his turn to be a big time player as he had been a substitute his first two years as he was a little undersized those first two years. He was always tough and quick and was a big time leader on this team as well. He did a very good job in any role where he was used, particularly as a lead blocker and runner from the vital HalfBack position.

Bobby Humphrey, OG and PK . . . As mentioned before, Bobby was a straight on kicker. He was very accurate and had a strong leg. His punting improved and was outstanding in the playoff win against Smyrna. Also, his trap blocking in that game was outstanding as the entire interior of our offensive line played a near perfect game that night and was outstanding the last several games of the season and post season.

Randy Smith, DE and backup QB . . . Randy was consistently the hardest hitter on the team, making many outstanding defensive plays throughout the year. As a backup QB, he did not play a lot of offense, but would have done a good job if we had needed to call on him.

Mark Gurr, OL and DL . . . Mark was our only two way starter in the lines and played the all important Strongside Tackle on Offense and Left Defensive Tackle. Like Greg Edwards, he had been a slightly undersized substitute on our previous two teams, but had learned his assignments and techniques and was ready to be a big time performer which he truly was on this team, manning two very important starting positions.

Guy Thacker, LB . . . Guy was small for a starter, but very smart and a leader of the Defense in 1978 and 1979. He actually was Jim Lineberger's defensive signal caller which required a lot of intelligence and understanding of the Defense as Jim had complicated signals which had to be interpreted by someone on the field in the defensive huddle in order to make the proper calls that Jim wanted.

Keith Tyson, TB . . . Keith was a little undersized for GYFC, and lacked breakaway speed, but he made up for those things with quickness, toughness and running instincts. He ran with great balance and also ran low behind his pads giving him exceptional tackle breaking strength, for a smaller player. He also read blocks well from the I formation, and hit his holes quickly and accurately from the twin back. He was a very good player, particularly toward the end of the year in the most important games.

James Reinstein, Center . . . James was the anchor of our Offensive Line, and did a great job all year, as we had a very good inside running game. The Center position is vital, particularly on the inside trap plays, which worked well all year.

1978 120 Lb. Atlanta Colts Record, 10-4-0

GYFC Runner-up, 2nd Place
Atlanta Colt Classic Champions
Holiday Bowl Champions

Colts 14 Forest Park 0
Colts 41 Sandy Springs 0
Colts 7 Central DeKalb 3
Colts 24 Briarcliff 0
Colts 0 North DeKalb 12
Colts 0 Northeast 7
Colts 15 Clairmont 6
Colts 41 South DeKalb 0
Colts 0 Smyrna 24
Colts 17 Tucker 0

GYFC Semi-Final, The Jim Brazier Bowl, St. Pius X High School, Atlanta, Georgia

Colts 21 Smyrna 0

GYFC Championship, The Bobby Dodd Bowl, Kiwanis Stadium, Forest Park, Georgia

Colts 17 Midway 21

Holiday Bowl, Pensacola, Florida

Colts 21 Brentwood 14

Atlanta Colt Classic, Colt Field, Murphy Candler Park, Atlanta, Georgia

Colts 14 Clearwater 6

1978 120 lb. Atlanta Colts Starting Lineups

OFFENSE

Strong End..........................Glenn Gandy
Strong Tackle.......................Mark Gurr
Strong Guard ....Richard NeSmith
Center...............................James Reinstein
Quick Guard.......................Bobby Humphrey
Quick Tackle ....John McMath
Quick End ....Lee Cawthon
Quarterback ....Kevin Anthony
Halfback ....Greg Edwards
Fullback ....Mike Ahern
Tailback..............................Keith Tyson

DEFENSE

Left End..............................Mike Stewart
Left Tackle...........................Mark Gurr
Nose Guard.........................Kenny Williams
Right Tackle ....David Rose
Right End ....Randy Smith
Left Linebacker ....Keith Killingsworth
Right Linebacker.................Mike Ahern
Strong Safety, or
"Monster" ....LB Guy Thacker
Left Cornerback ....Greg Webb
Right Cornerback...............Fred Mozzo
Safety ....Kevin Anthony

Coaches: Doug Bennett, Head Coach

Warren Watson, Offensive Line Coach
Jim Lineberger, Defensive Coordinator, Linebackers Coach
Fred Amtower, Defensive Backfield Coach
Frank Reeves, Offensive Backfield Coach

1978 Atlanta Colts 120 lb. Complete Roster

Keith Tyson	Dennis Campbell
Guy Thacker	Greg Edwards
Scott Miller	Kenny Williams
Bobby Kelly	Mark Brown
Jeff Craven	Randy Smith
Robert Harry	Richie NeSmith
Bobby Humphrey	David Rose
Keith Killingsworth	John McMath
Ken Duncan	Vince Graham
Greg Webb	Fred Mozzo
Mark Gurr	Troy Sadowski
Mike Stewart	Mark McLaughlin
Mike Ahern	Lee Cawthon
James Reinstein	Kevin Anthony
Glenn Gandy	

Cheerleaders

Tracie Wiggins	Robyn Smith
Christine Gammer	Kristin Schmitz
Janeen Hill	Cathy Reinkemyer
Kimberly Groves	Christi Clark
Dina Williamson	Tracie Jensen
Brittainy Harmon	Emily Reily

1978 100 lb. Atlanta Colts Record, 12-2

GYFC Runner-up
Holiday Bowl Champions

Colts 20 Forest Park 0
Colts 22 Sandy Springs 7
Colts 16 Central DeKalb 3
Colts 28 Briarcliff 0
Colts 28 North DeKalb 0
Colts 21 Northeast 0
Colts 23 Clairmont 14
Colts 40 DeKalb
Yellow Jackets 0
Colts 28 Smyrna 7
Colts 42 Tucker 0

GYFC Semi-Final, The Jim Brazier Bowl, St. Pius X High School, Atlanta, Georgia

Colts 42 Smyrna 6

GYFC Championship, The Bobby Dodd Bowl, Kiwanis Stadium, Forest park, Georgia

Colts 0 Glenwood 10

Holiday Bowl, Pensacola, Florida

Colts 19 Brentwood 6

Atlanta Colt Classic, Colt Field, Murphy Candler Park, Atlanta, Georgia

Colts 6 Clearwater 7

1978 100 lb. Atlanta Colts Complete Roster

Freddie Rosenthal	John Zagarella
Ward Murphy	Ray Carlisle
Scott Mischnick	Chris Sheffield
Craig Miller	Richie Locklear
Jim Ferguson	Jay Montgomery
Derek D'Alonzo	Dean Farber
Paul Pruitt	Jamie Mepham
Gary Humphrey	Tommy Thomas
Eric Kruel	Richie Combs
Roger Shadburn	David Myrick
Mark Soloman	Kevin Butcher
Sean McDonald	Greg Routt
John Duncan	Chuck Cianciolo
Todd Rampley	Brian Murphy
Ken Harmon	Steve Forsberg
Gary Ray	Frankie Doherty

Coaching Staff

Mac Scoggins Head Coach
Charlie Ragan
Pat Eder
Bob Carpenter
Bob Thomas

Cheerleaders

Maria Mischnick	Wendy Croft
Michelle Love	Jan Ragsdale
Lisa Sandusky	Rhonda Barras
Emily Heetderks	Susan Goode
Amy Blake	Teri Eder
Robyn Barto	Deidre Companik

1978 80 lb. Atlanta Colts Record, 9-3

Holiday Bowl Champions
Atlanta Colt Classic Champions

Colts 14 Forest Park 0
Colts 21 Sandy Springs 6
Colts 16 Central DeKalb 14
Colts 13 Briarcliff 7
Colts 0 North DeKalb 19
Colts 14 Northeast 0
Colts 21 Clairmont 7
Colts 13 DeKalb
Yellow Jackets 14
Colts 48 Smyrna 0
Colts 6 Tucker 20

Holiday Bowl, Pensacola, Florida

Colts 48 Brentwood 0

Atlanta Colt Classic, Colt Field, Murphy Candler Park, Atlanta, Georgia

Colts 29 Clearwater 0

1978 80 lb. Atlanta Colts Complete Roster

A.J. Paracsi	Robert Hayden
Steve Dodgen	Dale Leonard
Doug Cooper	Danny Healy
Wesley Clark	Doug Allvine
Davy Chandler	Britt Amtower
Chris Doyle	Doug Dykhuisen
Craig Goldberg	Brian Anderson
Tim Eigel	Jeff Mitchell
Kyle Waxman	Joseph Barras
Robbie Hynes	Randy Bassett
Craig McLaughlin	Curt Strahle
David Werner	Carig Wudi
Scooter Devine	Billy Schmitz
Charles Shepherd	Hamp Mepham
Billy Ray	Jimmy Hargis
Jay Martin	John Wischmeyer

Coaching Staff

John Ramsey Head Coach
Tom Hartley
Buddy Ragsdale
Bill Sanders
Bill Schmitz
Jay Williams

Cheerleaders

Lisa Schmitz	Suzanne Beeson
Kara Hiller	Lisa Boyd
Jill Reeves	Debbie Rutledge
Molly Papineau	Sheila Hartigan
Lorrie Gilbert	Regina Craven
Kim Jones	Dwana Duncan

1978 Coltettes Drill Team

Keri Musselman	Kim Halsell
Julie Bodenheimer	Rosie Hebert
Debbie Churchill	Jill Callahan
Keeley Gregorich	Karen Wilhelm
Diane McGuirk	Keri Sussman
Lorri Savage	Kay Patterson
Vanessa Lane	Alicia Wilfong
Tracy Bass	Sandy Jennings
Cindy Corbett	Susie Crowder
Holly Parker	Donna West
Charlotte Swygert	Jennifer Jewel
Stacy Stoutt	Diane Royal

Coaches

Lynn Britt
Liz Green

CHAPTER 14

1979, The Bill Sanders Era Begins

The Atlanta Colts did win their subdivision in all three weight classes, and placed two of our three varsity teams in the Bobby Dodd Bowl, with my 120 lb. group being the only Brazier Bowl loser, failing to make it to the Bobby Dodd Bowl for the first time in 8 tries.

However, both of the others fell short in the championship games. Jim Lineberger was Head Coach of the 100 lb team and he did a great job, but they just fell short in the Bobby Dodd Bowl, losing 6-0. His team came very close to scoring the winning TD, but were unable to get it in.

Their overall record was a very good 11-2-1. They were 8-1-1 in regular season, losing to Tucker, but they easily avenged that loss by beating Tucker soundly in the Jim Brazier Bowl game.

They were 2-0 in the post season Bowl games, easily beating Clearwater 30-0 in Clearwater. I'm sure this was gratifying to Jim because Clearwater was always very good, and also Jim had actually suffered a Tachycardia (rapid heart beat) during our 1976 game at Clearwater and had to be treated at a local hospital after that tough loss. His 100 lb Colt team also squeaked by Sarasota in the Colt Classic 14-12.

Bill Sanders was the first year Head Coach of the 80 lb Colts, and they also made the Bobby Dodd Bowl, but were defeated by speedy Glenwood, a rising power in GYFC.

The 80 lb Colts' regular season record was 8-2, and overall was 11-3. They won their post season bowl games as well over Clearwater in Clearwater and Savannah in the Colt Classic, a very successful first year for Bill and his staff, which included Jay Williams, Buddy Ragsdale, David Pugh and Tom

Hartley. They would lead the ACYA Varsity program into the 80's and were a terrific coaching staff. Bill Sanders also replaced John Ramsey as Athletic Director and had quickly become the new leader of the ACYA.

The overall Varsity record for 1979 was 28-10-3.

*   *   *

1979 120 lb. Atlanta Colts

We had to make some very significant changes in 1979, as our entire 120 lb. coaching staff turned over. Jim Lineberger became head coach of the 100 lb Colts, Warren Watson took some time off to work with his youngest son, Clayton's team, Frank Reeves went with Jim Lineberger to the 100 lb. team and Fred Amtower went to part time as he wanted to work with his two younger sons in Interleague.

I had known Doug Cooper and Billy Martin for a couple of years. They were two former Georgia Tech players from the glorious Bobby Dodd era, who had both played in the NFL. They both had younger kids in ACYA, and had been watching the Colts.

Knowing them and their backgrounds, I quickly asked them to be my assistants, with Doug Cooper running the defense and Billy Martin working with offensive and defensive ends, his former positions. Both of those guys came from the one platoon era of college football when players played both ways on offense and defense, so they both had a lot of playing experience from both sides of the football and thus a great deal of tactical and strategic knowledge.

I also knew Bill Schmitz, who had been around ACYA a long time as a dad and coach, having assisted Bob Johnson at one time. He knew most of the offense and the line blocking schemes and he was a perfect supplement to help fill in for Warren Watson in that job, so we were pretty well set with very knowledgeable and experienced football men on our staff, who also were familiar with the ACYA program.

We began with the good fortune of having Todd Rampley as our upcoming quarterback. He had been the previous year's starter for Mac Scoggins 100 lb team, and was a good one. Todd was big and strong, an excellent passer and runner. He later led Peachtree, his high school team, to the AAAA Georgia High School state championship game where they lost to the legendary Valdosta Wildcats, in a close game at Valdosta. He also started for Georgia Tech in their 1985 bowl game victory over Michigan State.

The ACYA program was still in slow decline in enrollment and numbers were dropping due to the same reasons stated in 1978. But this upcoming team had a great nucleus of outstanding Colt type players starting with Rampley and including lineman Chris Sheffield, End Frankie Dougherty, returning 120 lb. Colt Fullback Ken Duncan and many others. We had the full complement of 33 on our roster.

We also brought in size and speed in the Davis twins, Brian and Barry to run in the backfield. Richie Locklear and Scott Mischnik were good backs as was Jeff Craven, but they were all a little undersized, but good competitors. Eric Kruel was also a very good looking prospect and played extremely well on defense all year. So was Chris Duncan, a very good athlete, who averaged almost 30 points per game in his ensuing high school basketball career.

For some reason, this group never jelled offensively. It seemed like I could never come up with the right combinations or make the right play call at the right time. Also we never found a consistent Tailback. Both of the Davis twins were speedy and very capable, but both missed most of the year with nagging injuries and never got into prominent roles.

Scott Mischnick and Jeff Craven were both quick and could read their holes well. They both did some very good things, but they were both very small and running inside was difficult for them.

In retrospect, I should have run more out of the veer series, which would have better utilized their talents but for some reasons, I tried to stay in the Power I most of this particular year. Looking back, I can now see that mistake.

In reality, it was a bit of a bizarre year, starting with two losses, and included two ties, which is very unusual. A good example of our year came in the game with Sandy Springs, who ran a non-option wishbone. They had two speedy halfbacks, the left halfback's name was Scott Frank, and he was very good and very fast.

I knew from scouting them that the QB never kept on an option, he always took about two steps after the initial fullback dive fake and then pitched to Frank. The QB was small and not a running threat, in fact, to make him keep would have been good for us. My gut told me to have our Ends play pitch only and fire into the backfield at the pitch man, which would disrupt the pitch, thereby forcing the QB to keep.

But, taking a more conservative and traditional approach, we decided to play the more conventional end play and have our Ends play QB first, then pursue after the pitch. The first time they ran it, Frank took it all the way for a TD. We changed after that, and creamed their QB the rest of the night, but lost 13-9.

We also lost to Central DeKalb, 8-3, our first loss ever to them and I'm sure very gratifying to my friends, Eakin and Cunningham. And we had two 0-0 ties, a very strange year.

We somehow managed to win our subdivision despite a less than stellar regular season of 5-3-2, and qualified for the playoffs, but we lost to Tucker 7-0 in the Jim Brazier Bowl game, so the last season of the decade, we had a 5-4-2 GYFC record, but won our subdivision, and thereby tied for 3rd place overall in the conference.

Our two post season bowl games were just like the regular season. We lost at Clearwater, 22-0, but won the Colt Classic over Sarasota, 6-2. Our only TD came on a fumble recovery in the Sarasota end zone, adding more fuel to the unusual nature of this quirky season, which ended with a 6-5-2 record.

The sad thing about this team was that it had very good players, and nice kids, especially Todd Rampley. He was a championship capable QB and proved it in high school and college. We also had added very good new coaches in Cooper, Martin and Schmitz.

I really felt that I had let this group down. Rampley definitely deserved better, and I had badly wanted Coaches Cooper and Martin to participate as coaches in the game that bore the name of their legendary college coach, the Bobby Dodd Bowl, but we fell one game short.

But I also felt that I had given a good physical effort, and that realistically the GYFC was tougher than ever. We had practiced long and hard like usual, scouted all opponents and had good thoughtful preparation with some excellent football minds combining for those plans.

This had just been a mystifying year, and I felt that 1980 would be much better as our 100 lb. team had made the Bobby Dodd Bowl this year, and we hoped to do the same with that team as the nucleus of the upcoming 1980 120 lb. team.

1979 120 lb. Atlanta Colts Key Performers

Todd Rampley, QB . . . Todd was as good as any QB we ever had. He was a natural leader with a strong arm and good running ability. He went on to lead his high school team to the AAAA State Championship game where they lost to legendary Valdosta High

In a very close game. He also played at Georgia Tech and started in their 1985 Bowl game.

Chris Sheffield, OL and DL . . . Chris was big and tough and quick. He was very good on both Offense and Defense.

Richie Locklier, HB and DB . . . Richie was a smart player, very quick. He was a good blocker and runner from Halfback and played well in Doug Cooper's 4 deep secondary.

Chris Duncan, DB and PK . . . Chris was a natural athlete and was an outstanding defensive back. He was also a very good placekicker whose father was a high school coach. He went on to a fabulous high school basketball career where he averaged almost 30 points per game.

Frank Doherty, End . . . Frankie was a Pop Warner All American and played like one. He had sure hands and ran very good pass routes. We also used him as a passer on an end around pass play.

Ken Duncan, FB . . . Ken was a second year player on this team and had scored a long TD run in the previous year's playoff win over undefeated Smyrna. He was a team leader and turned in a very good performance from the Fullback position as runner and blocker.

Ray Carlisle, DL . . . Ray was a very consistent defensive player for this team. He had a good frame for a defensive lineman and was strong, quick and powerful. He was awarded the Colt Classic Governor's Medal for his outstanding play in that game, and it was well deserved.

1979 120 lb. Atlanta Colts Record 6-5-2

GYFC Subdivision Champions
Atlanta Colt Classic Champions

Colts 3 Central DeKalb 8
Colts 9 Sandy Springs 13
Colts 14 Smyrna 6
Colts 0 Northeast 0
Colts 28 Briarcliff 0
Colts 0 Tucker 0
Colts 17 Clairmont 6
Colts 31 Gresham Park 6
Colts 19 Forest Park 0
Colts 0 North DeKalb 3

GYFC Semi Finals, The Jim Brazier Bowl, Pebblebrook High School, Smyrna, Georgia

Colts 0 Tucker 7

Holiday Bowl Clearwater High School, Clearwater, Florida

Colts 0 Clearwater 22

Atlanta Colt Classic Colt Field, Murphy Candler Park, Atlanta, Georgia

Colts 6 Sarasota, Florida 2

1979 120 lb. Atlanta Colts Starting Lineups

OFFENSE

Strong End..........................Frank Doherty
Strong Tackle......................Chris Sheffield
Strong Guard ....Ricky Mitnitski
Center...............................Roger Shadburn
Quick Guard......................Dean Farber
Quick Tackle ....John Norris
Quick End ....Tommy Thomas
Quarterback ....Todd Rampley
Halfback ....Richie Locklier
Fullback ....Ken Duncan
Tailback.............................Scott Mischnick

DEFENSE

Left End.............................Kevin Butcher
Left Tackle.........................Steve Forsberg
Nose Guard........................Ray Carlisle
Right Tackle ....Mark Armistead
Right End ....Robert Whitmore
Inside Linebacker ....Guy Thacker
Inside Linebacker ....Richie Combs
Cornerback ....Jeff Craven
Cornerback ....Eric Kreul
Strong Safety ....Chris Duncan
Free Safety.........................Bob Chandler

1979 120 lb. Atlanta Colts Compete Roster

Dean Farber	Chris Sheffield
Tommy Thomas	Richie Locklier
Jeff Craven	Scott Mischnick
Bob Chandler	Ray Carlisle
Rob Sullivan	Rickie Mitnitsky
Richie Combs	Roger Shadburn
Kevin Butcher	Sean McDonald
Barry Davis	Jim Ferguson
Eric Kruel	Gary Humphrey
Guy Thacker	John Norris
Robert Harry	Mike Civis
Robert Whitmore	Mark Armistead
Steve Forsberg	Darrin Herringdyne
Ken Duncan	Frank Doherty
Todd Rampley	Brian Davis
Cedric Tucker	Chris Duncan

Coaching Staff: Doug Bennett, Head Coach
Doug Cooper, Defensive Coordinator, Secondary Coach
Warren Watson, Offensive Line
Bill Schmitz, Defensive Line
Billy Martin, Ends
Fred Amtower, Offensive Backfield Coach

1979 120 lb. Atlanta Colt Cheerleaders

Kristin Schmitz	Jan Jones
Denise Doherty	Debra Saliba
Christi Clark	Margie Inbau
Bonita Dozier	Lisa Majurek
Cathy Anton	Dina Williamson
Stacy McDonald	Lisa Schmitz

Cheerleader Coach

Judy Schmitz

1979 100 lb. Atlanta Colt Record 11-2-1

GYFC Division Champions
Holiday Bowl Champions
Atlanta Colt Classic Champions

Colts 17 Central DeKalb 0
Colts 10 Sandy Springs 8
Colts 27 Smyrna 0
Colts 24 Northeast 14
Colts 28 Briarcliff 7
Colts 7 Tucker 21
Colts 42 Clairmont 0
Colts 40 Gresham Park 6
Colts 27 Forest Park 6
Colts 13 North DeKalb 13

GYFC Semi Finals, The Jim Brazier Bowl, Pebblebrook High School, Smyrna, Georgia

Colts 23 Tucker 6

GYFC Championship, The Bobby Dodd Bowl, Kiwanis Stadium, Forest Park, Georgia

Colts 0 Midway 6

Holiday Bowl, Clearwater High School, Clearwater, Florida

Colts 30 Clearwater 0

Atlanta Colt Classic, Colt Field, Murphy Candler Park, Atlanta, Georgia
Colts 14 Sarasota 12

1979 100 lb. Atlanta Colts Complete Roster

Doug Cooper	A.J. Paracsi
Jim Hickman	John Wischmyer
Britt Amtower	Robbie Hynes
Mike Kester	Jeff Mitchell
John Zagarella	Ward Murphy
Craig Wudi	Billy Ray
Jeff Brown	Thad Barnes
Elliott Gatehouse	Randy Bassett
Jake Cotton	Craig Goldberg
Pat Standard	Mark Soloman
Craig Miller	Jamie Mepham
Derek Panek	Charles Shepherd
Hamp Mepham	Jay Montgomery
David Lerner	Billy Schmitz
Chuck Cianciolo	

Coaching Staff

Jim Lineberger Head Coach
Homer Doster
Frank Reeves
Tom Lucey
Buddy Waller
Jim Rudder

Cheerleaders

Sheila Hartigan	Jill Reeves
Penny Pressnal	Penny Nichols
Jan Ragsdale	Emily Heetderks
Susan Simpson	Sandy Majewski
Wendy Grimsley	Nancy Pittard
Maria Mischnick	Carrie Mepham

Cheerleader Coach

Tracy Jensen

!979 80 lb. Atlanta Colts Record 11-3

GYFC Division Champions
Holiday Bowl Champions
Atlanta Colt Classic Champions

Colts 7 Central DeKalb 6
Colts 0 Sandy Springs 6
Colts 26 Smyrna 0
Colts 19 Northeast 9
Colts 35 Briarcliff 0
Colts 0 Tucker 6
Colts 40 Clairmont 0
Colts 34 Gresham Park 20
Colts 35 Forest Park 0
Colts 21 North DeKalb 6

GYFC Semi Finals, The Jim Brazier Bowl, Pebblebrook High School, Smyrna, Georgia

Colts 21 Tucker 6

GYFC Championship, The Bobby Dodd Bowl. Kiwanis Stadium, Forest Park, Georgia

Colts 7 Glenwood 20

Holiday Bowl, Clearwater High School, Clearwater, Florida

Colts 22 Clearwater 0

Atlanta Colt Classic, Colt Field, Murphy Candler Park, Atlanta, Georgia

Colts 21 Savannah 8

1979 80 lb. Atlanta Colts Complete Roster

William Fratesi	Grady Dickens
Wesley Clark	Tim Eigel
Jay Martin	Craig McLaughlin
John Love	Chris Thompson
Trey Hollis	Scott Waller
Jeff Curtis	David Devine
Danny Handley	Jay Memory
Chris Hill	Doug Harof
Kyle Waxman	Richard Skaggs
Greg McDonnell	Steve Dodgen
Daniel Higgins	Bryant Spann
Orlando Strickland	Danny Healy
Rory Webster	Albert Burt
Davy Chandler	Bruce Hood
Doug Allvine	Phillip Glenn
Jack Manfredi	Ricky Turner

Coaching Staff:

Bill Sanders Head Coach
Jay Williams
David Pugh
Buddy Ragsdale
Walter Glenn
Harold Whitney

Cheerleaders

Caryn Sheffler	Denise Thomas
Sage Sanders	Colleen O'Connell
Kara Heller	Emily Reily
Kim Jensen	Molly Papineau
Laurie Love	Traci Johnson
Dawn Thomas	Missy Cleveland

Cheerleader Coaches:

Robyn Smith
Lisa Sandusky

1979 Atlanta Coltettes Drill Team

Michelle Madden	Cary Hunt
Debbie West	Heidi Brothers
Beth Powell	Renee Rogers
Darlene Jones	Jennifer Rolader
Joni Rausch	Diane Ruth
Kelly Churchill	Kay Patterson
Lorri Savage	Carrie Freeman
Melanie Knight	Mary Magnier
Tracy Ragland	Kim Thaxton
Mary Malone	Julie Sharkey
Kathleen Keown	Jennifer Abbott
Phyllis Harbison	Linda Kay McPherson
Dawn Lockwood	

Director

Shirley West

Coaches

Allison Sandberg
Winnie White

SECTION 3

The "Nuts and Bolts" of a Winning Football Team (Bob Johnson Style)

Author's Note: The following strategies were those used by my own team and were formulated by myself and those coaches who assisted me in the 1970's. Much of this was learned from Coaches Bob Johnson and Leonard Jones. The specific strategies used by the other Colt coaching staffs were similar, but each practiced, prepared and strategized in their own unique ways.

CHAPTER 15

Practice

I always looked forward to practice, both pre-season and regular season. When I started dreading practice, I knew it was time to quit coaching altogether.

We had a practice routine that we used the last 8 of our 9 years and I would repeat it if I were starting over today. I decided on this practice routine after spending time watching and talking about this with Bob Johnson. His practices were well planned and very precise. What I see of today's teams is so out of order! They start putting in plays way too early and do not spend near enough time on fundamentals

They will put in a play and tell their linemen who to block (no blocking rules or strategy) without taking the time to teach them HOW to make that block. It's no wonder that there is generally mass confusion and no one can run inside. In today's youth football that I have seen, it's either a wide run or reverse, or no gain. The primary strategy is often simply deception.

An inside running game was very important to our success, and we had to practice over and over to get the assignments right and to execute the different kinds of blocks that were necessary for the different position players. On most plays, there are different TYPES of blocks required by the various linemen and backs. To make the Offense work, you have to practice those blocks often and we did that every day.

The coaches I have talked to recently might want to learn some strategy, but they lose patience when trying to learn it and particularly when they try to teach it. Offensive football is about timing and execution, and that takes work and patience, but you have to build it one step at a time. The first step is the blocking ! Backfield blocking and line blocking ! You have to teach your players first how to block and second, what kind of block to use in each situation and third, how to execute that block, and finally against which defender or gap the block is to be made, play by play.

The same thing is true with passing offense. Even if you have a QB with a strong and accurate arm, you can't put in a pass play and expect it to work unless you practice it over and over. It takes timing and repetition to make the receiver's pass route run correctly and consistently. It takes repetition to get the passer accurate and the receiver to consistently make the catch without dropping the ball. If you work on it long enough, they will complete the pass out of habit as the Quarterback and Receiver become more familiar with each other and the Receiver learns to concentrate on the catch.

Defense is about recognition, positioning and alignment, attacking and tackling, all of which also require tedious repetition. You cannot get away with the occasional tackling drill, you must do it weekly if not daily. Defensive stunts are similar to offensive plays in that they require timing, and specific spacing and alignment. That also takes more than showing it to your players once and moving on. We practiced those things every Wednesday during regular season, and we would also use our Thursday practice time to work our second defense against our first offense on offensive practice Thursdays. That way our defensive reserves got close attention on offensive practice days to gain valuable experience and build depth for our team. Doug Perreault, Jim Lineberger and later Doug Cooper worked with the reserve defensive players on offensive practice days (Thursdays) just as hard as they did the first teamers on defensive practice days (Wednesdays).

As I stated earlier, our preseason practices were based on five things, fundamentals (blocking and tackling), quickness, toughness (hard hitting), timing and execution. During the season, a sixth and very important thing would be opponent preparation.

Here are the ways we worked on those necessary requirements.

Point One, Fundamentals . . . Almost every successful football coach, or coach in any sport will tell you the foundation for success is built on the fundamentals of that sport. In football, that generally boils down to blocking and tackling, supplemented by the individual playmaking skills of running, passing, pass receiving, pass defending, etc.

I will discuss blocking further on in this chapter, but we worked on this every day, most times in group work, as the backs and linemen had different kinds of blocks. The Oklahoma drill was a partial team drill and included a back and a lineman blocking in that same drill. It also required tackling and block shedding (use of forearm shiver and hands) on the defensive side. The Board Drill (or chalk line drill) is a similar drill.

In backfield group work, we used the trap/hook drill and linebacker block drill. In lineman group work, we used the sled, one on one blocking drill, quick read drill, cut/reach block drill and post and read drive drill. We used these drills almost every day.

In all drills in practice, if a player did a poor job, he was required to stay in the drill until at least giving his best effort if not making a perfect play. Once again, I recall Billy Todd in Bob Johnson's 1971 Oklahoma drill.

Point Two, Quickness . . . This may be an overused term by some, but it was something that was necessary for us, and we were serious about it. We emphasized quickness in every aspect of practice beginning with double time calisthenics during practice and game warm ups.

We felt that we had to have superior quickness in order have the running game we wanted. That meant our linemen had to get on their blocks quickly and our backs had to be quick to their holes.

We went on a quick snap count and tried to use that as our first advantage. We did our grass drills emphasizing quickness before and at the end of practice. By the end of the season, we were usually at peak quickness.

Point Three, Toughness . . . Another term that might be overused by some, but again, we were serious about this as well. We also worked on this in every part of practice. We wanted to be the hardest hitting team in GYFC and we felt that we were never outhit even in games we lost. We wore pads to every practice, including post season games, with the exception of an occasional morning of two a days. We hit in all of those practices.

My opinion is that the amount of contact necessary in practice decreases as you advance in age groups of football, but here's a good example of the need for contact in practice.

An example to point to is Georgia's former coach Vince Dooley. He believed in tough practices. In fact, some often referred to Georgia's regular season Tuesdays as "Bloody Tuesday" in reference to the intensity of those practice sessions. Often, you would hear UGA's radio announcer Larry Munson beg Coach Dooley on the radio to not go so hard on Tuesday to avoid potential practice injuries before a big game like a Florida or Auburn, but Coach Dooley, Bear Bryant, Bob Johnson and other successful coaches knew that tough practices helped you get ready for tough opponents.

Another example from UGA. The Bulldogs got off to a terrible 1-4 start in 2010, with sloppy tackling, crucial fumbles and just looked weak overall. After the 4th consecutive loss, Coach Richt called for a rare full pad practice on Monday, tougher than normal practice Tuesday and then routine the rest of the practice week. They soundly defeated Tennessee that week, and afterward Coach Richt stated that he had run summer practice with less contact than usual, particularly because of installing a new Defense. He also stated that Tuesday practices would continue with higher intensity, contact, etc. than before.

Point Four, Timing . . . The timing I am talking about relates to the coordination of players in the collective effort of making a play work on offense or defense. On offense, you want to work on the backs being quick and the linemen being quick, but you also want them to be coordinated with each other, backs together and line together, and ultimately backfield and line together. It does no good for the line to open a hole if the back with the ball does not get there at the right time to take advantage of it and the back that is blocking to be in synch also. Many plays require very precise timing and that does not happen without repetition. That is particularly true on plays that employ pulling linemen to trap or lead.

To accomplish this, we ran a lot of dummy plays against no defense to demonstrate how they needed that coordination. And we scrimmaged a good bit, defense on Wednesdays and offense on Thursdays to improve the timing in live conditions.

On some plays, particularly the outside veer series, it took a great deal of practice to enable the QB to get the handoff to the HB before the HB hit the hole. The HB is taught to hit the hole as fast as possible on this play and it was the QB's job to get there on time. They often had problems early on, but always became successful with the necessary practice.

On another of our plays, 50 Trap, described in Chapter 8, the QB handed off to the FB at an intersection point in the backfield, with his head turned away, a blind handoff. This had to be practiced often to ensure the proper paths were being run by both players and that the handoff could successfully be made by the QB without him looking at the FB. The blind handoff was part of the deception that made the play work so well. (Note: The FB was told to always adjust his path to the QB as he was looking and the QB was not)

With passing plays, as I stated earlier, our receivers caught the ball out of habit because they had to do it so often in practice. Their pass route running became more consistent as well due to that repetition in practice, and the QB's would be able to time their lead better and be familiar with the receiver's speed matching it to the velocity with which they threw the pass, all because of a lot of boring practice.

Defensive timing is also important, particularly the timing on stunts between the linemen with each other as well as between linemen and linebackers. A stunt requires coordination between two or more defenders and it is vital that their timing be consistent in order to not leave a hole in the defense.

Point Five, Execution . . . Execution goes along with timing, as the offensive plays were practiced often, the execution would be better. Similar to a pass route is the feel necessary on the handoff exchange between QB and RB on running plays, particularly difficult ones like the 86A's and 50 Traps that we ran. It is similarly important on option plays that require precise spacing between QB and pitch man (RB), and reverses (including our Punt Return) that require precision timing due to handoffs that occur with players running at full speed.

Same as offense, defensive execution goes along with repeated timing and tackling. It is imperative to keep proper gap control and spacing on your defense in order to surround the ballcarrier or receiver. Keeping proper angles in the secondary for tackling and pass defense are part of defensive execution as well.

On special teams, punt and kickoff coverage requires similar execution to defense as they require spacing and coverage lane maintenance. And certainly our Punt Return with the crossing reverse action required timing and execution as well, as I will describe in the chapter on special teams.

Point Six . . . Opponent preparation in practice is vital and something that may be under emphasized by some, but we strongly believed in scouting and making preparations based on that scouting. In Chapter 19, the chapter on game preparation, a lot of the chapter is devoted to this, but in summary, during the season, we would introduce preliminary opponent information on Monday, and then practice specifically our defense against opponent offense on Wednesday, and our offense against opponent defense on Thursday.

*   *   *

The GYFC had no time limit on preseason summer practice, but restricted regular season practice to 8 hours in 3 days after school started back, which was usually around Labor Day back in the 1970's. We followed those rules without any problem at all.

Preseason Practice

Our annual routine began in August with tryouts in which we used basic skills drills to determine player's positions. We tried to get everyone a position by the end of week one.

During part of this time, we also began to teach the basic blocks. For the line, Coach Watson, and later Coach Schmitz, would teach the following: quick read block, post and read drive block, cut block, reach block, trap block and pull and lead read block, much less emphasis was placed on pass blocking. We wanted our linemen to be quick and aggressive which is contrary to the passive nature of pass blocking.

For the backs, it was trap/hook block and linebacker lead block. The skills assessment drills would quickly indicate who your potential Quarterback and Tailback would be, and a combination of the running and blocking drills would identify the Fullback and Halfback positions. One policy we had was that anyone could try out for the backfield that wanted to. After a practice or two, the kids could tell who the best backfield would likely be, and therefore it was usually not hard to convince someone to be a starting lineman as opposed to a second string back. Even kids can tell when someone is a better fit in the backfield than themselves. Occasionally, a player who had played in the line in his previous career wanted to try out for a backfield position. Usually it would not work out for the player, but at least one occasion it did. Mike Ahern played offensive guard for our 1976 100 lb. Colts, and then tried out for and was switched to fullback his next two years. He was very good at all positions he ever played.

Other perfect examples were probably my best linemen in the 1976-1977 championship teams. Chuck Trense was our Strong Tackle, Dutch Minor our Quick Guard and Pete Stephens our Strong Guard. All three were fast and went on to successful high school careers as running backs, but they knew as kids that Caudill, Yancey, Wheaton and Malcolm (then Daugherty in '77) were better backs as 12 and 13 year olds, so they chose to be starters as linemen. And they were VERY good linemen. We could not have won without them. Jeff Anderson was another example. He was good enough to start as a 10 year old on our powerful 1973 11 year old/ 80 lb. team, but only as a quickside lineman. Yet, in his further Colt career, he was a fullback for our 1975 100 lb. team and then a star QB in high school at Peachtree that went on to a college career.

When we did start putting in plays it was gradual, and in group work. We would usually spend the first hour of practice with the whole team in one group and then divide into separate groups of backs and linemen for an hour or so, and then finish the rest of the day with the team back together. When putting in plays, Watson and Lineberger, and later Bill Schmitz, knew the plays and what blocking rules applied to each play for each position, and they would teach the line each play and the appropriate blocking rules over and over.

The backfield coaches would teach the backs the footwork and blocking, and work on the timing of handoffs, pitches etc. Our backs, particularly one of either the HB or FB had to block on almost every running play, sometimes, for example our TB power plays 26 and 84X, both backs had a blocking assignment. If they did not execute their blocks, the play would gain nothing.

The first three weeks in August were hard. It was hot, there was a lot of contact and conditioning work, and some two a day practices. It was just a lot of hard, boring work, but we knew it had to be done to lay a foundation of success.

In weeks two and three, we usually had two a day practices. In the early years, we would go two a day for the full two weeks, and in later years, we toned it down a little and skipped a day here and there. Some of our GYFC competitors went to camps, but we did everything right there on the practice and game fields of Murphy Candler Park.

Knowing what I know now, I would likely eliminate contact in the morning sessions of two a days and work strictly on strategy, offense play timing and kicking. We did taper off some the last few years. But, so much for hindsight as we also did a lot of morning contact most years.

By the fourth week, we usually had a fairly complete offense in place, although as I have said, we would always add things throughout the season. There was usually a preseason game the fourth week and the regular season started the 5th week. Many GYFC teams would scrimmage each other in preseason and we did that some years, but not every year. And some teams would play two preseason games, but Bob Johnson only wanted to play one. I agreed with him on that, in fact I agreed with him on almost everything.

The last part of summer, we would spend a lot of time polishing our teams on offense and defense with walk-throughs for defense and running offense plays, both run and pass, against no defense just to work on timing and coordinating backfield with line. Of course we did a lot of scrimmaging against ourselves and worked on kicking the last part of summer.

There is another thing we did that I see being done differently now. We wore full pads and did contact every day in practice. Again, my theory is the lower you go in age playing football, the more contact you need in practice. Today's kids miss blocks and tackles. We did not miss as many because we did them every day in practice. In the NFL, you see the least contact in practice, in college, a little more, high school still a little more, and finally in youth age football, I believe you need even more contact in practice.

We had a written schedule prepared before every practice of the year and we attempted to follow it to the minute. The written schedule provided organization to practice and helped to maximize our time and effort. By writing it down ahead of time and discussing it with the other coaches, we were able to concentrate each practice to the areas of play that needed emphasis at that particular point in the season.

A typical early summer practice would go something like this, with practice starting at 6 PM. We started late in the day before school started back due to the heat, and there were brief water and rest periods worked into the schedule daily through the year:

6:00-6:15 Warm up and calisthenics
6:15-6:30 Quickness Drills
6:30-7:00 Tackling (Various drills, for example the board drill where a blocker tries to knock a defender off a straddled board, or preferably chalk line, and the defender has to stay on the board or line and make a tackle) or other fundamental drills like Oklahoma or angle tackling
7:00-8:00 Group Work, as described below
8:00-8:45 Scrimmage new plays put in that day and previous days, emphasize Offense one day and Defense the next.
8:45-9:00 Conditioning, Sprints, up downs, grass drills

Group Work for Linemen:

7:00-7:20 Sled Drills . . . There are several drills on the blocking sled that are used, hit and roll, alternate shoulder, hand shivers, drive blocking etc.
7:20-7:40 Blocking Techniques for various types of blocks, Quick Read, Post/Read Drive, Cut, Reach, Trap etc. Coaches watch each player to make sure they use proper footwork, shoulder, head, hand and arm positioning etc.
7:40-8:00 Put in blocking assignments on the new plays for the day.
Group Work for backs:
7:00-7:10 3 man drill (a ball carrier hits a dummy, then a live forearm shiver and then a tackler in a row) the coaches make sure the ball carrier has the ball secure under the correct arm, and that he keeps his balance and that each of the three men in the row hit properly. I invented this drill and the idea of the drill is to teach the ballcarriers to run tough and low, behind their pads, deliver a blow as a runner and run with good balance. The tackler is being coached to tackle properly and the first and second men learn to deliver a good forearm blow, first man with a hand dummy and second man live.
7:10-7:20 Trap hook block drill (Coach holds a standup dummy in a simulated Defensive End position, and as the blocker approaches, coach moves dummy in or out, and the blocker adjusts to a hook block on the in move and a trap block on the out move)
The backfield coaches watch each blocker's technique and make sure he is executing each block properly as far as reading which block to use (trap or hook), and then footwork, shoulder and head position etc.
7:20-7:25 Linebacker Block Drill The players take turns practicing lead blocks, and defending lead blocks. Coaches watch for and instruct on hitting technique on Offense and Defense, proper pad level, etc.
7:25-7:40 Open field tackling drill concentrating on footwork, angle and head positioning
7:40-8:00 PM Install new offensive plays and work on timing
Whether in group work or together work, if a player made a poor play (block, tackle, missed assignment) we immediately made them repeat the play until done properly. Coaches I've seen today just accept the poor play and move on. That creates bad habits, players will make poor plays and half efforts as long as the coaches allow it!

A later summer practice (4ᵗʰ or 5ᵗʰ week) would probably be something like this:

6:00-6:15 Warm-up
6:15-6:30 Quickness drills
6:30-6:40 Place Kicking on a game field with goal post
6:40-6:50 Punting
6:50-7:00 Punt Return
7:00-8:00 Group Work
8:00-8:45 Scrimmage
8:45-9:00 Conditioning

The difference is that now we are closer to the season, so we will practice more like a regular season practice with some time allocated to each phase of kicking. We did not spend as much time on kick offs and kick off returns, except on occasional regular season Thursdays.

We spent a good deal of time in backfield group work on our passing game, particularly on Offense practice days during the season and late in preseason summer practice. I would try and use Colt Field for this, to allow our players to get accustomed to the turf conditions and the crown of the field, both of which are important to success in Offense.

The typical drill was to have the Quarterback simulate his play action steps and the receivers to run different pass routes from the correct spacing of the formation being practiced. This was essential to have the timing of the various plays to be perfected. We would often have the receivers catch with one hand, particularly in later season practices. As mentioned before, this one handed receiving stresses accuracy by the passer (it has to be a near perfect pass to be able to be caught with one hand), and it creates a high level of concentration by the Receiver, which generally creates a good habit for him. The QB's were taught to throw short length passes down hill or nose down and long passes nose up.

The timing and execution of pass plays being practiced translates to higher levels of football as well. For example, I attended the 2009 Independence Bowl where Georgia played Texas A & M. Watching the two QB's warm up was interesting and possibly revealing as well. The Texas A & M QB was relaxed, dropping back in slow motion and lobbing his passes to jogging receivers.

On the other hand, all 4 of Georgia's QB's were going full speed on every rep, simulating taking snaps from Center, simulating full speed play action, then setting up in perfect seven step drops, and throwing full velocity to full speed receivers. I cannot help but believe that the way you practice is indicative of how you play and this game may well have been proof of that. In general, Georgia has one of the best passing games in the SEC, and I suspect their weekday practices are conducted the same way.

Our group work was usually similar every day with a little variety from day to day. We worked on our blocking techniques every practice of the year! Later in the summer more time would be spent on play timing and execution. The whole idea of preseason summer practice is to have your team ready for game contact, in shape and executing better than your opening opponent, and then to build every week pointing to a post season peak.

*   *   *

Regular Season Practice

Our regular season schedule was Monday 2 ½ hours, Wednesday 3 hours and Thursday 2 ½ hours. GYFC had an 8 hour limit during the season.

The other Colt teams practiced on Tuesday instead of Wednesday, but I preferred the continuity of the back to back days on Wednesday-Thursday. It helped the players remember new things and stay focused on the week's opponent. That was significant as Wednesday and Thursday were the two days most important in game planning and preparing for the upcoming week's opponent. Also, we were usually the only Colt team out there on Wednesday which gave us complete access to the fields and we could spread out as much as needed.

Monday was for installing whatever new Offense or Defense we might put in for the current week, which allowed polish and scrimmage time on Wednesday-Thursday. The rest of Monday practice time was spent on fundamentals and heavy contact.

A typical Monday schedule would be something like this, starting at 5 or 5:30 PM due to an 8 PM GYFC curfew:

5:00-5:20 Warm-up and quickness drills
5:20-5:30 Place Kicking
5:30-5:40 Punting
5:40-5:50 Punt Return

Note here . . . . You will see that kicking was part of every practice in regular season, as you have already seen in previous chapters the successes that can be gained by excellence in place kicking, punting and punt returning. You cannot have that excellence without a lot of practice. Also note that these drills were in 10 minute increments. We tried to keep practice moving fast to better utilize the time allowed and to keep practice from becoming boring to players or coaches.

5:50-6:10 some kind of contact drill like angle tackling or board drill, varying from one week to the next
6:10-6:50 Group Work, similar to summer group work, with blocking every day, and play timing and execution every day. New plays would also be installed in group work.

6:50-7:20 Oklahoma Drill

7:20-7:30 Conditioning, sprints, up downs, grass drills (we worked on quickness in the grass drills as we found that working on quickness at the end of practice when the players are tired was very effective)

A typical 3 hour Wednesday would go like this:

5:00-5:20 Warm up and quickness drills

5:20-5:30 Place Kicking

5:30-5:40 Punting

5:40-5:50 Punt Return

5:50-6:20 Defense oriented team drills like tackling and Oklahoma

6:20-7:00 Group work, emphasizing defense

7:00-7:50 Full team defense game plan review and walk through, scrimmage first defense against this week's opponents offensive plays run by our second unit

7:50-8:00 Conditioning, sprints, up downs and grass drills emphasizing quickness

Wednesday group work would be focused on defensive individual skills like tackling, defensive line play techniques for line, and tackling and pass defense techniques for backs. The defensive coach would determine what specific areas he felt needed emphasis and put them in the day's schedule accordingly.

Final Practice of the week in Regular Season was 2 1/2 hours on Thursday, for example:

5:30-5:50 Warm up and quickness drills

5:50-6:00 Place Kicking

6:00-6:10 Punting

6:10-6:20 Punt Return

6:20-6:30 Kick off

6:30-6:40 Kick off return

6:40-7:15 Offense group work

7:15-7:50 Team back together for offense scrimmage

7:50-8:00 Conditioning, sprints, up downs, grass drills

Thursday group work would be blocking and new play review for line, and blocking, play timing and review, and passing and pass receiving drills for backfield.

In current times, I have seen youth teams of all ages have Thursday or Friday practice without pads. I would never do that, as stated before, I wanted full contact every day possible, with the exception of mornings in two a days. I suspect the no pad practice is to emulate high school or college routines, but as I have repeatedly said, the younger the player, the more contact they need in practice. (In my opinion)

These schedules or others very similar were what we went by for our last eight years, and they proved to be successful, fun and not too boring for our teams.

*   *   *

The sum and substance of this chapter is borne out in the results we achieved most years. We generally played our best at the end of every year, and generally started a little slow, particularly on points production. I believe the reasons for that are simple. We took a lot of practice time on fundamentals, quickness and timing from the beginning of the year to the end, installing the offensive plays gradually. The gradual installation led to increasing point production as the season went on, as did the consistent work on the fundamentals, timing and quickness with improvement consistently through the year. This emphasis also was probably the reason we started a little slow, with plays being put in gradually, the entire Offense was not fully ready early in the year.

By the end of the season, we were the quickest, had the results of consistent work on timing and were fundamentally strong with our blocking techniques, leading to a high level of play during the playoff and bowl seasons.

The same would be true of the Defense. After working all season in practice on stunt timing, gap protection, pass rushing, pass defending, pursuit angles and the fundamentals of tackling, shedding blockers and quickness, we were ready to defend at a high level as well, leading to consistent post season play for most years.

I believe all of that success was primarily based on the way we practiced.

With all of the discussion about hitting and contact in practice as well as game action, I want to comment on injuries. Fortunately we had very few. In nine varsity years, we had one serious knee injury in practice and that player walked off the field with a slight limp. It turned out that he had a torn ligament that did require surgery. Our most common injury was a broken wrist and we had three or four of those over the years, which cost one missed game usually, if any. We did have one concussion to a 9 year old in 1971, but never another.

Players would often twist or sprain a knee or ankle in practice or game, but they never turned out serious with that one exception. I believe it's hard to incur a serious injury at these ages because the younger kids must have more pliable joints due to growth patterns.

That's not a medical theory as much as it is practicality based on real experience of seeing all of these violent collisions causing some pain, but very rarely injury.

So based on my experience, I would tell parents contemplating football, but fearing injury, that they should not be too worried about injury until kids are closer to fully grown, usually 10th grade or older.

*   *   *

CHAPTER 16

The Offense

This will be an interesting chapter as I look forward to going over the basics of the Leonard Jones/Bob Johnson Offense, and the things we added to it over the years.

100 lb. Colt Receiver Jimmy Costlow hauls in a pass from Mike Yancey in the 1976 Bobby Dodd Bowl. This was not a TD, but many passes between the two resulted in Colt Touchdowns. Moving Costlow into a Split End was typically effective for the passing game.

The bases for the Offense are the Power I and the Split (Twin Back) Veer. The line blocking techniques are called quick read (option) blocking, cross blocking, angle blocking, trap blocking, post and read drive (double team) blocking and pull and lead read (option) blocking. Other techniques are cut block, which is inside gap protection and reach block, which is outside or play side gap blocking. Veer blocking is a combination of the others, generally a post and read drive or angle block to the inside of an unblocked defensive lineman. The backs only had to learn and execute two blocks, a trap/hook option block and a linebacker lead (head on) block.

The entire offense is based on six principles:

1. I formation lead plays with FB leading TB and "option" or "quick read" blocking at the point of attack,
2. Trap plays over center, which are run from any of the formations by any of the backs, including QB. Either Offensive Guard would pull and trap the first defensive lineman on the opposite side of center. You also have the ability to trap and read a defensive end (see "20 Countertrap Outside" in Chapter 9)
3. Veer dive plays, which are straight handoffs to one of the "Twin" backs with veer blocking at the point of attack, which means a defensive linemen is left unblocked,
4. QB Options from any of the formations,
5. Play action passing attack based on bootlegs from the Power I, or any split formation,
6. Drop back or short rollout (moving pocket) passing from the split formations.

The most basic plays are the inside running plays. 26, which is the base off tackle play actually is a double team on the point of attack Defensive Tackle, and a trap/hook option block on the Defensive End by the Halfback, and a read and linebacker lead block on the first defender in the hole by the Fullback. Everyone else in the line has play side gap protection. The play is fully described in chapter 13.

I used the term double team for simplicity, but we (taught by Leonard Jones) actually called it post and read drive. That meant the following, the post man would have the primary responsibility to block the Defensive man opposite him, usually a defensive guard or tackle, he would be assisted by the read drive player, usually an offensive end or interior lineman. This would allow for the read driving player to watch for a stunting linebacker entering the gap to his inside as he moved toward his double team. He would automatically pick up this gap on this read drive move. In that same event, the Post man would have his head up responsibility which also covered the gap to his inside. If one defender was stunting to his outside, that usually meant another would be stunting to his inside. The post man always had gap protection for the gap away from where the read drive came. (I.E. on 26, the End had read drive, so he came through the gap outside the Tackle, therefore knowing that, the Tackle was responsible for the gap to his own inside) thus, the post and read drive technique always covered both gaps. It was very effective against a "Stack" (defensive lineman with linebacker stacked directly behind).

A quick read or option block by a lineman simply gives the offensive lineman the option of blocking his man in or out (right or left), whichever way is easier. If his man is gapped inside or out, the play is "pre-read" to take advantage of the angle the gapped alignment offers.

A trap/hook block by a running back gave the running back the option of blocking his man the easier of two ways (in or out) as well.

Plays where we ran inside over Tackle or Guard were called inside isolation or lead option read plays, and exactly where they went depended on the defensive line alignment. Against an odd defense (five man line, with nose guard) we called it 24 Strongside and 34 Weak or "Quick" side, and the point of attack quick read block was Offensive Tackle on Defensive Tackle. Against an even defense, 4 or 6 man line, no nose guard, we called it 22 strongside and 32 quickside and the point of attack was a quick read block by whichever Offensive Guard we wanted to run over against a defensive lineman either head up on him or in either gap to his inside or outside.

There was always a post and read drive on the next defensive down linemen to the inside (toward Center) of the quick read. That was to provide a "seal" providing a barrier to pursuit and second level blocking whereby the read drive man would slide off onto a linebacker after hitting the preliminary double team. For example on a 24 or 34, reading Offensive Tackle on Defensive Tackle, the post and read drive block was on the nose man, who would be the next down man to the inside. To the outside of the quick read there was a natural advantageous angle that required a one on one block automatically made easier by the natural defensive alignment, creating the "alley" where the quick read was taking place. Also the quick read and post and read drive covered any potential movement or "stunts" that the defensive line and linebackers might be doing.

Using those basic plays, we could gain a blocking advantage in any situation, by "reading" the point of attack, and going whichever way the defense allowed. Building off of those basic plays, there was a quickside option, off of a 32/34 fake, with the HB looping back around the fake, and an option on the Defensive End to that side with the QB and HB in option position. This was a very good play which, used sparingly and at the right time, was very effective.

It was the crucial play in Bob Johnson's 1971 win over Midway, accounting for the winning TD. We had similar success with it for a 50 yard TD run by QB Kevin Anthony, in our 1978 win, 7-3 over Central DeKalb. Also, the play was very similar to a play UGA used for a two point conversion to beat Georgia Tech in 1978, when freshman QB Buck Belue option pitched to Amp Arnold for the winning two points. I believe Arnold had lined up as a Wingback on that play, and the play works equally well to a HB lined up in his usual backfield position or a wingback position.

Bob Johnson called it 28 A, and we called it 98 A.

Seeing that difference, this might be a good time to go over play numbering. Leonard Jones's system used some logic I could never figure out. His TB running plays started with numbers in the 70's, and I thought it depended more on memory than logic. Being a logic thinker, I thought the players could better utilize more familiar numbering, so I changed it to a more traditional system as follows:

Our line had a strong side and a weak (we preferred to call it quick) side. I numbered the backs as follows: a Tailback carrying to the strongside play begins with 2, Tailback quickside play begins with 3. Fullback strongside play begins with 4, Fullback quickside play begins with 5. Halfback strongside play begins with 8, Halfback quickside play begins with 9.

We did not number holes or gaps, we numbered the offensive player we wanted to run over. 0 was center over nose guard, 2 was guard over guard or tackle, 4 was tackle over tackle, 6 was HB or FB over end, 8 was an outside option, to either strongside or quickside.

So, the play 24 was TB over strong tackle. 34 was TB over quick tackle, and so on. This system worked for the Power I plays and the Veer plays as well. Our players knew that any play beginning with an even number was a strongside play and anything beginning with an odd number, a quickside play, then the second number indicated which offensive player was the point of attack blocker.

Our base Power I formation was a power right with the halfback at right HB lined up directly behind the Guard, and the FB and TB in the

"I" formation directly behind the QB, at a usual backfield depth. The strongside of the line was also to the right, unless otherwise specified. If we wanted to run to a strong left 26 (or any other play), we called the play "L left" 26. That meant the HB switched to the left side and the line flip flopped with strongside left and quickside right, and we did that a lot early in games as we tried to find advantages and probe for defensive weak points in our opponents.

Occasionally for post season, I would put in a set where we would line up with two halfbacks (one on either side behind the Guards) and a tailback. This would give us the option to shift into Power I right or left. The QB would lift his heel and one of the HB's (pre-designated by the play call) would shift to FB creating the Power I. This allowed us to disguise the formation's strength until right before the ball was snapped and prevent a defense from lining up against our strength. The strength and any Power I play we wanted to run would be precalled in the huddle, but the shift did give us the element of surprise. It required the HB and FB to know both positions, but by the end of the year they usually did know that.

The rest of the Power I was also simple. We had a 42 or 44, which was the HB leading the FB ballcarrier over the strong guard or tackle's quick read block. Whether it was a 42 or 44 depended on the defense being even or odd, and we had audibles or automatic check-offs to change into the proper play. The audibles also worked for the other inside read plays 32-34 and 22-24 that were changeable based on the same different defense alignments.

For example if we called a 42 or 22 in the huddle, that meant we wanted to Quick Read over the Strong Guard, anticipating an even defense (4 or 6 man line). If we came up to the line and the QB saw an odd defense (3 or 5 man line with a Nose Guard) the QB would simply yell "Automatic" and everyone knew that meant the play would now change to 44 or 24, meaning that the Quick Read block would now be over Strong Tackle.

We had a 50 Trap (plays ending in 0 went directly over center and were almost always trap blocking) as described earlier in the book in chapter 6. The only exception that I recall to that was in 1974 when we changed from trap blocking to cross blocking in the middle to combat the Tucker Middle Linebacker that was so good.

Then there was the Halfback Series, which were the 98A quickside option described earlier, a 94 Trap which trap blocked to the quickside (94 Outside was a trap block on the end) and the 96 quickside power sweep. 90 Countertrap was a HB trap into the middle.

I stated that the trap plays ending in 0 went over Center, which is not completely accurate. They actually went slightly to the opposite side of center from where the pulling guard vacated. How far to that opposite side depended on the defensive alignment and our players were taught how to read where the running path should go based on where the defensive lineman being trapped was lined up combined with where the linebacker lined up on that side. Usually a trap play created a path for the ballcarrier between two of our blockers, usually the Guards blocking in a crossing action, but sometimes, particularly against an odd defense the crossing action was between the pulling guard and our offensive tackle on the side of the trap. That play actually went a little further out on the weak side.

The HB plays to the strongside were the Veer plays. Veer blocking is different and it is based on leaving a linemen unblocked and having the QB and HB "reading" his move to determine a handoff to the HB or a keep by the QB. I considered that reading above our heads and too risky for our age level, so we predetermined that an 84A was a handoff to the HB, and our Strong Tackle would let his man go and block to the inside.

The play was a quick handoff, and we practiced the speed relentlessly with the idea that the HB would be past the unblocked defensive Tackle before he could close down the hole. "Reading" the tackle on that play was actually the basis for the Veer Offense the college teams ran. We actually had better success with 86A which left an end unblocked. It is described in chapter 13.

84B was a fake of the handoff and an option off of the Defensive End, and 84X was an off tackle power play behind cross blocking, with the cross blocking giving us superior angles to make a hole, and as usual, reading option blocks at the point of attack. 84X is described in detail in Chapter 11.

The passing game in the Power I was play action off of the base running plays. They were numbered with the play to be faked, such as 26, and another number 2, 4, 6, and up as the pass route to be run. An even route number was a strong side pass and an odd route number was a quick side pass. We did not have many routes. We had 26-2 described in Chapter 7. We also had 22-1, 22-3, 32-2, 32-4 and 32-10.

22-1, and 32-2 were combination routes with the two Ends. 22-1 was a fake of the strongside play, 22 and a bootleg back to the weakside (weakside and quickside are synonymous) with the Quick End running a deep corner and the Strong End running a crossing pattern. This generally called for the QB to bootleg to his left creating a difficult pass with a right handed

QB running to his left. 32-2 and 32-4 were easier passes for the right handed QB as they were bootlegs to the right. 22-3 and 32-4 were similar to 22-1 and 32-2, but they called for the FB to slip through the line and into the flat creating a flood pattern.

This was especially effective on 22-3 as it flooded the weakside which was usually one defender short and the FB was often wide open. To make it easier on a right handed QB, we would run L left 22-3. This meant the strongside would be left, and the defense would overload left. Running 22-3 out of the L left formation meant the QB would be bootlegging to his weakside RIGHT, making the pass much easier for a right handed QB. That is a perfect example of dictating the defense's positioning to your offense's liking and we did that frequently!

32-10 was a pass that we would use against a 4 deep or twin safety defense (usually called "Cover 2"). The QB faked a 32, weakside TB over guard, do a short bootleg into a pocket behind the strong guard. The Ends would run right at the safeties and then go wide, taking safeties with them, and the FB would go deep up the middle after his 32 fake. He would usually be wide open often for a long gain and sometimes TD.

This 32-10 was a play similar to the "Hobnail Boot" pass play that Mark Richt called for Georgia to beat Tennessee in 2001, for his first significant win at UGA. Coach Richt said afterwards that the pass play would only work if UT were in a Cover 2 defense which they were on that particular play. (Scouting had indicated that UT usually used the cover 2 near their own goal line) In fact, QB David Greene was instructed by Coach Richt to either change the play or throw the ball away if UT had been in a single safety. But true to form, UT was, as usual, in the Cover 2 on the goal line as that play was only about an 8 yard pass for the winning TD. The UGA wide receivers took the UT safeties to the outside and the UGA FB, Verron Haynes was wide open for the easy pass, after faking a TB running play up the middle and slipping through the line into the end zone, exactly like our 32-10.

This was our entire offense for 1973 and 1974. It was 1975 after being held to 7 points in our opener that I decided to add a more wide open playbook.

In reality, the thing we did to diversify was to add formations, more than actual plays. I decided to "break" the I formation some of the time and go to a twin back set, by leaving the halfback behind the strongside guard and putting the tailback or fullback behind the quickside guard, putting extra emphasis on the Veer portion of the Offense.

That allowed much more diversification in play calling. For example 86A was one of our bread and butter most reliable plays. I started to run it from split back formations, the only requirement being a Tight End to the side the play was run. By using "twin" backs, both lined up behind the offensive guards, we could also run it to the weakside of a slot formation or a two Tight End Set, and call it 36A or 56A, as described in Chapter 12.

The one new play and series of plays that we did add was 90 Countertrap. It was blocked the same way as 50 Trap, but with a halfback carrying. It could be run from the Power I or any Split Back formation. We also added the same play from the other split back, such as FB Slot (or wing or flank), 20 Trap, or TB slot, 40 Trap. This just meant that the QB would pivot the other way, and our Quickside Guard would trap to his strong side. The line blocking was exactly the opposite as a 50 or 90 trap play.

The other very successful new play in that series was TB Slot, 48, the counter option that Ken Duncan scored on against Smyrna in the 1978 playoff upset, detailed in Chapter 13. We could also play action pass from that set, after faking a 90 Countertrap, as also described in Chapter 13 in that same game against undefeated Smyrna.

The new formations also allowed straight options (colleges called them "Track" Options) from the I or twin sets, and drop back and short rollout passing plays. These pass plays were not necessary very often, but became helpful in situations where we had to pass and play action would not be deceptive. We used these pass plays in two minute situations, some 3rd and long yardage and the rare occasions we might have been behind late in a game.

Two examples were the Clearwater bowl game in 1976 on the last series as we tried to catch up in the last two minutes. The other was in 1977 Jim Brazier Bowl, where we the game plan was passing and veer series plays against Forest Park. In that game, we did not want to use the play action, and when we were also trying not to reveal our Power I plays to the next game's opposing scouts.

Passing out of any of the twin back sets was easier than the Power I formations as you have a back in an outside position, often at least one Split End and additionally, the Running Backs can enter the pass routes quicker and easier from the "twin" positions. We really liked passing from the FB Slot formation as it allowed our Tailbacks to be in the pass routes and these players were usually the best offensive athlete on our team. Mark Wheaton was particularly effective in 1976 and 1977 as a slot receiver. The two favorite plays to him were an out pattern and a delay throwback as he circled back over the middle to the weak side.

197380 lb. Colt Tailback Neil Brewer into a hole against Sandy Springs Saints led by Fullback Preston Coleman on a "L Left, 26" Power I Isolation Play

So there you have it. The Offense did not have that many plays, but when you combine the different plays with all of the different formations and looks, it became very versatile, and also not predictable, a combination which produced offense that consistently averaged 23 points per game for several (8) years, totaling 1,953 points in 85 games played. Considering that GYFC only played 40 minute games, that 23 points per game average would interpolate to 28 points in a high school length game (48 minutes) or over 34 points in a college length game (60 minutes).

*   *   *

Offensive Play Calling

I think this might be a good time to talk about what I call "sequential" offensive play calling which had been significant in many of our games. In our offense, as in most good ones, plays feed off of each other. Many plays start with the same action making them difficult to diagnose. Play action passes come off of fakes of real running plays that are being used in the game, such as our 26-2, which is a fake of our base and most frequently used running play, 26 run out of our base Power I formation.

Sequential by my definition is to "set up" a big play, by faking another play that has already been successful, and to run plays out of a series, such as our 84 series which had about five or six different plays in it. Many times, as offensive play caller, I would set up such a scenario. Reverses can work the same way, by faking a successful play and having the runner or QB hand off to another speedy runner crossing and going the opposite direction.

As many times as we scored on 26-2 through the years, probably over 30 TD's, it continually worked because the 26 running play was already working for yardage in the game where the 26-2 then worked! The running play 26 had to work for us or we could not win. We practiced it constantly and repeatedly. No play action works unless you are successfully running the ball.

26 is a simple play out of the base Power I formation. I consider it the most important play in our Offense, and it is the most frequently run. It's a straight off tackle handoff to the TB, behind HB and FB as lead blockers. It starts with a post and read drive (double team on the Defensive Tackle by our Strongside Tackle and End.) If executed properly, this blocking technique eliminates the Tackle and seals off inside linebacker pursuit, or a "second level" block by the End. This blocking technique is also designed to handle stunts or "twists" between the defensive line and linebackers by having every gap and man accounted for with a good blocking angle.

The HB leads first and has a trap/hook block assignment on the Defensive End to our strong side. If the end plays wide, the HB "Traps" or blocks him out, if the end plays tight, the HB "Hooks" or blocks him in. The FB reads the HB block and leads the TB into the hole created by the End-Tackle double team and HB trap/hook option block. The FB picks up the first defender in the hole and the TB breaks whichever direction is open off the FB block.

Our bootleg series was similar. It was off of a fake of 24 or 34, our inside running plays, and the QB keeping and "bootlegging" with a run/pass option, which was a staple of the Leonard Jones Offense.

Bob Johnson's famous "28A" (we called it 98), as previously described in this chapter was a classic sequentially called play. It came off of a fake of the TB over quickside guard and the ran an option to the HB around the quickside end. When it started the play action simulated a running play which could be converted to a play action bootleg pass or the option.

The plays out of the Twin or Veer series are called sequentially as well, with the dive handoff plays and countertrap plays being the basic plays, and options and passes being the "home run" or set up plays capable of bigger yardage. A reverse can be created from almost any running play.

As I mentioned once before, if coaching today, I would incorporate more motion into the offense. This would create further uncertainty in opposing defenses, but more importantly, it would allow the motion man to attain very good blocking angles, as well as quick entry into pass routes from a player on the move.

Motion also helps to determine the opposing defense's secondary coverage. If a Defensive Back or Linebacker follows a man-in-motion that generally indicates a man-to-man coverage, particularly if the following defensive player passes Center. On the other hand, if the linebackers and secondary shift or realign to a man-in-motion, that generally indicates a zone coverage by the defense.

197380 Ib Quarterback Jeff Lineberger about to pitch on an "84B" option play. Pitchman Neil Brewer is outside the view; Fullback Preston Coleman (#34) is the lead blocker. Lineberger is showing excellent footwork in stepping his right foot toward the pitchman target.

100 lb. Colt Tailback Mark Wheaton runs through a gaping hole in the Tucker defense in the 1976 Bobby Dodd Bowl, behind key blocks by Jimmy Caudill, Pete Stephens and Don West.

CHAPTER 17

The Defense

80 lb. Colt defenders swarm the Tucker ball carrier in the 1973 Chattahoochee Bowl GYFC Playoff Game. That year's 4-4 defense coached by Doug Perreault, was famous for pursuit and gang tackling.

This chapter will be short, unless I can get Doug Perreault, Doug Cooper and/or Jim Lineberger to help write it.

We used three base defenses, the 4-4 under Doug Perreault, the 5-2 Monster under Jim Lineberger and the 5-2, with 4 deep under Doug Cooper. Doug Cooper always said that you want your opponent to run against a 4 deep and throw into a 3 deep coverage. Cooper's 5-2 with 4 deep would roll into 3 deep pass coverage.

Those defenses allowed a total of 528 points in 109 games, an average of less than 5 points per game and exactly 66 points per year in 8 years, translating into80 points per year at high school length and 99 points per year at college length games.

My description of the difference in the base defenses is that the 5-2 with either secondary coverage was based on a lot of stunts between linemen and linebackers. It was more of a "man up" defense and the 4-4 is more of a gap control defense. Stunts out of the 4-4 went through gaps and the 5-2 stunts went through the offensive linemen positions.

If I were coaching a defense today, I would likely use a base 6-2. I think it's better for youth football teams, and I would use "gap control" strategy. By that I mean that each of the front eight is responsible for a gap first and then pursuit. This 6-2 is versatile and particularly so with the type of players and capabilities we had in the GYFC of the 70's and 80's.

None of these defenses used a single middle linebacker, which I prefer due to the importance of that single player. Ours always had two "inside" linebackers, each responsible for a side, but players that usually had the ability to cover both sides of an offensive play.

In 3 deep coverage, basically two corners each had zone coverage responsibility for a deep outside 1/3 of the secondary and the free safety had the middle deep 1/3. Linebackers had "underneath" coverage zones, depending on stunts or blitz calls, and an occasional End might have pass coverage responsibility, as in today's "zone" blitzes used in College and the NFL.

There are many good defensive strategies and they all work if executed properly. The main things to work on are similar to offense. They are fundamentals, in this case tackling, and then positioning and timing. The main differences in offense and defense are obvious. The defense must react to what the offense does, as only the offense knows what is going to happen before a play starts.

So an offense must execute, but a defense must react (Positioning, sometimes before the ball is snapped, but always after), and then execute (timing and tackling). The way you teach that is scouting and preparation. When I talk about timing on defense, I mean the movement between the players involved in a stunt, or just the way a player attacks his blocker or his gap.

Our defensive strategy was always to have a lot of information about the opponent, and then prepare a defense to stop their strengths. This is exactly what we did to prepare for Smyrna in that 1978 Jim Brazier Bowl upset victory. You cannot always line up in a base defense and expect to counteract every offensive strength. You must have versatility in your players and where they line up going into a game.

Our pass defense was pretty simple, based on the three deep zone and linebackers covering the underneath or short zones. The amount of short zone coverage would vary and occasionally leave spots open if there was a stunt or blitz called. Jim Lineberger liked to stunt his 5-2 front more than Doug Cooper. Doug preferred movement or rotation in the secondary and to involve safeties in run support, which is how Jim's "Monster" or 3rd linebacker was used. Jay Williams, who coached with Bob Johnson, then John Ramsey and Bill Sanders was also a very good Defensive Coordinator and secondary pass coverage coach.

The 4-4 under Perreault was simpler, at least I think it is. I would call it a form of gap 8, in that each of the front 8 had gap responsibility. The fact that you had 4 linebackers allowed for more pursuit, but provided less bulk against inside running plays. Doug's 4-4 in 1973 only allowed 15 points all year, and those players were all fast and pursued extremely well. This led to very effective gang tackling, and produced a lot of turnovers.

It was very effective in the 11 year old 80 lb. division, but less effective in the older leagues, where offenses were more capable of attacking its interior weak points.

It's easier to run inside and off tackle against the 4-4, but in younger groups, the 4-4 works very well, as outside running is more prevalent in the offensive football played by teams of younger aged players.

Doug Cooper could have coached at any level. He had tremendous knowledge, particularly of defensive secondary strategies and player fundamentals. He did an excellent job of teaching to the young players as well. He preferred a straight up strategy most of the time, with less emphasis on stunts and blitzes, and more emphasis on reading keys and strategic player positioning.

Jim Lineberger loved the 5-2 Monster, using the monster as a 3rd Linebacker in various ways, including blitzes to counteract an offense's strengths. Jim loved to stunt the linebackers and linemen on twists and had a great ability to put a Linebacker right into the hole being attacked by the opposing offense.

Perreault was strictly a 4-4 coach. He did like to move his down linemen around in different gaps or head up positions. He also used linebacker stacks and twists to move the players into position to make their plays. As previously reported, his 1973 defense only allowed 15 points in 13 games.

There were times, when preparing to defend an option or wing T type, attack that we would design some man to man responsibility, assigning certain linemen, linebackers and even secondary players to certain players (numbers or positions) from the opposing Offense. That is the way that is used to defend an option style attack in higher levels of football. I did not even know that at the time, but it made a lot of sense and we did it that way. And that strategy always resulted in a high level of defensive success.

100 lb . Colt Defense preparing to stop a North DeKalb ball carrier in the 1974 Bobby Dodd Bowl GYFC Championship game, which was played at Georgia Tech's Grant Field Bobby Dodd Stadium . Bob Johnson always told his defenders to "build a fence around the football" in using the 5-2 Defense he employed as Coach Jim Lineberger's group is doing here.

CHAPTER 18

Special Teams

As emphasized throughout the book, special teams play is very important as there are many plays in every game involving special teams. Good special teams play was a big reason for our success over the years.

I cannot start a chapter about our experiences and philosophy on special teams without beginning with Punt Return. As I mentioned in chapter 6, we used a twin safety, criss cross punt return system for all the Colt years. I had first seen Decatur High School use it in the 1950's while I was in grammar school in Decatur, Georgia.

Also, as you have read in the earlier chapters, we had many long returns for touchdowns through the years, especially by Richie Guerin, Mike Coveny and. Mark Wheaton.

The first most obvious thing you have to have is two guys who can catch a punt, which is not the easiest thing to do. The higher level you go in football, the longer and higher punts get, and different punts have different kinds of spin and ball movement, so it becomes more difficult in advanced ages of play. I really liked having a left footed punter like Bobby Humphrey in 1978. Similar to facing a left handed pitcher in baseball, the left footed punt spun differently, faded the opposite direction of a typical punt, and was overall just more difficult to catch.

In our punt return system, the second thing is we had to have two guys who could think quickly and judge space and distance, as well as the kicking opponent's oncoming punt coverage, all while the punted ball was in the air. We spent a lot of practice time on this. In fact, instead of having a player punt to our return team in practice, I would always pass the ball the approximate height and distance that I expected an opposing punter to be able to achieve. This prevented wasting valuable practice time, and kept things moving at a decent pace.

That way, I could throw to either return man, short or long, high or low, and between them or away from either to a side. The purpose of this was to teach the returners to get the right space and alignment as the ball was being caught, thus preparing for the criss cross. I wanted the players to be on the same yard line, and about 8 yards apart when the ball was caught. Too close together would make coverage easier, and too far apart would take too much time. I wanted the return men to be running almost full speed when they crossed and made the handoff or fake. This also helped with the timing between the return men, and the blockers retreating to set up the blocking wall.

The opponents' punts were not always useable for this play, but enough were that it was worth the effort to have it and spend the appropriate practice time on it. The play was predetermined a right return or left return from the bench. If it were called a right return, the left safety would always wind up with the ball. So, on a right return if the right safety caught the ball, he would handoff to the left safety on the criss cross, and if the left safety caught it, he would fake a handoff on the criss cross, and keep the ball. The exact opposite would be the case on a left return.

Very importantly, our rule was whoever caught the punted ball went in front on the criss cross to avoid collisions and forward handoffs. This had to be practiced a lot to work, so we practiced it a lot and it did work! The safeties were taught to call the ball kicked to their side, and it was predetermined that a ball kicked in the middle between them would always be caught by the left safety. Whoever was not catching the ball was responsible for getting the correct spacing and yard line depth to set up the correct 8 yard separation and spacing required for the criss cross action.

The blocking was simple. We used a 5-2 front with two halfbacks about ten yards off the ball. It was the two halfbacks' job to make sure there was not a fake punt run or pass, and then to pick off the first two coverage men to protect the safeties from being hit as they made the catch and began running toward each other.

Further to prevent a fake by the punting team, our two ends met in front of the punter after the kick and then retreated to the end of the "wall" that was set up on the return side. Our linebackers played as loose as five yards depending on the 4th down yardage required, and the front three did not penetrate, but tried to hold up the offensive line from coverage. Above all, the front 9 had to make sure the ball was kicked.

In order, the linebackers, three interior defensive linemen and ends created a blocking wall, or picket line. The linebacker on the return side, was assigned to the first coverage man endangering the return man and the rest formed the picket line barrier to block the coverage.

I usually tried to call the return to the right, which was the returning side of Left Safety Guerin, Coveny or Wheaton, but their partners (the other or right punt return safety) were also dangerous runners. Guerin was paired with Neil Brewer, Coveny with Neil Gifford and Wheaton with Mike Yancey, and I would call the left side return on occasion just for a changeup and to prevent our return side from becoming too predictable.

When we had to punt ourselves, we used a spread punt with a 9 man line, single personal protector and punter about 10-12 yards deep, depending on the ages of the team that year. The 80 lb. team used a 10 yard snap, and the120 lb team used a 12 yard snap. We worked on punting every day in practice. I considered kicking so important that it was my own duty in pregame warmups to take the kickers, first warming up place kicking and then punting. The return men would also practice catching punts during pregame warmups as well, and also, the deep snapper would be practicing with this group. The deep snapper is a particularly crucial position that is generally greatly undervalued, as is the holder on place kicks. The snapper and holder also needed adequate warmup and pre-game practice to work on the timing between snapper, holder and kicker.

On our punt team, each of the nine linemen had inside gap responsibility. We took wide splits, as wide as possible, but just wide enough where we could not get beat to any inside gap. We released anyone outside our nine man line, as we could get the punt off before it could be blocked by an outside rusher. Over the Colt years, I think we had one punt blocked and none returned for a TD against us. Each of the front nine released as soon as the ball was kicked, or before if no defender was head up or inside them.

Kicking off, we spread the field with our coverage team and used a squib kick. I wanted the kick to be a low line drive as a football will bounce unpredictably when kicked that way. We always kicked away from a dangerous return man like Soles of Central DeKalb, and in fact, I usually tried to find a hole in the opposing return formation to tell our kickers to try and kick toward, hoping the ball would roll deep into the receiving team's territory before it could be picked up and returned.

On our own kickoff return, I used a 5-2-2-2 formation, with the five front spread out across the field by rule between the 45 and 50 yard lines, and the next two ten yards deep behind around the 40, and a little inside the widest of the front five. The next two about ten yards deeper around the 30 and still closer inside and the final two about the 20 yardline about ten yards apart. Again the depth of the final two would be dependent on age group of that particular team and year. The alignment looked like an inverted trapezoid.

The idea of this formation was to cover the field with as little room as possible for a kick off to roll free in our end. I wanted someone to get on the kickoff ASAP. I used running backs or defensive backs as kickoff returners. I wanted to have the ball fielded cleanly most of all, and then usually called for a middle return with cross blocking.

Our placekicking team used the traditional seven man line with wingbacks and the holder about 6 yards deep. Everyone had inside gap responsibility and we would also release anyone from outside our widest man. Again, the snapper was vital, and repeated practice was necessary to keep the place kicking team sharp, including the timing between snapper, holder and kicker.

Identifying the kickers was at times difficult. We only had true place kickers in Scott Young in '75, Bobby Humphrey in '78 and Chris Duncan in '79. The other years we found someone like a Mike Yancey or Neil Brewer who had a little ability and wanted to do it. We then practiced a lot and worked on their skills with repetition. The same was true with punters. Coaches Doug Perreault and Fred Amtower were good punters themselves, and helped with the teaching of that skill. I knew the proper technique on punting as well, but none of our coaches had a clue about soccer style place kicking, which is part of why we had to practice it so hard. It also tells a little about our ages.

Kickoff was a little easier. We just tried to find the best person that could kick off low and hard, and be able to kick a directional kick that would go to a designated area in the return formation where we wanted it kicked. It was a fun job and the early practice competition was fun as we tried a lot of players before deciding on the final kickoff candidate. Coverage was five players spread out on each side of the kicker. Coverage emphasis on kickoff and punt was for each player on the coverage unit to maintain the proper lane and separation, and not over run the return man.

CHAPTER 19

Game Preparation and Management

I have mentioned several times in previous chapters about the importance I saw and emphasis we placed on scouting and using information to prepare for our upcoming opponents.

The GYFC had very strict rules about this. You were not allowed to view a film unless your own team was playing in that film. You were not allowed to view another team's practice at all, preseason or regular season.

Some of the other GYFC coaches would call me on occasion during the season to ask about a team that I had already played, which was legal and within the GYFC rules. I would always talk to them, but I really did not like to help anyone else, and I never called anyone else for information. We also never broke any of the film rules, practice rules etc. I would rather not win than win by cheating or deliberately breaking any rules. Bob Johnson was the same way, no thought whatsoever of breaking any rules.

So, the only way we were ever able to get any information was by scouting opponents' games. At the beginning of the year, I would look at the entire conference schedule, and create a lineup of games each week that we needed to have scouted. All of the coaches participated and we even swapped out with the other Colt team coaches for scouting purposes.

Bob Johnson had told me in the early years that he felt that his Defense could stop anybody else's Offense, but that he wanted to know ahead of time what kind of defense his Offense needed to prepare for. I felt the opposite. I felt that we could move the ball on any defense because of our offense's ability to block any kind of front, in addition to the diversity we had in plays and formations. On the other hand, I wanted a good book on the opposing Offense, so we would know what special plays and players to prepare our defense to defend.

Ideally, I wanted to see every opponent myself, or at least as many as I could, so I created the schedule around my own ability to do that when it did not conflict with our own game schedule, as best as I could. When I scouted, I would chart the opponent's plays including formation, including the numbers of players in the key positions, and write them down in sequence including down and distance, focusing on diagramming the best plays and highlighting the players that made long gains or TD's.

Sometimes, we might have three or four scouting reports on a key opponent from myself and the other coaches. Every Saturday, our coaches would head out in different directions to look at other GYFC games, either before or after our own game. This was quite a commitment for these other coaches with families, as scouting and then our own games would occupy most Saturday afternoons and usually into the night from Labor Day until almost Thanksgiving week. It didn't bother me, I was single the entire time I coached. It was what I wanted to be doing. The others enjoyed it too, but had families that also required their time. Their wives graciously understood and since their children either were involved in ACYA at the same time, or had been previously involved with ACYA, they understood the value and service their husbands' involvement meant to the ACYA and community. They also knew it was necessary to have our best chances to teach and prepare our players and ultimately to win.

On the occasions where we would play a team a second time in a season, which always occurred in first round GYFC Playoffs, we would go over that regular season game film in detail. However, if the regular season game had been a few weeks earlier, I would still scout that team again to see if they had added anything new. With Tucker in 1974, we shut them out in regular season, but by playoff time, their passing offense was outstanding, and we almost got beat by it, as they scored 20 points against us, to our 21.

We were not prepared to face that passing game at that time, it really caught us by surprise, and I am not sure to this day how that happened except for the simple fact that they were very good and that Larry Rakestraw really knew how to communicate his own great capability and knowledge to those 12 year old kids on his Tucker team.

In preparing for an opponent's offense, the obvious thing to do was to stop their home run plays and their best players. As discussed, we knew if we could stop Tracy Soles in the 1975 Bobby Dodd Bowl, we would win if we could score. Same with Glenwood's Alfred McKerson in 1977. In the 1978 Playoff game with Smyrna, we knew if we could do a better job of neutralizing their offensive line, we would have a better chance, but were not sure how much we could score against them. But in that case, superior defensive planning, good punting and offensive patience led to 21 points and a shutout.

Also while scouting, we would look for offensive tendencies in play calling, which was why I charted every play's down and distance. In preparing our offense, we would chart opposing defenses by down and distance, watching for stunts, blitzes, coverage types, etc., making sure we noted how they covered wideouts, and adjusted to different formations, etc.

During game week practice, we would show our players the upcoming opponent's plays and formations in group work in every practice, and then also scrimmage live with our first defense against their offensive plays on Wednesday and our first Offense against the opponent's defensive sets on Thursday. When running the opponent's offensive plays, I would often be the QB to simulate the best execution possible, using our remaining players to run the plays.

When preparing our offense, we were confident that we could block any kind of defensive front, so we would usually have one or two plays we could change by switching automatically to a different play if we had something called that we knew would not work against a certain alignment. We would just tell the QB to say "Automatic" and the play would change to something we had pre-determined. The 86A-84B combination call I described earlier in Chapter 9 is a good example of that.

Also, as mentioned in previous chapters, on occasion, we would put in something special on offense for a certain opponent that might appear vulnerable defensively in a certain way. We would also do that occasionally with our defense, particularly that '78 playoff game with Smyrna, and other times against opponents who might do some unusual things offensively.

When the games actually started, I was the Offensive play caller. I used certain plays, like our base running plays to start most games. The inside running was used to set up our bootlegs and play action passes. There might be other plays I would try and set up like the 84 Reverse we used against Tucker in the '74 playoff game. Often, I would start games by running the same plays with Strongside Right and then Strongside Left, looking for defensive weak points, or places where we might find a manpower advantage. As I previously mentioned, for most years, Coach Frank Reeves would be our upstairs eyes and would give me information on defensive alignments via headset.

Doug Perreault, then Jim Lineberger, and then Doug Cooper would call the defensive plays, deciding when to stunt or blitz, use different secondary coverages, etc. Frank Reeves or another coach would advise them from upstairs as well.

There were a few occasions, like the '75 Central DeKalb Bobby Dodd Bowl, the '78 playoff with Smyrna come to mind where I actually went in with the philosophy of playing "not to lose." You often hear criticism by the TV pundits about that strategy, but I can easily defend that. I never did that for an entire game, but I certainly started some that way.

In the games where I used that strategy I simply had a lot of respect for my opponent and did not want to do anything to help them early in the game. My thought was to play conservative, be patient, kick for field position, and wait for a break, or at least superior field position, then take the shots and open up the playbook after the team is into the feel of the game.

A good example of where UGA should have used the "play not to lose" strategy occurred in 1995, Coach Ray Goff's last year. UGA had a very good team, but had lost future NFL TB Robert Edwards and starting QB and current UGA Offensive Coordinator Mike Bobo to season ending injuries. But they still had a very good defense headed by veteran coordinator Joe Kines. Into Athens comes a good Alabama team, who, similar to UGA were very good on defense also, and mediocre on Offense.

After losing Bobo the previous week, Coach Goff converted the great Hines Ward (Super Bowl MVP in 2008) to QB from his WR position as Ward had played QB in high school. UGA had a decent backup QB named Brian Smith who Goff overlooked for this crucial game, obviously thinking he needed more athleticism and firepower that a great athlete like Ward provided. In my opinion, knowing the UGA defense matched up very well against the Bama offense, UGA should have started Smith with a very conservative "not to lose" strategy and hoped to keep it close and win in a low scoring squeaker.

Instead, Ward started at QB, and made a few mistakes against the Tide's great defense due to his lack of experience at QB. Predictably, the Alabama defense forced costly turnovers and Bama scored all its points on defense or from a short field, including three interceptions and a blocked punt, none of which should have occurred if the proper strategy had been employed. After the 31-0 loss to Alabama, Smith started the following week in an upset win over Clemson. This allowed Ward to ease into the QB picture in easier situations over a few games, and by the season ending game against Georgia Tech, Ward was playing sensationally and led a great victory for UGA over Tech at Grant Field.

Back to our strategy, on the other hand, there were many times I was so confident in my plan, that I couldn't wait to get the ball and open up. In those cases, we would frequently score on the first drive.

I have seen that very often in college football as well. Today's offenses are so good, that it is not unusual for a well coached offensive team with a good game plan, Florida, Georgia, Alabama, Georgia Tech to score before the opposing defense knows what hit them.

Today, whenever I see a team win the coin toss and elect to receive rather than defer to the second half, that makes me think they have an offensive plan to start the game whereby they are pretty confident of scoring, or at least moving the ball well. For example, in the 2009 Georgia-Georgia Tech game at Tech's Grant Field, UGA won the toss. Every other time that year that they won the toss, they deferred to the second half. Against Tech, they chose to receive in the first half. That made me think they were very confident in their offensive game plan, which they were, as they scored a TD on the first possession of the game and never trailed.

Sometimes, even often, teams will have their first few plays "scripted," leading to immediate success. I only recall "scripting" once or twice, although I usually had a good idea of what the first few offensive plays of a game were going to be, with the only variable being starting field position. That's the problem with scripting, you never know what your first drive's field position will be, and I, for one, would alter my plans if starting field position was less than optimal.

When I go to football games now (usually UGA or Atlanta Falcon), I hear a lot of criticism of play calling, also on the rare occasion I might listen to talk radio. Those handing out this criticism usually think a run play should be a pass play or vice versa. They generally have no idea of the thought processes that created a particular play call. Play calling starts with the scouting report, goes through the game plan preparation, evaluation of practice results during the week, and then the current information the play caller sees/has seen in the current game or has received from his other coaches. The second guessers also have the ultimate advantage. They hand out that criticism AFTER the play. So a 3rd and 7 draw play is a great call WHEN IT WORKS, but stinks otherwise!

Two current 2010 examples from the UGA-Mississippi State game, which UGA lost and the critics have howled for the UGA play callers scalp. I personally think he does a very good job at play calling.

Example 1, 3rd and 8 from about the MSU 20 in the 1st half. UGA ran a simple delay pass to the TB because MSU had been blitzing and applying good pressure to the UGA QB. The play went all the way to the MSU one yard line where it was fumbled into the end zone and recovered by MSU. It was a great play call, but no one recognized it due to the fumble.

Example 2, 3rd and long again in the 2nd Half, from about the MSU 40. This time a Wide Receiver "Tunnel" Screen was called, resulting in a 40 yard TD, called back due to the other WR holding. Another great play call, resulted in nothing because of the penalty.

Example 3, from the 2006 Chick-fil-a Bowl, UGA vs Virginia Tech, V-Tech heavily favored. UGA down 21-3 at half. Early in Q3, 3rd and goal from about the VT 8. UGA runs a sprint draw from the shotgun formation for a TD. Imagine the UGA fan reaction if the play goes for no gain. UGA went on to an upset win.

There is more to play calling than meets the eye! The UGA play caller is the same guy that called the plays when UGA finished number 2 in the nation in 2007. I just cannot believe he has forgotten what he knows! or gotten dumber!

I have also given examples in earlier chapters about special preparations in the kicking game, whether faking a punt, returning a kick, or just defending a special play. You have to be prepared in all phases of the game. We won more than once because of our kicking preparations and execution. So did Bob Johnson.

Time management and awareness are also very important aspects of play calling and overall game management. I cite two examples, one good, one bad.

A good Bob Johnson example: In the 1972 Holiday Festival Bowl Game against Hialeah, Florida, played on a cold, extremely windy mid-December night in Lakeland, Florida. It was late in the game, the Colts holding on to a tight 7-6 lead against this very good Hialeah team, who had a super running back named Barney Underwood. Underwood also returned punts. Bob's 120 lb. team had a 4th and about 2 with time running out in Q3 close to mid-field. They lined up in normal formation against a very stiff wind, which would have been very difficult to punt against, but Bob noticed that the referee marked the ball ready for play with 24 seconds remaining in the Quarter so he wisely told his QB to let the time run out. The 24 seconds seemed like an eternity, but the clock finally ran out. Then, after the field was flipped going into the 4th Quarter, with the wind now at their back, the Colts lined up in normal formation again, appearing to go for it on the 4th and short. As the play developed, the Colts quick kicked the ball with the wind, completely flipping field position and avoiding a potential return by the dangerous Underwood. Bob's team then held on to the 7-6 win. Might Hialeah have called a timeout to save the wind advantage if Bob had lined his team up in punt formation? I would have had I been the Hialeah coach, but the brilliant Bob Johnson's deceptive quick kick WITH the wind, and with Underwood NOT in return position undoubtedly saved that game.

A bad example by Coach Ray Goff of the 1993 Georgia Bulldogs: Georgia held a slim

4 point lead against South Carolina in Sanford Stadium, but were backed up to their goal line with time running out, less than a minute to play in the game. South Carolina was out of timeouts and a field goal would not help them. Georgia punted with the clock running, but they snapped the ball with about 15 seconds on the play clock. Why not run it down to one or two seconds?? With that extra time given to them by UGA, USC scored the winning TD as time expired. Burning that extra ten or twelve seconds would have won the game for UGA!!

You have to be aware of those details like when the ball is marked ready. Ray Goff had the advantage of the play clock, but he (or his team on the field) didn't realize that he had time to burn. Bob Johnson didn't even have or need a play clock, he saw the game clock and noted when the ref whistled "ready to play," and used the clock to his advantage, by one tiny second, getting the severe wind behind his kicker, and pulled the surprise quick kick that allowed the Colts to hold on to the victory.

Most people think of time management as using timeouts at the right time, but managing the play clock is just as important. Getting plays called timely is also important and generally is a result of your game week preparation and communication ability.

Paying attention to little details is one of many things at which Bob Johnson excelled.

EPILOGUE

The decade of the 1970's (1970-1979) saw our ACYA program win 17 1/2 (the ½ was a tie game and co-championship in the 1975 80 lb. class) of 30 possible GYFC championships, with five runner-up or second place finishes. I was fortunate to be the coach of 6 of those GYFC Champions, Bob Johnson 4 (he retired after 1976), Mac Scoggins 2 ½, David Johnson 2 (in his only two years 1970-71), Jim Wilson 1, Mike Sellers 1, and John Ramsey 1. The Johnson brothers and Coach Pete Combs also accounted for four (1 Bob, 2 David, 1 Combs) in the late 1960's.

The last championships came in a sweep of all three weight classes in 1977. In 1978 and 1979, two Colt teams finished second, losing close games in the Bobby Dodd Bowl. The only other Bobby Dodd Bowl loss occurred in 1976 in Bob Johnson's last game. There were at least two Colt teams in the Bobby Dodd Bowl every year in the decade, and all three made it twice, winning all three games both times. We had two teams win subdivisions in the 70's and lose in the Round One Jim Brazier Bowl, my 120 lb. team in 1979 and Mac Scoggins's first 80 lb. team in 1974.

So in summary, we had participated in a total of 23 out of 30 possible Bobby Dodd Bowls, winning 17, losing five, with the one tie for a co-championship in the 1975 80 lb. division for Mac Scoggins. Only 7 (of 30) Bobby Dodd Bowl GYFC championship games were played in the decade without a Colt team participating in a 16 team league! It's no wonder why Bob Johnson called it "our" game. We had also won 25 out of 30 possible subdivision titles in that decade.

There were several undefeated Colt teams that won the GYFC and more. Bob Johnson's 120 lb. Colts in 1970 at 13-0-1, the 1971, 1973, and 1974 teams all at 14-0; David Johnson's 100 lb. Colts in 1971 at 14-0; Mac Scoggins's 1976 80 lb. Colt National Champions at 13-0 and 1977 100 lb. Colt National Champions at 14-0; Jim Wilson's 1972 100 lb. Colts at

14-0; John Ramsey's 1977 80 lb. Colt National Champions at 14-0 and my 1973 80 lb. Colts at 13-0 and 1974 100 lb. Colts at 13-0-1.

The ACYA had also won four GYFC (or its predecessor, the DYFC) championships in its earlier years in the 1960's. One was won by Bob Johnson's 115 lb. Colts in 1967, two by David Johnson's 95 lb. Colts in 1968 and 1969 and another by Pete Combs's 75 lb. Colts in 1969.

The 100 lb. Colt Team had a streak of winning 9 of the 10 GYFC championships between 1968 and 1977, with David Johnson coaching four straight from 1968-1971 before retiring from coaching in his early 30's.

There were also numerous Pop Warner All American players. Among them were:

Doug White
Brad Reese
David Campbell
Jimmy Wilson
Frank Baynham
Ron Barto
Steve Noles
Mike Yancey
Frankie Dougherty

Between 1970 and 1979, the Atlanta Colts had a conference record of 302-39-10 in the tough 16 team GYFC, including playoffs, and a post season record of 45-9-2 while playing in difficult intersectional bowl games. This created an overall record of 347-48-12 in the 1970's, a remarkable winning percentage of .853.

That ends the decade of the '70's.

*   *   *

Going into the 1980 season, I felt that I wanted to coach one more year, and I wanted it to be a good one. The ACYA was experiencing a "changing of the guard" with a new administration led by super businessman Bill Sanders. I liked and respected Bill very much. But I felt that it was time to let some new blood take over, plus the ACYA was not the same to me without Bob Johnson involved. I would probably still be coaching today if he was.

My incoming 120 lb. team was shaping up well for the 1980 season. Craig Goldberg had been the Tailback on the previous year's 100 lb. Bobby Dodd Bowl runner-up team and he was a good one, capable of being as good as any we had ever had. He was our leader. Craig Wudi would be a good quarterback and there were several other good experienced players like Ward Murphy, Pat Standard and Chuck Cianciolo.

With this group, I truly felt that we could get back to the Bobby Dodd Bowl and win. Our coaching staff was intact from the previous year and we added Bob Thomas who had been a Colt assistant coach for Bob Johnson and others through the years.

Our crucial game of the year was with Briarcliff, a typically good GYFC 120 lb. team, similar to those I described at the end of Chapter 13. They defeated us 19-17, as we missed a game winning field goal attempt at the end. We went on to a record of 10-2-1, with the key loss to Briarcliff keeping us out of the GYFC playoffs. That was how important those crucial regular season intra-subdivision games were, and this year was the only time we ever lost one, having won our subdivision the previous eight straight years. This time a failure in the kicking game helped beat us, once again proving the importance of that phase of football.

The rest of the record shows that this was a very good 120 lb. Colt team, and I still believe was championship worthy winning both post season games as well as a non-conference game against Larry Morris's NYO team. Larry Morris was also a former Georgia Tech and NFL player and a good friend of our coaches Martin and Cooper.

I retired from being a youth football head coach after that 1980 season. After the 1979 season, I had been pretty sure 1980 would be my last year. So, in preparing for coaching retirement, I had become a University of Georgia contributing booster earlier that year, and had also purchased season tickets for the 1980 UGA season. Luckily, the schedules allowed me to go to most of the UGA home games that season, while still coaching the Colt team.

In fact, I went into the pre-game warm-ups for my final Colt regular season home game in 1980, thinking Georgia had lost to Florida, and I was told by the Referee in our pregame officials' conference about the famous Buck Belue to Lindsay Scott pass play right after it had happened. And of course, UGA went on to win the National Championship that year.

Also, at the 120 lb. Colts post season banquet, UGA Coach Vince Dooley was our special guest featured speaker, a real treat for us Bulldog fans, especially as he had just won the National Championship. Beginning the next 1981 season, I began following that team with great enthusiasm, rarely missing a game, home or away, as I still do today.

I also went to a 1982 UGA home game with Kevin Anthony and his father on a recruiting trip that they made while Kevin was being recruited as a high school senior. Kevin was being recruited by many schools, and as previously mentioned, chose the University of North Carolina, where he went on to be the starting QB for the Tar Heels as a Junior.

Although I always missed coaching, being a Georgia booster kept me involved and interested in football. I had met Coach Dooley a few more times and also had the pleasure of meeting Coach Erk Russell and some of the other UGA assistant coaches.

I also met Mark Richt the summer before his first season as Head Coach at UGA.

I had always said that if I ever went back into coaching, I would like to do it with some of my former Colt players as assistants. In the summer of 2005, the year after Bob Johnson's death, I received a letter from Chuck Trense, my former player from 1976-77. He was now 40 years old and writing to me because he could not find my telephone listing. He was now coaching at ACYA and he wanted to get in touch with me to learn some of our old strategies, blocking techniques etc. after 28 years.

I had stayed in pretty close touch with Mark Wheaton, who had been a teammate of Chuck's on my 1976-77 teams, over the years, for occasional golf and UGA games, so I suggested the three of us have lunch to help Chuck out and talk over old times. By the end of lunch at the Pig 'n Chik in Buckhead, we had agreed that Mark would assist Chuck with his team as Assistant Coach for Offense and that Mark's son Will would be a player on Chuck's 8 year old Colt team. Chuck's son Charlie III was also a player on that team. I also committed as much time as I could give to help that season.

Will Wheaton would become the starting QB for this team and he displayed many of the same capabilities as his father Mark had done in the mid-70's for me. He was a naturally gifted runner with great speed and natural running moves and instincts. Guy Thacker, another former player and key performer and leader from my 1978-79 120 lb. Colt teams was also a coach on that team. His son Carter looks just like Guy did as a kid, and displayed the same gritty and determined qualities his dad did as well.

The conference was totally different, called North Metro and the travelling teams started with 8 years old. The GYFC was now down to about four teams on the south side of Atlanta, as the growth in Atlanta and related traffic had caused competition to become more localized to the various sections around metro Atlanta.

Since my current business requires a good bit of week night travel, I was actually more of a consultant than a coach, as I could only be at about 1/2 of the practices, but it was a lot of fun. I was able to contribute in practice by showing them (players and coaches) some of the old contact drills I had used in the past, and also some of the quickness and conditioning drills that we had used. Many of the parents expressed their gratitude to me for my contributions which made me feel very good.

During that season, I also designed special defenses that helped win two crucial games. One was against a wishbone team and then the other against a single wing or shotgun team, both of which led to shutout victories that season. Chuck's son Charlie III was also a chip off the old block, being the leading tackler and hardest hitter. He was also the backup QB and smart enough to play any position on the team.

I ran into many old friends, parents and former players alike during that year, including ¾ of my 1975 100 lb. Colt starting backfield. Jeff Anderson was a parent/coach in the program, Mike Rosing a parent and Mike Coveny was just there watching as he lived close by.

It was a great feeling seeing these grown men that I had known as 12 year old kids from my 1975 team of exactly 30 years ago. And it was especially gratifying to see them back living nearby as adults, and participating in the program where they had learned the game themselves and now wanted to teach it to their own kids. Or like Mike Coveny, a Princeton graduate, who simply enjoyed being there, "hanging on the fence," observing practices and games and remembering his own experiences of the past. He actually thanked me for spending that time with him 30 years ago. Believe me, coaching kids like Mike Coveny was MY pleasure.

I also learned some tragic news. Roger Rubinson from our 1976-'77 teams had been killed in an auto accident a few years back and Hal Moore, from the same two teams as Roger had died tragically as well. Roger was a great kid and Hal was too. They were both good football players as kids and more importantly, they were both parts of great families.

I saw recently this year (2009) where Bill Carlson, a reserve football player, but a gritty and determined young man from our teams of '73 and '74, had died of cancer. Bill was in his mid-40's and the newspaper article about him said that he had lived a competitive, adventuresome adult life and had also remained in the North Atlanta area as an adult.

Coach Warren Watson, a close friend for so many years, and the oldest member of our coaching staffs, also passed away a few short years ago in 2001, and he is missed by everyone that knew him. He was a dedicated family man, a true friend and outstanding coach, and a retired high school football official. I also mentioned earlier the 2010 death of Coach Pat Eder, the father and husband of another great ACYA family. He and Katie were married 57 years.

While writing this book, I have named many of the people that were involved with our program, but have left out many more that I would love to hear from or see. It was an honor for me to have worked with every single child that was entrusted to me and our other coaches, whether they were the best player or the last substitute.

That reminds me of one last humorous story. In the 1976 Colt Classic, with the U.S.

Bi-centenniel theme, part of the pre-game pageantry was for each player to step up to a p.a. microphone and announce their name, home town and position to the crowd. The idea was to show how many states and towns from across the U.S.A. were represented in the ACYA program.

The players came out in numerical order starting with number 5, "Mike Yancey, hometown (I believe Charlotte, NC ?), Quarterback." Close to the end of our team, stepped up number 76 who announced "Wade McKinney," then his home town, and then, "Bench" as his position. The crowd roared in laughter.

Wade was one of those players good enough to make the varsity team, but not quite good enough to be a starter. But he came to every practice, worked as hard as anyone and was proud to be a Colt. He was also a funny and entertaining kid, who made that joke at his own expense announcing his position as Bench.

There are many great youth programs and sports related activities for kids of all kinds all over the U.S. and the world. There are soccer, hockey, baseball, football and basketball teams and golf, tennis and other individual sports activities as well. But this one, the ACYA, was very special. It had great influence on the families involved, and now it is in the extended generations of many of its original families.

I have to believe that it was and is so special because of the original values that were instilled in it by one man. That man had great influence on me and everyone that ever knew him. That man was Robert M. "Bob" Johnson, who was truly "One of a Kind."

THE END

Made in the USA
Lexington, KY
17 October 2012